Christmas

Taste of Home BOOKS

RDA ENTHUSIAST BRANDS, LLC
MILWAUKEE, WI

Contents

GET SOCIAL WITH US!

 LIKE US
facebook.com/tasteofhome

 PIN US
pinterest.com/taste_of_home

 FOLLOW US
@tasteofhome

 TWEET US
twitter.com/tasteofhome

To find a recipe
tasteofhome.com
To submit a recipe
tasteofhome.com/submit
To find out about other
Taste of Home products
shoptasteofhome.com

Taste of Home

© 2021 RDA Enthusiast Brands, LLC.
1610 N. 2nd St., Suite 102, Milwaukee WI
53212-3906

International Standard Book Number:
D 978-1-61765-991-1
U 978-1-61765-992-8
International Standard Serial Number:
1948-8386
Component Number:
D 119600100H
U 119600102H

Executive Editor: Mark Hagen
Senior Art Director: Raeann Thompson
Editor: Hazel Wheaton
Art Director: Maggie Conners
Designer: Arielle Jardine
Senior Editor, Copy Desk: Dulcie Shoener

Cover:
Photographer: Dan Roberts
Food Stylist: Shannon Norris
Set Stylist: Melissa Franco

Pictured on front cover:
Rosemary Roasted Turkey, p. 57;
Molded Cranberry-Orange Salad, p. 63;
Honey Garlic Green Beans, p. 133

Pictured on back cover:
Acorn Squash Slices, p. 75;
Mashed Peppery Turnips, p. 67

Holly illustration:
Shutterstock/Leigh Prather

Printed in U.S.A.
1 3 5 7 9 10 8 6 4 2

Relish the spirit of the holidays with Taste of Home Christmas

1. FIZZY & FESTIVE
With sparkling beverages and an elegant array of appetizers to match, you're on your way to hosting a Christmas or New Year's party that will have your friends buzzing.

2. BEST OF THE BUFFET
Welcome your party guests with a fabulous spread of 19 appetizers, mains, breads, side dishes and desserts—all ideal for buffet dining.

3. HOLIDAY FEASTS
Choose one of three special menus planned around a ham, duck, or surf & turf entree—or choose from tasty a la carte recipes to create your own feast.

4. TIMESAVING SIDES
When you're planning your holiday dinner, scheduling kitchen time is crucial. Take advantage of these 19 delicious side dishes—all with prep time of 20 minutes or less!

5. 12 DAYS OF CHRISTMAS TREATS
From breakfast treats to sweet afternoon snacks to decadent desserts, these recipes deliver a different flavor every day for 12 days. Spoil yourself and your family!

6. SNOW DAY!
When school closes unexpectedly, these 16 recipes—each one made with on-hand ingredients—will keep the kids happy and make the day off a celebration for everyone!

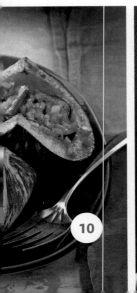

FIZZY & FESTIVE

Celebrate the holiday season with a party that brings the bubbly! These delicious appetizers and fizzy drinks are just the thing, whether you're hosting a Christmas party or gathering with friends for New Year's Eve.

SERVING CHAMPAGNE & FIZZY COCKTAILS

- If you're serving it straight, a quality champagne is worth the money. But for mixed drinks, a less expensive brand or a sparkling wine is fine. Go for a drier instead of a sweeter wine—the additions you'll be making to create the cocktail will make it sweet enough.

- Any drink made with fizzy ingredients should be stirred, not shaken. Just like shaking a soda can, vigorous shaking can lead to a messy carbonation explosion.

- When serving champagne, let the bottle sit in the refrigerator for 2-3 hours or chill it in an ice bucket for 30 minutes. The target temperature is between 39° and 48°. And remember—chill the champagne, never the glass.

- If mixing cocktails in batches, as with a pitcher of sangria, add ice to the glasses when serving, not before. Melting ice can dilute any cocktail, but it's even worse for sparkling cocktails—they'll go flat.

- For cold drinks, add the fizzy bit last. Whether it's wine, soda or tonic, add the sparkling ingredient just before serving to keep the effervescence alive for your guests.

- Use a flute for champagne—or not! Champagne flutes are elegant and traditional, but wine experts are split. Some say the tall, slender glass makes the champagne taste better; others say a tulip-shaped glass is actually better for bringing out the aromas. So choose what you like...you'll have an expert in your corner either way.

CRAN-APPLE SPRITZER

This is an easy and enticing drink to serve your guests—tart orange and cranberries, sweet honey and earthy cinnamon all come together to make a perfect holiday blend. You can serve it warm out of the slow cooker, or refrigerate it and serve it cold.
—Courtney Stultz, Weir, KS

- -

PREP: 10 min. • **COOK:** 3 hours
MAKES: 12 servings

1. bottle (2 liters) lemon-lime soda
6. medium apples, peeled and chopped
1. medium navel orange, sliced
1. cup fresh or frozen cranberries
5. cinnamon sticks (3 in.)
2. to 4 Tbsp. honey
   Optional: Apple slices and additional cinnamon sticks

In a 4- or 5-qt. slow cooker, combine the first 6 ingredients. Cover and cook on high 3-4 hours or until heated though. If desired, strain before serving. Garnish with apple slices and additional cinnamon sticks, if desired. Serve hot or cold.
¾ CUP: *137 cal., 0 fat (0 sat. fat), 0 chol., 17mg sod., 35g carb. (31g sugars, 2g fiber), 0 pro.*

SPICY PICKLED GRAPES

I love sweet and spicy flavors, so I created these pickled grapes. They are excellent as an appetizer, a sneaky addition to salads or a topper in your favorite Bloody Mary.
—*Carla Hinkle, Memphis, TN*

PREP: 10 min. • **COOK:** 10 min. + chilling • **MAKES:** 8 cups

- ½ cup sugar
- ½ cup white vinegar
- ½ cup cider vinegar
- 1 banana pepper, sliced
- 2 jalapeno peppers, sliced
- 1 red chili pepper, sliced
- 4 cinnamon sticks (3 in.)
- 2 in. fresh gingerroot, peeled and thinly sliced
- 1 Tbsp. coriander seeds
- 1 tsp. whole allspice
- 4 drops hot pepper sauce
- 1½ lbs. green grapes, halved
- 1½ lbs. seedless red grapes, halved

In a large saucepan, bring the first 11 ingredienwts to a boil. Reduce heat; simmer until sugar is dissolved, 3-5 minutes. Remove from heat and cool slightly. Place grapes in a large bowl; add pickling liquid. Refrigerate, covered, at least 12 hours before serving.
¼ CUP: 33 cal., 0 fat (0 sat. fat), 0 chol., 6mg sod., 8g carb. (7g sugars, 0 fiber), 0 pro.

VANILLA BEAN FIZZ

A homemade vanilla bean syrup adds a cozy touch to plain champagne. Once you've made the drink, save the vanilla beans to make vanilla sugar—just dry overnight and mix into a couple cups of sugar in an airtight container. Store at least one week for fragrant, flavorful sugar.
—*Taste of Home Test Kitchen*

PREP: 10 min. + cooling • **MAKES:** 8 servings

- 2 cups water
- 1 cup sugar
- 4 vanilla beans, split
- 4 cups champagne or sparkling white wine, chilled

1. In a small saucepan, bring water and sugar to a boil. Add vanilla beans. Reduce heat; simmer, uncovered, for 10 minutes. Remove from the heat; cool to room temperature. Remove beans.
2. For each serving, pour ¼ cup vanilla syrup into a champagne flute; add ½ cup champagne or sparkling wine.
¾ CUP: 137 cal., 0 fat (0 sat. fat), 0 chol., 0 sod., 26g carb. (25g sugars, 0 fiber), 0 pro.

SPARKLING SANGRIA

While on vacation with friends we enjoyed the best sangria at a Pennsylvania inn. When we got home, I tried to re-create it—and we all think my version is even better!
—Pam Mele, Franklin, NJ

PREP: 30 min. + chilling
MAKES: 32 servings (6 qt.)

- ¾ cup sugar
- ¾ cup water
- ½ vanilla bean, split

SANGRIA
- 1 pkg. (12 oz.) frozen unsweetened strawberries
- 2 medium peaches, peeled and sliced
- 2 medium kiwifruit, peeled and sliced
- 1 can (11 oz.) mandarin oranges, undrained
- 1 jar (10 oz.) maraschino cherries, undrained
- 1 can (8 oz.) unsweetened pineapple chunks, undrained
- 1 medium orange, thinly sliced
- 1 medium lime, thinly sliced
- 1 medium lemon, thinly sliced
- 2 bottles (750 ml each) dry red wine
- 2 cups orange juice
- ⅔ cup orange liqueur
- ⅔ cup Cognac or brandy
- ¼ cup lemon juice
- 3 Tbsp. lime juice
- 1 bottle (1 liter) carbonated water, chilled

1. In a small saucepan, combine the sugar, water and vanilla. Bring to a boil over medium heat. Reduce heat; simmer, uncovered, for 3-5 minutes or until sugar is dissolved, stirring occasionally. Remove from the heat; cool to room temperature. Discard vanilla bean.
2. Divide the fruits between 2 large pitchers. Add the half the wine, orange juice, liqueur, Cognac, lemon juice, lime juice and vanilla mixture to each pitcher. Refrigerate for at least 4 hours. Just before serving, stir in carbonated water.
¾ CUP: 126 cal., 0 fat (0 sat. fat), 0 chol., 4mg sod., 19g carb. (16g sugars, 1g fiber), 0 pro.

CURRIED BEEF BITES

These appetizers are fast and easy to prepare, and they are always the first to disappear at any party!
—Karen Kuebler, Dallas, TX

PREP: 15 min. • **BAKE:** 15 min.
MAKES: 3 dozen

- 12 slices white bread, crusts removed
- 3 Tbsp. butter, melted
- ½ lb. ground beef
- 5 celery ribs, chopped
- ½ cup seasoned bread crumbs
- 2 tsp. curry powder
- ½ tsp. garlic salt
  Cucumber raita and chopped fresh cilantro, optional

1. Preheat oven to 400°. Flatten bread slices with a rolling pin; brush tops with butter. Set aside.
2. In a large skillet, cook beef and celery over medium heat until the beef is no longer pink and the celery is tender, 8-10 minutes, breaking up beef into crumbles; drain. Stir in bread crumbs, curry powder and garlic salt.
3. Spoon the beef mixture evenly among bread slices. Roll up bread slices; secure with toothpicks. Place rolls on a greased baking sheet. Bake until golden brown, 12-15 minutes. When cool enough to handle, discard toothpicks and cut each roll crosswise into 3 slices. If desired, serve warm with cucumber raita and top with chopped fresh cilantro.
1 ROLL-UP: 52 cal., 2g fat (1g sat. fat), 6mg chol., 114mg sod., 6g carb. (1g sugars, 0 fiber), 2g pro.

CITRUS & WHITE GRAPE PARTY PUNCH

I found this when I was looking for a punch that wouldn't stain expensive prom dresses and tuxedos. Everyone loved it, and now it's a regular at house parties. You can mix the first four ingredients ahead of time, refrigerate, and add the soda right before serving.
—Karen Ballance, Wolf Lake, IL

TAKES: 5 min. • **MAKES:** 32 servings (4 qt.)

4 cups white grape juice, chilled
1 can (12 oz.) frozen lemonade concentrate, thawed
1 can (12 oz.) frozen orange juice concentrate, thawed
2 bottles (2 liters each) lemon-lime soda, chilled
  Lemon slices, orange slices and green grapes, optional

In a punch bowl, combine grape juice, lemonade concentrate and orange juice concentrate. Add soda; serve immediately. If desired, garnish with fruit.
½ **CUP:** 119 cal., 0 fat (0 sat. fat), 0 chol., 17mg sod., 30g carb. (26g sugars, 0 fiber), 0 pro.

LOBSTER TARTLETS

I love lobster, so I created these little gems. They are the perfect cocktail party or dinner appetizer, and elegant enough for a special occasion. Top with chives or green onions for color.
—Lorraine Caland, Shuniah, ON

TAKES: 25 min. • **MAKES:** 25 servings

½ cup shredded white cheddar cheese
½ cup shredded provolone cheese
½ cup cooked lobster meat or 1 can (6½ oz.) flaked canned lobster meat, drained
⅓ cup finely chopped sweet red pepper
2 Tbsp. finely chopped green onion (white portion only)
2 Tbsp. mayonnaise
  Dash seafood seasoning
2 pkg. (1.9 oz. each) frozen miniature phyllo tart shells
  Paprika, optional

Preheat oven to 350°. In a small bowl, combine the first 7 ingredients. Spoon into tart shells. Place on an ungreased baking sheet. Bake until shells are lightly browned and filling is heated through, 12-15 minutes. If desired, sprinkle with paprika before serving.
1 **TARTLET:** 76 cal., 4g fat (1g sat. fat), 8mg chol., 78mg sod., 6g carb. (0 sugars, 0 fiber), 3g pro.

BASIL & CASHEW PESTO PIZZAS

I love making pesto with basil from my garden; I use cashews to give it a deliciously different taste. To save time, make the pesto one day and finish the pizzas the next.
—Charlotte Rogers, Virginia Beach, VA

TAKES: 25 min. • **MAKES:** 12 servings

- 4 oz. Parmesan cheese, cut into chunks
- 2 cups loosely packed basil leaves
- ½ cup salted cashews
- 4 garlic cloves, halved
- ⅓ cup olive oil
- 3 Italian herb flatbread wraps
- 1½ cups (6 oz.) shredded part-skim mozzarella cheese
- ¾ tsp. coarsely ground pepper

1. Preheat oven to 350°. Place Parmesan cheese, basil, cashews and garlic in a food processor; pulse until chopped. Continue processing while gradually adding oil in a steady stream.

2. Place flatbreads on ungreased baking sheets; spread with pesto. Sprinkle with mozzarella cheese and pepper. Bake until cheese is melted, 8-10 minutes.

1 PIECE: *204 cal., 15g fat (5g sat. fat), 15mg chol., 351mg sod., 9g carb. (1g sugars, 1g fiber), 10g pro.*

CHICKEN BACON TRIANGLES

We host an annual Christmas party, and I whip up a new menu item every year. These golden appetizers were an absolute hit.
—Annette Fecht, Sorrento, BC

PREP: 60 min. + chilling
BAKE: 15 min. • **MAKES:** 4 dozen

- ½ lb. bacon strips, chopped
- ¾ lb. boneless skinless chicken breasts, cubed
- ½ cup condensed cream of mushroom soup, undiluted
- 4 oz. cream cheese, cubed
- 2 garlic cloves, minced
- 1½ tsp. dried minced onion
- ⅛ tsp. pepper
- 1 cup shredded part-skim mozzarella cheese
- ½ cup shredded Parmesan cheese
- 24 sheets phyllo dough, 14x9 in.
- ¼ cup butter, melted
  Ranch dip, optional

1. In a large skillet, cook bacon over medium heat until crisp. Remove to paper towels with a slotted spoon, reserving drippings in pan. Saute chicken in drippings until no longer pink; drain.

2. Add soup, cream cheese, garlic, onion, pepper and bacon to the skillet; cook and stir until blended. Remove from the heat. Stir in mozzarella and Parmesan cheeses; cool slightly. Cover and refrigerate for at least 2 hours.

3. Lightly brush 1 sheet of phyllo dough with butter; place another sheet of phyllo on top and brush with butter. (Keep the remaining phyllo covered with a damp towel to prevent it from drying out.) Cut into four 14x2¼-in. strips.

4. Preheat oven to 375°. Place a scant Tbsp. of filling on the lower corner of each strip. Fold the dough over filling, forming a triangle. Fold triangle up, then fold over, forming another triangle. Continue folding until you come to the end of the strip. Brush the end of the dough with butter and press onto the triangle to seal. Repeat with remaining strips of dough and with remaining sheets of phyllo.

5. Place triangles on a greased baking sheet. Bake until golden brown, 15-17 minutes. If desired, serve with ranch dip.

FREEZE OPTION: *Freeze unbaked triangles on baking sheets; when frozen, transfer to resealable freezer containers. Bake frozen triangles until golden brown, 18-22 minutes.*

1 APPETIZER: *70 cal., 5g fat (2g sat. fat), 13mg chol., 121mg sod., 4g carb. (0 sugars, 0 fiber), 3g pro.*

CHICKEN CAKES WITH AVOCADO MANGO SAUCE

These savory little cakes with their creamy dipping sauce make a great party appetizer. You don't have to save them for the holiday season, though. You can serve them for dinner anytime with a side of rice and your favorite vegetable.
—Rachael Nodes, La Barge, WY

PREP: 15 min. • **BAKE:** 15 min.
MAKES: 48 servings

- 2 lbs. ground chicken
- 1 cup dry whole wheat bread crumbs
- ½ cup unsweetened crushed pineapple
- ½ cup finely chopped sweet red pepper
- ½ cup finely chopped red onion
- 1 garlic clove, minced
- 1 tsp. salt
- ½ tsp. pepper

AVOCADO MANGO SAUCE

- 1 medium ripe avocado, peeled and pitted
- ½ cup chopped peeled mango
- 3 Tbsp. unsweetened crushed pineapple
- 2 Tbsp. chopped red onion
- 1 garlic clove, halved
- ½ tsp. salt
- ¼ tsp. ground cumin
- ¼ tsp. pepper

1. In a large bowl, combine the first 8 ingredients, mixing lightly but thoroughly. Shape mixture into 48 ½-in.-thick patties. Heat oil in a nonstick skillet over medium-high heat; fry the patties in batches until a thermometer inserted in the center of a patty reads 165°, 3-5 minutes on each side.
2. Meanwhile, place sauce ingredients in a blender; cover and process until smooth. Serve with chicken patties.
1 CAKE WITH 2 TSP. SAUCE: *43 cal., 2g fat (0 sat. fat), 13mg chol., 98mg sod., 3g carb. (1g sugars, 1g fiber), 3g pro.*

SKINNY HUCKLEBERRY COCKTAIL

I re-created an amazing concoction we enjoyed while on a vacation to Idaho and Wyoming. The flavor of vodka and the drink mix can be varied according to personal preference and availability.
—Susan Franck, Rapid City, SD

TAKES: 10 min. • **MAKES:** 14 servings

- 5 bottles (12 oz. each) light beer
- 2 cups huckleberry flavored vodka
- 1 can (12 oz.) diet lemon-lime soda, chilled
- 4 tsp. (2 packets) Crystal Light raspberry lemonade drink mix
  Fresh blackberries and raspberries, optional

In a large pitcher, combine beer, vodka, soda and drink mix, stirring until the mix is dissolved. Serve with ice and garnish with berries as desired.
¾ CUP: *121 cal., 0 fat (0 sat. fat), 0 chol., 23mg sod., 8g carb. (0 sugars, 0 fiber), 0 pro.*

JELLIED CHAMPAGNE DESSERT

This refreshing treat is a beautiful, festive optical illusion—it looks just like bubbling champagne, with a fresh berry floating in the glass. But it's really a sweet dessert your guests eat with a spoon.
—*Vickie McLaughlin, Kingsport, TN*

- -

PREP: 20 min. + chilling • **MAKES:** 8 servings

- 1   envelope unflavored gelatin
- 2   cups cold white grape juice, divided
- 2   Tbsp. sugar
- 2   cups champagne, sparkling wine or club soda
- 8   fresh strawberries, hulled

1. In a small saucepan, sprinkle gelatin over 1 cup cold grape juice; let stand for 1 minute. Heat over low heat, stirring until gelatin is dissolved. Stir in sugar. Remove from heat; stir in the remaining grape juice. Let cool to room temperature.
2. Transfer the gelatin mixture to a large bowl. Slowly stir in champagne. Divide half of the champagne mixture between 8 champagne or parfait glasses. Add 1 strawberry to each glass. Refrigerate glasses and the remaining champagne mixture until almost set, about 1 hour.
3. Place reserved champagne mixture in a blender; cover and process until foamy. Pour into glasses. Chill until set, about 3 hours.
1 SERVING: *96 cal., 0 fat (0 sat. fat), 0 chol., 9mg sod., 13g carb. (12g sugars, 0 fiber), 1g pro.*
DIABETIC EXCHANGES: *1 starch.*

GREEN CHILE PROSCIUTTO ROLLS

I created these spicy rolls for my husband, who loves green chiles. He loves these so much he could eat a whole pan!
—*Paula McHargue, Richmond, KY*

- -

PREP: 10 min. • **BAKE:** 15 min. • **MAKES:** 14

- 1   tube (8 oz.) refrigerated crescent rolls
- 3   oz. cream cheese, softened
- 1   can (4 oz.) chopped green chiles, drained
- 1   Tbsp. sweet hot mustard
- ½   cup thinly sliced prosciutto, cooked and crumbled
- 1   large egg, beaten
- 3   Tbsp. grated Parmesan cheese

1. Preheat oven to 375°. Unroll crescent dough into 1 long rectangle; press the perforations to seal. In a small bowl, beat cream cheese, green chiles and mustard. Spread over the dough to within ½ in. of edges. Sprinkle with prosciutto. Roll up the left and right sides toward the center, jelly-roll style, until the rolls meet in the center. Cut into 1-in. slices.
2. Place slices on a parchment-lined baking sheet. Brush with egg; sprinkle with Parmesan cheese. Bake until golden brown, 12-15 minutes. If desired, top with additional grated Parmesan cheese.
1 ROLL: *98 cal., 6g fat (2g sat. fat), 23mg chol., 258mg sod., 8g carb. (2g sugars, 0 fiber), 3g pro.*

ORANGE-FENNEL SALSA

I love salsa! Everyone enjoys this variation. Its sweet and tangy flavor profile goes well with ham, pork and poultry around the holidays.
—Nancy Heishman, Las Vegas, NV

PREP: 20 min. + chilling • **MAKES:** 3 cups

- 3 large navel oranges
- 1 medium fennel bulb, finely chopped plus 1 Tbsp. chopped fennel fronds
- ½ cup finely chopped red onion
- ⅓ cup minced fresh cilantro
- 1 jalapeno pepper, seeded and finely chopped
- 4 large fresh basil leaves, finely chopped
- 2 tsp. rice vinegar
- 2 tsp. olive oil
- ¼ tsp. garlic salt

Cut a thin slice from the top and bottom of each orange; stand orange upright on a cutting board. With a knife, cut off peel and outer membrane from orange. Working over a bowl to catch juices, cut along the membrane of each segment to remove fruit. Finely chop oranges; add to bowl with reserved juices. Add the remaining ingredients; toss to coat. Refrigerate, covered, until ready to serve.

½ CUP: 77 cal., 2g fat (0 sat. fat), 0 chol., 130mg sod., 16g carb. (11g sugars, 4g fiber), 2g pro.

AUNT KAREN'S SHRIMP SALAD

When company calls during the holidays, this salad is the perfect fit. It's quick to put together, too, leaving you plenty of time to spend with your guests.
—Karen Moore, Jacksonville, FL

PREP: 10 min. • **COOK:** 10 min. + chilling • **MAKES:** 24 servings

- 2 lbs. uncooked shrimp (26-30 per lb.), peeled and deveined and halved
- 1 Tbsp. white vinegar
- 1 Tbsp. lemon juice
- ⅓ cup plus 1 Tbsp. mayonnaise, divided
- ½ tsp. garlic salt
- 2 celery ribs, chopped
- 5 hard-boiled large eggs, chopped
- ¼ cup chopped sweet red pepper
- 24 Bibb lettuce leaves or Boston lettuce leaves
   Sliced green onions, optional

1. In a large saucepan or Dutch oven, bring 6 cups water to a boil. Add shrimp; cook, uncovered, until the shrimp turn pink, 3-5 minutes. Drain. Transfer to a large bowl. Add vinegar, lemon juice, 1 Tbsp. mayonnaise and garlic salt; toss to coat. Refrigerate, covered, at least 4 hours or overnight.
2. To serve, stir in remaining ⅓ cup mayonnaise, celery, eggs and red pepper. Serve in lettuce leaves. If desired, top with sliced green onions.

¼ CUP: 74 cal., 4g fat (1g sat. fat), 85mg chol., 120mg sod., 1g carb. (0 sugars, 0 fiber), 8g pro.
DIABETIC EXCHANGES: 1 lean meat, 1 fat.

3. Bake until golden brown, 12-15 minutes. Remove from pans to wire racks to let cool slightly. Serve warm.

FREEZE OPTION: *Cover and freeze unbaked triangles on parchment-lined baking sheets until firm. Transfer to a freezer conatiner; return to freezer. To use, bake as directed.*

1 APPETIZER: *97 cal., 6g fat (3g sat. fat), 8mg chol., 70mg sod., 8g carb. (0 sugars, 1g fiber), 2g pro.*

FRUITY WHITE SANGRIA

This lovely and refreshing white sangria is given a holiday-worthy spin with the unexpected addition of brandy, and a touch of bubbly fizz with club soda.
—Sharon Tipton, Casselberry, FL

- -

PREP: 15 min. + chilling • **MAKES:** 6 servings

- 1 **bottle (750 ml) Chablis wine**
- ¼ **cup sugar**
- 2 **oz. brandy**
- 1 **medium lemon, sliced**
- 1 **cup sliced fresh strawberries**
- 1 **medium pear, sliced**
- 1 **medium peach, sliced**
- 1½ **cups club soda, chilled**

In a 2-qt. pitcher, stir wine, sugar and brandy until the sugar is dissolved; add lemon, strawberry, pear and peach slices. Chill for at least 2 hours. Just before serving, stir in club soda. Serve over ice.

¾ CUP: *194 cal., 0 fat (0 sat. fat), 0 chol., 20mg sod., 22g carb. (16g sugars, 2g fiber), 1g pro.*

Holiday Helper
If you like, partially muddle the strawberry slices before adding them to the sangria. The drink will have a hazier appearance and a stronger strawberry flavor.

MUSHROOM PUFFS

These tender, golden puffs make the perfect finger food. I even freeze them for a quick appetizer for unexpected guests.
—Marion Ruzek, Jeffersonvlle, IN

- -

PREP: 15 min. • **BAKE:** 15 min.
MAKES: 3 dozen

- 2 **Tbsp. butter**
- ½ **lb. fresh mushrooms, chopped**
- 1 **small onion, finely chopped**
- 1 **garlic clove, minced**
- ¼ **tsp. pepper**
- 1 **pkg. (8 oz.) cream cheese, softened**
- 1 **pkg. (17.30 oz.) frozen puff pastry, thawed**

1. Preheat oven to 400°. In a large skillet, heat butter over medium heat. Add mushrooms and onion; cook and stir until tender, 3-5 minutes. Add garlic and pepper; cook for 1 minute longer. Stir in cream cheese until melted; remove from heat.

2. Unfold 1 pastry sheet; cut into 9 squares, then cut each square diagonally in half. Place a scant tsp. of filling on 1 half of each triangle. Brush the edges of the pastry with water; fold over to form a triangle. Seal edges with a fork; place triangles 1 in. apart on parchment-lined baking sheets. Repeat with the second pastry sheet and the remaining filling.

BEST OF
THE BUFFET

*When you create a stunning spread of gorgeous holiday
food, your guests are free to choose their dishes...
and with a selection this impressive,
they'll want to taste it all!*

LET IT SNOW!

To make a beautiful display for your buffet, the best option might be the thrift store! This display of homemade snow globes was created from a collection of old glass items—cookie jars, glass hurricanes and candlesticks—found in secondhand shops. Vintage ornaments, Christmas decor and toys were selected and arranged to create charming scenes. Cotton batting and bagged snowflakes from the craft store fill the bottom of the containers, and carefully trimmed bottle brushes make the perfect white trees. Let your imagination run wild—if you prefer everything at your party to be edible, create scenes using gingerbread cutouts, with sanding sugar as snow!

EASY BATTER ROLLS

The first thing my guests ask when they come for dinner is if I'm serving these dinner rolls. The buns are so light, airy and delicious that I'm constantly asked for the recipe.
—Thomasina Brunner, Gloversville, NY

PREP: 30 min. + rising • **BAKE:** 15 min. • **MAKES:** 1 dozen

- 3   **cups all-purpose flour**
- 2   **Tbsp. sugar**
- 1   **pkg. (¼ oz.) active dry yeast**
- 1   **tsp. salt**
- 1   **cup water**
- 2   **Tbsp. butter**
- 1   **large egg, room temperature**
     Melted butter

1. In a large bowl, combine 2 cups flour, the sugar, yeast and salt. In a saucepan, heat water and butter to 120°-130°. Add to the dry ingredients; beat until blended. Add egg; beat on low speed for 30 seconds, then on high for 3 minutes. Stir in the remaining flour (batter will be stiff). Do not knead. Cover and let rise in a warm place until doubled, about 30 minutes.
2. Stir dough down. Fill 12 greased muffin cups half full with batter. Cover and let rise until doubled, about 15 minutes.
3. Bake at 350° until golden brown, 15-20 minutes. Cool for 1 minute before removing from pan to a wire rack. Brush tops with melted butter.
FREEZE OPTION: *Freeze cooled rolls in airtight containers. To use, microwave each roll on high until warmed, 30-45 seconds.*
1 ROLL: *147 cal., 3g fat (1g sat. fat), 21mg chol., 219mg sod., 26g carb. (2g sugars, 1g fiber), 4g pro.*

PECAN DATE PUDDING

This recipe was passed down from my great -grandmother to my grandmother. They lovingly served it with whipped cream on top. We never had a holiday without it.
—*Patricia Rutherford, Winchester, IL*

PREP: 20 min. • **BAKE:** 50 min. • **MAKES:** 8 servings

- 1 cup all-purpose flour
- 2 cups packed brown sugar, divided
- 1½ tsp. baking powder
- ¼ tsp. salt
- 2 Tbsp. butter, divided
- ¾ cup whole milk
- 1 cup chopped dates
- 1 cup chopped pecans
- 2 cups water
  Whipped cream, optional

1. Preheat oven to 350°; In a bowl, combine flour, 1 cup brown sugar, the baking powder and salt. Melt 1 Tbsp. butter; combine with milk. Stir into flour mixture until smooth. Fold in dates and walnuts. Transfer to a greased 8-in. square baking dish.
2. In a large saucepan, bring the water and the remaining 1 cup brown sugar to a boil. Cook and stir until sugar is dissolved. Remove from heat; stir in the remaining 1 Tbsp. butter until melted. Pour over batter.
3. Bake until a toothpick inserted near the center of cake comes out clean, 50-60 minutes. Serve warm. If desired, top pudding with whipped cream.
1 SERVING: *452 cal., 14g fat (3g sat. fat), 10mg chol., 213mg sod., 83g carb. (67g sugars, 3g fiber), 4g pro.*

SNOW PEA HOLIDAY WREATH

Santa himself might stop to sample this pretty-as-a-picture finger food! Crunchy green pea pods and juicy red tomatoes give the buffet table a naturally fresh, festive holiday look.
—*Carol Schneck, Lodi, CA*

TAKES: 25 min. • **MAKES:** 20 servings

- ½ lb. fresh snow peas, strings removed
- 3 oz. cream cheese, softened
- ¼ tsp. garlic powder
- ¼ tsp. seasoned salt
- 2 cups grape tomatoes

1. In a large saucepan, bring 6 cups water to a boil. Add snow peas; cook, uncovered, just until they're bright green and crisp-tender, 1-2 minutes. Drain and immediately drop into ice water. Drain and pat dry.
2. In a small bowl, combine cream cheese, garlic powder and seasoned salt. Place bowl in the center of a serving platter. Arrange snow peas and tomatoes around the bowl.
1 SERVING: *23 cal., 2g fat (1g sat. fat), 5mg chol., 33mg sod., 2g carb. (1g sugars, 0 fiber), 1g pro.*

ITALIAN BREAD SALAD WITH OLIVES

This quick and flavorful panzanella-style salad always gets rave reviews from my friends and family. It makes a colorful addition to a buffet spread, and the toasted bread holds its crunch. If you like, you can make this ahead of time; just keep the bread cubes separate and add them right before serving.
—Angela Spengler, Niceville, FL

TAKES: 30 min. • **MAKES:** 9 servings

- 1 loaf (14 oz.) ciabatta bread, cut into ½-in. cubes (about 10 cups)
- ¾ cup olive oil
- 3 garlic cloves, minced
- ¼ tsp. pepper
- ¼ cup balsamic vinegar
- ¼ tsp. salt
- 2 large tomatoes, chopped
- ¼ cup sliced olives
- ⅓ cup coarsely chopped fresh basil
- 2 Tbsp. chopped fresh Italian parsley
- ¼ cup shredded Parmesan cheese

1. Preheat oven to 350°. Place bread cubes in a large bowl. In another bowl, mix oil, garlic and pepper; drizzle 3 Tbsp. over bread and toss to coat. Reserve remaining oil mixture. Spread bread cubes in a single layer on two 15x10x1-in. baking pans.
2. Bake until crisp and light brown, stirring occasionally, 12-18 minutes.
3. Meanwhile, whisk vinegar and salt into the reserved oil mixture. Add tomatoes, olives and herbs; toss to coat.
4. Cool bread cubes slightly. Add to the tomato mixture; toss to combine. Sprinkle with cheese; serve immediately.
1 CUP: 316 cal., 21g fat (3g sat. fat), 2mg chol., 345mg sod., 31g carb. (5g sugars, 2g fiber), 5g pro.

PEPPERY ROAST BEEF

With its spicy coating and creamy horseradish sauce, this roast will be the star of any meal, whether it's a potluck or a sit-down dinner.
—Maureen Brand, Somers, IA

PREP: 15 min. • **BAKE:** 2½ hours + standing
MAKES: 12 servings

- 1 Tbsp. olive oil
- 1 Tbsp. seasoned pepper
- 2 garlic cloves, minced
- ½ tsp. dried thyme
- ¼ tsp. salt
- 1 boneless beef eye round or top round roast (4 to 5 lbs.)

HORSERADISH SAUCE
- 1 cup sour cream
- 2 Tbsp. lemon juice
- 2 Tbsp. milk
- 2 Tbsp. prepared horseradish
- 1 Tbsp. Dijon mustard
- ¼ tsp. salt
- ⅛ tsp. pepper

1. Preheat oven to 325°. In a small bowl, combine oil, seasoned pepper, garlic, thyme and salt; rub over roast. Place fat side up on a rack in a shallow roasting pan.
2. Bake, uncovered, for 2½-3 hours or until meat reaches desired doneness (for medium-rare, a thermometer should read 135°; medium, 140°; medium-well, 145°). Let roast stand for 10 minutes before slicing.
3. In a small bowl, combine the sauce ingredients. Serve with roast.
4 OZ. COOKED BEEF WITH ABOUT 1 TBSP. SAUCE: 228 cal., 10g fat (4g sat. fat), 83mg chol., 211mg sod., 3g carb. (1g sugars, 0 fiber), 30g pro.

ORANGE-PISTACHIO QUINOA SALAD

Add this fresh and healthy salad to your holiday spread. Its citrusy, nutty taste is simply delicious.
—Jean Greenfield, San Anselmo, CA

- -

PREP: 15 min. • **COOK:** 15 min. + cooling • **MAKES:** 8 servings

- 1⅓ cups water
- ⅔ cup quinoa, rinsed
- 2 cups chopped romaine lettuce
- 1 can (15 oz.) garbanzo beans or chickpeas, rinsed and drained
- 1 can (15 oz.) mandarin oranges, drained
- 1 medium cucumber, halved and sliced
- 1 cup shelled pistachios, toasted
- ½ cup finely chopped red onion
- 1 medium navel orange
- 2 Tbsp. olive oil
- ½ tsp. salt
     Pinch pepper

1. In a large saucepan, bring water to a boil. Add quinoa. Reduce heat; simmer, covered, for 12-14 minutes or until the liquid is absorbed. Remove from heat; fluff with a fork. Cool.
2. In a large bowl, combine romaine, beans, mandarin oranges, cucumber, pistachios, onion and cooled quinoa. In a small bowl, finely grate zest from orange. Cut orange crosswise in half; squeeze juice from orange and add to zest. Whisk in oil, salt and pepper. Drizzle over salad; toss to coat.
1 CUP: *257 cal., 12g fat (1g sat. fat), 0 chol., 287mg sod., 31g carb. (10g sugars, 6g fiber), 8g pro.*
DIABETIC EXCHANGES: *2 starch, 2 fat.*

PUFF PASTRY HOLLY LEAVES

These elegant holiday appetizers look like you've put in tons of hard work in the kitchen, but they can be assembled in a jiffy. Guests always love these when I set them out at a party.
—Angela King, Walnut Cove, NC

- -

PREP: 30 min. • **BAKE:** 15 min. + cooling • **MAKES:** 2 dozen

- 1 pkg. (17.3 oz.) frozen puff pastry, thawed
- 1 large egg
- 1 Tbsp. water
- 4 oz. cream cheese, softened
- 1 cup (4 oz.) crumbled feta cheese
- ½ cup minced fresh parsley
- ½ cup prepared pesto
- 24 pimiento pieces

1. Preheat oven to 400°. Unfold pastry sheets onto a lightly floured surface. With a floured 3½-in. leaf-shaped cookie cutter, cut out 12 leaves from each sheet. Place leaves on ungreased baking sheets. With a toothpick, score veins in leaves. In a small bowl, beat egg and water; brush over pastry.
2. Bake for 12-14 minutes or until golden brown. Remove from pans to wire racks to cool.
3. In a large bowl, combine the cheeses, parsley and pesto. Split pastry leaves in half. Spread 1 Tbsp. of the cheese mixture over bottom halves; replace tops. Add a pimiento piece on each for a holly berry. Refrigerate leftovers.
1 APPETIZER: *151 cal., 10g fat (3g sat. fat), 15mg chol., 191mg sod., 13g carb. (0 sugars, 2g fiber), 3g pro.*

TAPAS MEATBALLS WITH ORANGE GLAZE

Crisp on the outside, moist on the inside, these cheese-stuffed baked appetizers are drizzled with a sweet-and-sour glaze.
—Bonnie Stallings, Martinsburg, WV

PREP: 25 min. • **BAKE:** 20 min.
MAKES: 16 meatballs

- 1 large egg, lightly beaten
- ¼ cup ketchup
- 1 small onion, finely chopped
- ½ cup soft bread crumbs
- ¼ cup minced fresh parsley
- 3 tsp. paprika
- 2 garlic cloves, minced
- ½ tsp. salt
- ½ tsp. pepper
- 1 lb. lean ground beef (90% lean)
- 2½ oz. feta cheese, cut into sixteen ½-in. cubes

GLAZE
- 1 jar (12 oz.) orange marmalade
- ¼ cup orange juice
- 3 green onions, chopped, divided
- 1 jalapeno pepper, seeded and chopped

1. Preheat oven to 400°. In a large bowl, combine the first 9 ingredients. Crumble beef over the mixture and mix well. Divide into 16 portions; flatten. Top each portion with a cheese cube; form the beef mixture around the cheese into meatballs.
2. Place on a greased rack in a shallow baking pan. Bake, uncovered, until cooked through, 20-25 minutes. In a small saucepan, heat marmalade, orange juice, half of the green onions and the jalapeno.
3. Place meatballs in a serving dish; pour glaze over top and gently stir to coat. Garnish with the remaining green onions.
FREEZE OPTION: *Freeze cooled meatball mixture in freezer containers. To use, partially thaw meatballs in refrigerator overnight. Microwave, covered, on high in a microwave-safe dish until heated through, gently stirring and adding a little water if necessary. Meanwhile, combine and heat glaze ingredients as directed. Serve over meatballs.*
1 MEATBALL: *127 cal., 3g fat (2g sat. fat), 33mg chol., 206mg sod., 18g carb. (15g sugars, 1g fiber), 7g pro.*

PASTA WITH PROSCIUTTO, LETTUCE & PEAS

This elevated pasta dish is easy, elegant and downright delicious—it's the perfect holiday dish without a lot of work.
—Amy White, Manchester, CT

PREP: 20 min. • **COOK:** 15 min.
MAKES: 8 servings

- 1 lb. uncooked campanelle pasta
- 2 Tbsp. butter
- 3 Tbsp. olive oil, divided
- 12 green onions, sliced
- 1 shallot, finely chopped
- ½ cup white wine or chicken broth
- ½ cup reduced-sodium chicken broth
- ¼ tsp. salt
- ⅛ tsp. pepper
- 1 head Boston lettuce, cut into ¾-in. slices
- 2 cups fresh or frozen peas
- 1 cup grated Parmesan cheese
- 4 oz. thinly sliced prosciutto or deli ham, cut into ½-in. strips

1. Cook pasta according to the package directions for al dente.
2. Meanwhile, in a large skillet, heat butter and 2 Tbsp. olive oil over medium-high heat. Add green onions and shallot; cook and stir until tender. Stir in wine. Bring to a boil; cook and stir until liquid is almost evaporated, 6-8 minutes.
3. Add broth, salt and pepper. Bring to a boil. Reduce heat; stir in lettuce and peas. Cook and stir until lettuce is wilted. Drain pasta; add to pan. Stir in Parmesan cheese and prosciutto; drizzle with the remaining oil. If desired, top with additional cheese.
1¼ CUPS: *220 cal., 13g fat (5g sat. fat), 29mg chol., 629mg sod., 14g carb. (5g sugars, 5g fiber), 13g pro.*

HERBED ROAST TURKEY BREAST

I made this turkey breast for my first formal dinner party as a newlywed. It was such a success that it's become a standby on all my entertaining menus.
—Lisa Mahon Fluegeman, Cincinnati, OH

PREP: 10 min. • **BAKE:** 2 hours + standing
MAKES: 12 servings

- 1 bone-in turkey breast (5 to 6 lbs.)
- 5 tsp. lemon juice
- 1 Tbsp. olive oil
- 1 to 2 tsp. pepper
- 1 tsp. dried rosemary, crushed
- 1 tsp. dried thyme
- 1 tsp. garlic salt
- 1 medium onion, cut into wedges
- 1 celery rib, cut into 2-in. pieces
- ½ cup white wine or chicken broth

1. Preheat oven to 325°. With fingers, carefully loosen the skin from both sides of turkey breast. Combine lemon juice and oil; brush under the skin. Combine the pepper, rosemary, thyme and garlic salt; rub over turkey.
2. Place onion and celery in a 3-qt. baking dish. Top with turkey breast, skin side up. Pour wine into the dish.
3. Bake, uncovered, for 2-2½ hours or until a thermometer reads 170°. (Cover loosely with foil if turkey browns too quickly.) Cover and let stand 15 minutes before carving.

5 OZ. COOKED TURKEY: *285 cal., 11g fat (3g sat. fat), 102mg chol., 241mg sod., 2g carb. (1g sugars, 0 fiber), 40g pro.*
DIABETIC EXCHANGES: *5 medium-fat meat.*

Holiday Helper
When you want a different flavor, you can often use lemon and lime juice interchangeably in recipes. If you want to use orange juice, however, you'll need to keep a little lemon or lime juice as well. Orange juice is more subtle and won't give your dish the same brightness.

CARROT, PARSNIP & POTATO GRATIN

Thanks to a Taste of Home community challenge a few years back, my husband and I tried parsnips and discovered that we liked them! I now grow them in my garden and we have fun experimenting with them—which is how this tasty beauty was born.
—Sue Gronholz, Beaver Dam, WI

PREP: 20 min. • **BAKE:** 50 min.
MAKES: 8 servings

- 1 lb. medium carrots, thinly sliced
- ½ lb. medium parsnips, peeled and thinly sliced
- ½ lb. Yukon Gold potatoes, peeled and thinly sliced
- 1 small onion, halved and sliced
- 2 garlic cloves, minced
- 1½ tsp. minced fresh rosemary
- ½ tsp. salt
- ½ tsp. ground nutmeg
- 1 cup half-and-half cream
- ¼ cup heavy whipping cream

Preheat oven to 400°. In a large bowl, combine all the ingredients. Transfer to a greased 3-qt. baking dish. Bake, covered, until the vegetables are tender, 40-45 minutes. Uncover and continue baking until the cream has thickened and is beginning to turn golden brown, 10-15 minutes longer. Let stand for 5-10 minutes before serving.

¾ CUP: *141 cal., 6g fat (4g sat. fat), 23mg chol., 208mg sod., 19g carb. (6g sugars, 3g fiber), 3g pro.*

BRUSSELS SPROUTS BROWN BETTY

I had the idea to make a savory version of the family-favorite brown Betty using vegetables in place of fruit, while keeping the classic crunchy bread crumb topping. The result is a creamy, decadent side dish that is a surefire way to turn anyone into a Brussels sprouts fan.
—*Shauna Havey, Roy, UT*

PREP: 30 min. • **BAKE:** 40 min. • **MAKES:** 8 servings

* 1½ lbs. fresh Brussels sprouts, sliced
* 1 small onion, chopped
* 4 garlic cloves, minced
* 2 Tbsp. olive oil
* 1 tsp. salt
* ½ tsp. pepper
* 1½ cups shredded Swiss cheese
* 1 cup heavy whipping cream
* 8 bacon strips, cooked and crumbled
* 3 slices whole wheat bread, torn
* 2 Tbsp. butter, melted
  Minced fresh thyme, optional

1. Preheat oven to 425°. In a large bowl, combine the first 6 ingredients; toss to coat. Transfer to a greased 13x9-in. baking dish. Bake, uncovered, for 20 minutes. Stir in the cheese, cream and bacon. Bake until casserole is bubbly and starting to brown, 12-15 minutes longer.
2. Meanwhile, place bread in a food processor or blender. Cover and pulse until crumbs form. Transfer to a small bowl and stir in butter. Sprinkle over casserole. Bake until the topping is golden brown, 8-10 minutes longer. If desired, top with thyme before serving.
¾ CUP: 301 cal., 25g fat (13g sat. fat), 62mg chol., 554mg sod., 9g carb. (3g sugars, 3g fiber), 12g pro.

SPINACH DEVILED EGGS

Spinach adds unexpected color and flavor to this tasty variation on deviled eggs. They're so easy to make and such an attractive addition to a party spread.
—*Dorothy Sander, Evansville, IN*

TAKES: 15 min. • **MAKES:** 2 dozen

* 12 hard-boiled large eggs
* ¼ cup mayonnaise
* 2 Tbsp. white vinegar
* 2 Tbsp. butter, softened
* 1 Tbsp. sugar
* ½ tsp. pepper
* ¼ tsp. salt
* 4 bacon strips, cooked and crumbled
* ½ cup frozen chopped spinach, thawed and squeezed dry

Cut eggs in half lengthwise. Remove yolks; set whites aside. In a small bowl, mash yolks. Add the mayonnaise, vinegar, butter, sugar, pepper and salt; mix well. Stir in bacon and spinach. Stuff or pipe mixture into egg whites. Refrigerate until serving.
2 EGG HALVES: 146 cal., 12g fat (4g sat. fat), 221mg chol., 194mg sod., 2g carb. (2g sugars, 0 fiber), 7g pro.

CHUNKY POTATO LEEK SOUP

My family and I love a steaming bowl of potato soup on a cold winter evening, but we don't love the butter and fat content of regular soup recipes. So I created this lighter version. I have shared it with many folks, and everyone who has tried it loves it for the robust, satisfying flavor, not just the lighter ingredients.
—*Christine Frye, Odessa, MO*

PREP: 20 min. • **COOK:** 25 min.
MAKES: 8 servings

- 2 medium leeks, coarsely chopped
- 1 medium onion, chopped
- 3 Tbsp. all-purpose flour
- ½ tsp. garlic powder
- 2 Tbsp. olive oil
- 4 cups reduced-sodium chicken broth or vegetable broth
- 2 bay leaves
- ¾ tsp. salt
- ½ tsp. pepper
- ⅛ tsp. hot pepper sauce
- ⅛ tsp. Worcestershire sauce
  Dash ground nutmeg
- 5 cups diced potatoes
- 1½ cups fat-free milk
- 1 can (12 oz.) fat-free evaporated milk

1. In a nonstick skillet coated with cooking spray, cook leeks and onion for 5 minutes or until vegetables are tender and just beginning to brown; set aside.
2. In a large saucepan, cook flour and garlic powder in oil for about 2 minutes or until lightly browned. Gradually whisk in broth. Stir in bay leaves, salt, pepper, pepper sauce, Worcestershire sauce and nutmeg. Bring to a boil; cook for 1-2 minutes or until thickened.
3. Stir in potatoes and the leek mixture; return to a boil. Reduce heat; cover and simmer 15-20 minutes or until potatoes are tender. Stir in milk and evaporated milk; heat through. Discard bay leaves.
1 CUP: *197 cal., 4g fat (1g sat. fat), 3 mg chol., 593mg sod., 32g carb., 2g fiber, 10g pro.*
DIABETIC EXCHANGES: *2 starch, ½ fat.*

CRANBERRY EGGNOG BRAID

With its rich holiday flavors, this delicious bread is great for parties. It's sweet enough to be a seasonal indulgence, but not so sweet to be sent to the dessert table.
—*Mary Lindow, Florence, WI*

PREP: 25 min. + rising
BAKE: 25 min. + cooling
MAKES: 1 loaf (10 slices)

- 3 to 3½ cups all-purpose flour, divided
- ¼ cup sugar
- ½ tsp. salt
- 1 pkg. (¼ oz.) active dry yeast
- ½ tsp. ground nutmeg
- 1¼ cups eggnog
- ¼ cup butter
- ½ cup dried cranberries

GLAZE
- 1 cup confectioners' sugar
- 1 to 2 Tbsp. eggnog
- ¼ tsp. vanilla extract
  Dash nutmeg

1. Combine 1½ cups of flour, the sugar, salt, yeast and nutmeg; set aside. In a saucepan, heat eggnog and butter to 120°-130° (butter does not need to melt); add to flour mixture. Beat on low until moistened; beat on medium for 3 minutes.
2. Stir in cranberries and enough of the remaining flour to make a soft dough. Turn onto a floured surface; knead until smooth and elastic, 6-8 minutes. Place in a greased bowl, turning once to grease top. Cover and let rise in a warm place until doubled, about 1 hour.
3. Punch dough down; divide into thirds. Shape each third into a 16-in. rope. Braid ropes on a greased baking sheet; seal ends. Cover and let rise until nearly doubled, about 30 minutes.
4. Bake at 350° for 25-30 minutes or until golden. Immediately remove from pan to a wire rack to cool completely. Combine the first 3 glaze ingredients; drizzle over braid. Dust with nutmeg.
1 SLICE: *257 cal., 6g fat (4g sat. fat), 27mg chol., 153mg sod., 46g carb. (21g sugars, 1g fiber), 5g pro.*

3. For frosting, in a saucepan, combine sugar and water. Bring to a boil; cook over medium-high heat until a thermometer reads 244° (firm-ball stage).

4. Meanwhile, beat egg whites and cream of tartar in a bowl on high speed until foamy. Slowly pour hot sugar syrup over the egg whites while beating continuously. Continue beating on high until stiff glossy peaks form, about 7 minutes. Add vanilla; beat until the frosting cools slightly and reaches desired consistency.

5. Place 1 cake layer on a serving plate; spread with ¾ cup frosting. Sprinkle with ¼ cup coconut. Repeat layers. Top with remaining cake layer. Frost top and sides of cakes with remaining frosting; sprinkle with the remaining coconut.

1 SLICE: *376 cal., 12g fat (8g sat. fat), 97mg chol., 195mg sod., 62g carb. (45g sugars, 1g fiber), 5g pro.*

RAW CAULIFLOWER TABBOULEH

This recipe is super easy to make, so you can have it chilling in the fridge and take it out when guests arrive. I love that I can offer it to friends with dietary restrictions.
—Maiah Miller, Montclair, VA

- -

PREP: 10 min. + chilling • **MAKES:** 6 cups

- 1   medium head cauliflower
- ½   cup oil-packed sun-dried tomatoes
- 12 pitted Greek olives
- 2   cups fresh parsley leaves
- 1   cup fresh cilantro leaves
- 1   Tbsp. white wine vinegar
      or cider vinegar
- ¼   tsp. salt
- ¼   tsp. pepper

Core and coarsely chop cauliflower. In batches, pulse the cauliflower in a food processor until it resembles rice (do not overprocess). Transfer to a large bowl. Add the remaining ingredients to food processor; pulse until finely chopped. Add to cauliflower; toss to combine. Refrigerate for 1 hour before serving to allow flavors to blend.

¾ CUP: *55 cal., 3g fat (0 sat. fat), 0 chol., 215mg sod., 7g carb. (2g sugars, 2g fiber), 2g pro.*

HOLIDAY SNOWFLAKE CAKE

The coconut sprinkled on this old-fashioned fluffy white cake gives the impression of snow inside the house without the cold. It's a beautiful dessert that makes a fitting end to a delicious winter meal.
—Lynne Peterson, Salt Lake City, UT

- -

PREP: 40 min. • **BAKE:** 15 min. + cooling
MAKES: 12 servings

- 2   large eggs plus 4 large egg yolks, room temperature
- 1½   cups sugar
- 1   cup 2% milk
- ½   cup butter, cubed
- 2½   cups all-purpose flour
- 1   Tbsp. baking powder
- 1   tsp. vanilla extract
- ½   cup chopped nuts, optional

FROSTING
- 1¾   cups sugar
- ½   cup water
- 4   large egg whites
- ½   tsp. cream of tartar
- 1   tsp. vanilla extract
- 2   cups sweetened shredded coconut

1. Preheat oven to 350°. In a large bowl, beat the eggs, egg yolks and sugar until light and fluffy, about 5 minutes. In a small saucepan, heat milk and butter until butter melts. Combine flour and baking powder; add to egg mixture alternately with milk mixture. Beat until well mixed. Add vanilla. Fold in nuts if desired.

2. Pour into 3 greased 9-in. round baking pans. Bake until a toothpick inserted in the center comes out clean, 15-18 minutes. Cool in pans 10 minutes before removing to wire racks to cool completely.

ROASTED RED PEPPER GREEN BEANS

This oh-so-easy recipe showcases a creamy sauce with shallot and chive cheese. The toasted pine nuts add crunch, and the bright bursts of red pepper with the green beans makes a lovely holiday dish.
—Becky Ellis, Roanoke, VA

- -

TAKES: 20 min. • **MAKES:** 10 servings

- 2 **lbs. fresh green beans, trimmed**
- 1 **Tbsp. butter**
- ½ **cup pine nuts**
  Dash salt
- 1 **pkg. (5.2 oz.) shallot-chive spreadable cheese**
- 1 **jar (8 oz.) roasted sweet red peppers, drained and chopped**

1. In a pot of boiling water, cook green beans until tender, 6-8 minutes.
2. Meanwhile, in a large skillet, melt butter over medium heat. Add pine nuts; cook and stir until lightly browned, 3-4 minutes. Remove from heat; sprinkle with salt.
3. Drain beans; return to pot. Place cheese over warm beans to soften; toss to coat. Add the roasted red peppers; toss to combine. Sprinkle with pine nuts and serve immediately.
¾ CUP: *152 cal., 12g fat (5g sat. fat), 18mg chol., 341mg sod., 9g carb. (3g sugars, 3g fiber), 4g pro.*

Holiday Helper
Once the cheese is stirred into these beans, it thickens quickly as it cools off. Keep the beans warm, then add the cheese right before setting them out on the buffet.

TOFFEE TURTLE SQUARES

Here's an easy way to make turtle candy for a large group. These bars are very rich, so a little square will do ya—ideal for setting out in a bowl or on a pretty platter for party guests.
—Glenna Tooman, Boise, ID

- -

PREP: 15 min. • **BAKE:** 15 min. + cooling
MAKES: 4 dozen

- 2 **cups all-purpose flour**
- 1½ **cups packed brown sugar, divided**
- 1 **cup plus 3 Tbsp. softened butter, divided**
- 1½ **cups coarsely chopped pecans**
- 1½ **cups semisweet chocolate chips**

1. Preheat oven to 350°. Line a 13x9-in. baking pan with parchment, letting the ends extend up the sides of the pan.
2. Beat flour, 1 cup brown sugar and ½ cup of the butter until well blended (the mixture will be dry and crumbly). Firmly press into prepared pan. Sprinkle pecans over the flour mixture.
3. In a small saucepan, combine the remaining butter and remaining brown sugar. Bring to a boil over medium heat. Stirring constantly, boil until sugar is dissolved, about 1 minute. Carefully pour mixture over pecans. Bake until bubbly and edges start to brown, 15-20 minutes.
4. Remove from oven. Immediately sprinkle with chocolate chips. Let stand until chocolate begins to melt; spread evenly. Cool completely in pan on a wire rack. Lifting with parchment, remove from pan. Cut into squares.
1 BAR: *134 cal., 9g fat (4g sat. fat), 12mg chol., 39mg sod., 15g carb. (10g sugars, 1g fiber), 1g pro.*

HOLIDAY FEASTS

The heart of the holiday is when loved ones gather for the celebratory feast. Three full menus—built around surf & turf, a formal duck, or a traditional ham—are complemented by a wealth of delicious a la carte choices.

Surf & Turf

GRILLED LOBSTER TAILS

I had never made lobster at home until I tried this convenient and deliciously different grilled recipe. It turned out amazing and has left me with little reason to ever order lobster at a restaurant again.
—Katie Rush, Kansas City, MO

PREP: 15 min. + marinating • **GRILL:** 10 min.
MAKES: 6 servings

- 6 frozen lobster tails (8 to 10 oz. each), thawed
- ¾ cup olive oil
- 3 Tbsp. minced fresh chives
- 3 garlic cloves, minced
- ½ tsp. salt
- ½ tsp. pepper

1. Using kitchen scissors, cut the shell of the lobster tail and loosen the meat (see instructions at right).
2. In a small bowl, combine remaining ingredients; spoon over lobster meat. Cover and refrigerate for 20 minutes.
3. Place lobster tails, meat side up, on grill rack. Grill, covered, over medium heat for 10-12 minutes or until meat is opaque.

NOTE: *You can also prepare these under the broiler. After preparing and marinating lobster, preheat broiler. Place lobster on a foil-lined 15x10x1-in. pan. Broil 5-6 in. from heat until meat is opaque, 5-8 minutes.*

1 LOBSTER TAIL: *446 cal., 29g fat (4g sat. fat), 215mg chol., 869mg sod., 2g carb. (0 sugars, 0 fiber), 43g pro.*

HOW TO PREP A LOBSTER TAIL

- Using kitchen scissors, cut and remove a 2-in.-wide rectangle from the top shell of each lobster tail, leaving the tail fin intact. (If the shell is still tight, cut 3 to 4 lengthwise slits in the underside of the tail to loosen it slightly.)
- Pull away the shell's edges to release the meat.
- Gently pry the lobster meat loose from the shell, keeping it attached at the tail end. Lift the meat and let it lie on top of the shell.

BROWN RICE WITH ALMONDS & CRANBERRIES

I'm always looking to switch things up during the holiday season. This rice salad fits the bill, as it's on the lighter side and it uses ingredients I always have on hand.
—Joan Hallford, North Richland Hills, TX

PREP: 35 min. • **BAKE:** 1¼ hours
MAKES: 10 servings

- 3 cans (14½ oz. each) beef broth
- ¼ cup butter, cubed
- 1 large onion, chopped
- 1 cup uncooked long grain brown rice
- ½ cup bulgur
- ½ cup slivered almonds
- ½ cup dried cranberries
- ¾ cup minced fresh parsley, divided
- ¼ cup chopped green onions
- ¼ tsp. salt
- ¼ tsp. pepper

1. Preheat oven to 375°. In a large saucepan, bring broth to a simmer; reduce heat to low and keep hot.
2. In a large skillet, heat butter over medium heat. Add onion; cook and stir until tender, 3-4 minutes. Add rice, bulgur and almonds; cook and stir until rice is lightly browned and has a nutty aroma, 2-3 minutes.
3. Transfer rice mixture to a greased 13x9-in. baking dish. Stir in cranberries, ½ cup parsley, green onions, salt and pepper. Stir in the hot broth. Bake, covered, 45 minutes. Uncover and continue to cook until liquid is absorbed and rice is tender, 30-35 minutes longer.
4. Remove from oven and fluff with a fork. Cover; let stand for 5-10 minutes. Sprinkle with remaining parsley before serving.
¾ **CUP:** *207 cal., 8g fat (3g sat. fat), 12mg chol., 658mg sod., 29g carb. (7g sugars, 4g fiber), 5g pro.*
DIABETIC EXCHANGES: *2 starch, 1½ fat.*

HORSERADISH-ENCRUSTED BEEF TENDERLOIN

Wow friends and family with this tender beef in a golden horseradish crust. Roasted garlic boosts the robust flavor even more.
—Laura Bagozzi, Dublin, OH

PREP: 35 min. + cooling
BAKE: 45 min. + standing
MAKES: 8 servings

- 1 whole garlic bulb
- 1 tsp. olive oil
- ⅓ cup prepared horseradish
- ¼ tsp. salt
- ¼ tsp. dried basil
- ¼ tsp. dried thyme
- ¼ tsp. pepper
- ⅓ cup soft bread crumbs
- 1 beef tenderloin roast (3 lbs.)

1. Remove papery outer skin from garlic bulb (do not peel or separate cloves). Cut top off bulb; brush with oil. Wrap in heavy-duty foil. Bake at 425° until softened, 30-35 minutes. Cool for 10-15 minutes. Lower oven setting to 400°.
2. Squeeze the softened garlic into a small bowl; stir in the horseradish, salt, basil, thyme and pepper. Add bread crumbs; toss to coat. Spread over top of the tenderloin. Place on a rack in a large shallow roasting pan.
3. Bake until the tenderloin reaches desired doneness (for medium-rare, a thermometer should read 135°; medium, 140°; medium-well, 145°), 45-55 minutes. Let stand for 10 minutes before slicing.
5 OZ. COOKED BEEF: *268 cal., 11g fat (4g sat. fat), 75mg chol., 119mg sod., 4g carb. (1g sugars, 1g fiber), 37g pro.*
DIABETIC EXCHANGES: *5 lean meat.*

DUCHESS POTATOES

Present your potatoes in an attractive new way! Swirled towers of creamy goodness make the whole plate look more elegant.
—Taste of Home *Test Kitchen*

PREP: 35 min. • **BAKE:** 20 min.
MAKES: 6 servings

- 2 lbs. russet potatoes, peeled and quartered
- 3 large egg yolks
- 3 Tbsp. fat-free milk
- 2 Tbsp. butter
- 1 tsp. salt
- ¼ tsp. pepper
- ⅛ tsp. ground nutmeg
- 1 large egg, lightly beaten

1. Place potatoes in a large saucepan and cover with water. Bring to a boil. Reduce heat; cover and simmer 15-20 minutes or until tender. Drain. Over very low heat, stir potatoes 1-2 minutes or until steam has evaporated. Remove from heat.

2. Preheat oven to 400°. Press potatoes through a potato ricer or strainer into a large bowl. Stir in the egg yolks, milk, butter, salt, pepper and nutmeg.

3. Using a pastry bag or heavy-duty resealable plastic bag and a large star tip, pipe potatoes into 6 mounds on a parchment-lined baking sheet. Brush with beaten egg. Bake 20-25 minutes or until golden brown.

1 SERVING: *158 cal., 7g fat (3g sat. fat), 134mg chol., 437mg sod., 21g carb. (2g sugars, 1g fiber), 4g pro.*
DIABETIC EXCHANGES: *1½ fat, 1 starch.*

CREAMY CREMINI-SPINACH SOUP

This vegetable soup is the perfect accompaniment to any multicourse feast. It can even be made ahead, then warmed and quickly finished on the day of your party.
—Susan Jordan, Denver, CO

PREP: 15 min. • **COOK:** 30 min. • **MAKES:** 6 servings

- ¼ cup butter, cubed
- ½ lb. sliced baby portobello mushrooms
- 2 Tbsp. finely chopped celery
- 2 Tbsp. finely chopped onion
- 2 Tbsp. all-purpose flour
- 2½ cups vegetable stock
- 1 pkg. (6 oz.) fresh baby spinach, chopped
- 1½ cups half-and-half cream
- ½ cup sour cream
- 1½ tsp. salt
- ¼ tsp. pepper
- 1 Tbsp. minced fresh parsley

1. In a large saucepan, heat butter over medium-high heat. Add mushrooms, celery and onion; cook and stir 4-6 minutes or until tender. Stir in flour until blended; cook and stir 2-3 minutes or until lightly browned. Gradually whisk in stock. Bring to a boil. Reduce heat; simmer, covered, 10 minutes.

2. Add spinach; cook and stir 2-4 minutes or until wilted. Gradually stir in cream, sour cream, salt and pepper; heat through (do not allow to boil). Sprinkle with parsley.

¾ CUP: *219 cal., 18g fat (11g sat. fat), 55mg chol., 952mg sod., 8g carb. (4g sugars, 1g fiber), 5g pro.*

SHRIMP SALAD WITH WINE VINAIGRETTE

This veggie and seafood salad is light and versatile—you can use whatever vegetables you prefer.
—Cecilia Flowers, Nashville, NC

- -

PREP: 45 min. • **COOK:** 35 min.
MAKES: 5 servings

4	large artichokes
1	lb. fresh asparagus, trimmed
1	cup chopped fresh cauliflower
1	cup fresh broccoli florets
½	cup dry red wine
2	shallots, finely chopped, divided
¼	cup olive oil
¼	cup red wine vinegar
2	tsp. Dijon mustard
¼	tsp. salt
¼	tsp. pepper
6	cups spring mix salad greens
1	bunch watercress
20	large shrimp, peeled, deveined and cooked
1	small fennel bulb, thinly sliced, fronds reserved
½	cup julienned sweet red pepper

1. With a sharp knife, level the bottom of each artichoke and cut 1 in. from the top. With kitchen shears, snip off tips of outer leaves. Place in a steamer basket in a large saucepan over 1 in. of water. Bring to a boil; cover and steam until leaves near the center pull out easily, 20-25 minutes. Add asparagus, cauliflower and broccoli; cover and cook until crisp-tender, 3-4 minutes. Drain. With a spoon, carefully remove and discard the fuzzy centers of the artichokes. Thinly slice artichoke hearts.
2. In a small saucepan, combine wine and 1 shallot. Bring to a boil; cook until liquid is reduced to about 2 Tbsp. Whisk the oil, vinegar, wine mixture, mustard, salt, pepper and remaining shallot; set aside.
3. Place salad greens and watercress on a large platter. Top with cooked vegetables, shrimp, fennel, red pepper and artichoke slices. Drizzle with dressing and sprinkle with reserved fennel fronds.
2 CUPS: *277 cal., 12g fat (2g sat. fat), 79mg chol., 446mg sod., 27g carb. (7g sugars, 11g fiber), 19g pro.*
DIABETIC EXCHANGES: *2 starch, 2 lean meat, 2 fat.*

PEAR OLIVE OIL CAKE

This flavorful cake is a lovely, understated way to finish your grand meal. That it doesn't take a lot of time to prepare is a bonus during the busy holidays.
—Andrea Potischman, Menlo Park, CA

- -

PREP: 15 min. • **BAKE:** 55 min. + cooling
MAKES: 12 servings

1¼	cups plus 2 tsp. packed brown sugar, divided
½	cup extra virgin olive oil
3	large eggs, room temperature
2	Tbsp. 2% milk
2	tsp. vanilla extract
1	cup all-purpose flour
¾	cup almond flour
2	tsp. baking powder
	Dash salt
3	medium red pears, peeled and thinly sliced
¼	tsp. ground cinnamon
	Sweetened whipped cream, optional

1. Preheat oven to 325°. Grease a 10-in. springform pan. Place the pan on a baking sheet. In a large bowl, beat 1¼ cups brown sugar, the oil, eggs, milk and vanilla until well blended. In another bowl, whisk the flours, baking powder and salt; gradually beat into the sugar mixture.
2. Transfer batter to the prepared pan. Arrange the pears over top; sprinkle with the remaining 2 tsp. brown sugar and the cinnamon. Bake until a toothpick inserted in center comes out clean, 55-60 minutes. Cool completely in pan on a wire rack. If desired, serve with whipped cream.
1 SLICE: *294 cal., 14g fat (2g sat. fat), 47mg chol., 121mg sod., 40g carb. (28g sugars, 2g fiber), 4g pro.*

Duck Feast

DUCK WITH ORANGE HAZELNUT STUFFING

For over 60 years, this elegant entree has graced my family's holiday table. The zesty stuffing with its nutty crunch complements the slices of moist duck, while the hint of orange in the gravy sets it apart.
—Donna Smith, Fairport, NY

PREP: 30 min. • **BAKE:** 2 hours
MAKES: 8 servings

- 2   domestic ducklings (4 to 5 lbs. each)
- 2   tsp. salt
- 1   tsp. grated orange zest
- ½   tsp. seasoned salt

STUFFING
- 4   cups coarse soft bread crumbs
- 2   cups chopped peeled tart apples
- 2   cups chopped toasted hazelnuts
- 1   cup chopped celery
- ½   cup chopped onion
- ½   cup orange juice
- 2   large eggs, beaten
- ¼   cup butter, melted
- 2   to 3 Tbsp. lemon juice
- 2   tsp. grated orange zest
- 1½ tsp. grated lemon zest
- 1   tsp. seasoned salt
- ½   tsp. pepper
- ½   tsp. dried thyme
- ¼   tsp. ground nutmeg

GRAVY
- 3   Tbsp. all-purpose flour
- ¼   tsp. salt
- ⅛   tsp. pepper
- 2   cups chicken broth
- ⅓   cup orange marmalade

1. Preheat oven to 350°. Sprinkle the inside of ducks with salt; prick skin lightly several times, being careful not to cut into the meat. Rub skin with grated orange zest and sprinkle with seasoned salt; set aside. Combine the stuffing ingredients; spoon stuffing into the ducks. If desired, secure legs with baker's twine.

2. Place with breast side up on a rack in a large shallow roasting pan; pour enough water below rack to thinly cover bottom of pan. Bake duck, uncovered, until a thermometer reads 180° in the thickest part of the thigh and 165° for stuffing, 2-2½ hours, rotating pan halfway through and tenting with foil if needed to prevent overbrowning.

3. For gravy, combine 3 Tbsp. of pan drippings, the flour, salt and pepper in a saucepan; stir until smooth. Heat until bubbly, stirring constantly. Gradually add broth. Bring to a boil; cook for 1-2 minutes, stirring constantly. Add marmalade; stir until smooth.
1 SERVING: *973 cal., 73g fat (20g sat. fat), 207mg chol., 1452mg sod., 34g carb. (16g sugars, 5g fiber), 45g pro.*

MULLED MERLOT

Our delightful recipe is sure to warm up your holiday guests! Keeping it ready to serve in the slow cooker means that you can enjoy the party.
—Taste of Home *Test Kitchen*

PREP: 10 min. • **COOK:** 1 hour
MAKES: 9 servings

- 4   cinnamon sticks (3 in.)
- 4   whole cloves
- 2   bottles (750 ml each) merlot
- ½   cup sugar
- ½   cup orange juice
- ½   cup brandy
- 1   medium orange, thinly sliced

1. Place cinnamon sticks and cloves on a double thickness of cheesecloth; bring up corners of cloth and tie with string to form a bag.

2. In a 3-qt. slow cooker, combine wine, sugar, orange juice, brandy and orange slices. Add spice bag. Cover and cook on high until heated through, about 1 hour. Discard spice bag and orange slices. Serve warm; if desired, garnish with orange wedges and additional cinnamon sticks.
¾ CUP: *143 cal., 0 fat (0 sat. fat), 0 chol., 4mg sod., 15g carb. (13g sugars, 0 fiber), 0 pro.*

LEEKS AU GRATIN

Leeks are too delicious to stand only as an enhancement. Here, they're the star of a side dish, with a bit of French flair.
—Chuck Mallory, Chicago, IL

PREP: 35 min. • **BAKE:** 15 min. + standing • **MAKES:** 8 servings

- 6 medium leeks (white and pale green portion only)
- 1½ cups heavy whipping cream
- 1 tsp. kosher salt
- ½ tsp. pepper
- ½ cup grated Pecorino Romano cheese

1. Preheat oven to 375°. Cut off the root end and the tough leaf ends, then cut leeks lengthwise in half; cut halves crosswise into 3-in. pieces. Place cream, salt, pepper and leeks in a large cast-iron or other ovenproof skillet; bring to a boil over medium-high heat. Reduce heat; simmer, covered, 5 minutes. Uncover; simmer 15 minutes. Remove from heat; sprinkle with cheese.
2. Bake, uncovered, until top is golden and leeks are tender, 15-20 minutes. Let stand 5-10 minutes before serving.
½ CUP: *224 cal., 19g fat (12g sat. fat), 52mg chol., 378mg sod., 11g carb. (4g sugars, 1g fiber), 5g pro.*

Holiday Helper

Leeks are part of the onion family, although their flavor is much more subtle. Once you've cut the leeks in half, be sure to wash them thoroughly under cold water—leeks trap a considerable amount of dirt between the layers of their leaves.

GERMAN-STYLE CABBAGE & BEANS

This is one of my greatest hits for a potluck dish at church suppers. If you use some red cabbage, it will have very festive colors, light pink with green. It looks so pretty.
—Winifred Winch, Wetmore, MI

TAKES: 30 min. • **MAKES:** 6 servings

- 1 lb. fresh green beans, cut into 1½-in. pieces
- 3 bacon strips, cut into 1-in. pieces
- ½ cup cider vinegar
- ¼ cup sugar
- 3 Tbsp. chopped onion
- ½ tsp. salt
- ¼ tsp. pepper
- 3 cups shredded red cabbage

1. Place 1 in. of water in a large saucepan; add beans. Bring to a boil. Reduce heat; cover and simmer for 8-10 minutes or until crisp-tender. Drain and set aside.
2. In a large skillet, cook bacon over medium heat until crisp. Remove to paper towels; drain, reserving 2 Tbsp. drippings. Add vinegar, sugar, onion, salt and pepper to the drippings. Bring to a boil.
3. Add cabbage. Reduce heat; cover and simmer for 5 minutes. Add beans; cook 3-5 minutes longer or until heated through. Stir in bacon.
¾ CUP: *87 cal., 1g fat (0 sat. fat), 3mg chol., 284mg sod., 16g carb. (12g sugars, 3g fiber), 3g pro.*
DIABETIC EXCHANGES: *2 vegetable, ½ starch.*

TINY TIM'S PLUM PUDDING

We first read about this English tradition in A Christmas Carol. *In the story, everyone clapped for plum pudding. Since then, we've made this cakelike "pudding" every year, and it really is something to clap for!*
—Ruthanne Karel, Hudsonville, MI

PREP: 30 min. • **COOK:** 2 hours
MAKES: 12 servings (1½ cups sauce)

- ½ cup butter, softened
- ¾ cup packed brown sugar
- 3 large eggs, room temperature
- ¾ cup dry bread crumbs
- ½ cup all-purpose flour
- 1 Tbsp. grated orange zest
- 1 tsp. ground cinnamon
- ½ tsp. baking soda
- ½ tsp. ground nutmeg
- ¼ tsp. salt
- ¼ tsp. ground cloves
- 2 cans (15 oz. each) plums, drained, pitted and chopped
- 1¾ cups chopped dates
- 1 cup golden raisins
- 1 cup shredded carrots
- ½ cup dried currants

HARD SAUCE
- ½ cup butter, softened
- 3 cups confectioners' sugar
- ¼ cup dark rum or orange juice

1. Generously grease an 8-cup pudding mold, metal gelatin mold or ovenproof bowl; set aside.

2. In a large bowl, cream butter and brown sugar until light and fluffy, 5-7 minutes. Add eggs, 1 at a time, beating well after each addition. In another bowl, mix bread crumbs, flour, orange zest, cinnamon, baking soda, nutmeg, salt and cloves; gradually add to the creamed mixture. Fold in the plums, dates, raisins, carrots and currants.

3. Transfer to prepared pudding mold. Cover tightly with heavy-duty foil; tie foil with kitchen string to secure.

4. Place on a rack in a stockpot; add 3 in. of hot water to the pot. Bring water to a gentle boil; steam pudding, covered, until a toothpick inserted in center comes out clean, 2-2½ hours, adding more water to pot as needed. Remove pudding from pot; let stand 5 minutes before unmolding.

5. Meanwhile, in a bowl, beat hard sauce ingredients until smooth and creamy. Unmold pudding onto a serving plate; serve warm with sauce.

1 SLICE WITH 2 TBSP. SAUCE: *550 cal., 17g fat (10g sat. fat), 93mg chol., 292mg sod., 98g carb. (80g sugars, 5g fiber), 5g pro.*

MINTED BEET SALAD

My interest in Mediterranean food inspired this beet salad recipe. The vinegar and oil dressing with fresh mint tones down the sweetness of the beets, and the kalamata olives add a salty touch.
—Barbara Estabrook, Appleton, WI

PREP: 20 min. • **COOK:** 15 min. + chilling
MAKES: 6 servings

    5   medium fresh beets (about 2 lbs.)
    2   Tbsp. water
    2   Tbsp. champagne vinegar
        or rice vinegar
    2   Tbsp. olive oil
    ½   tsp. salt
    ¼   tsp. coarsely ground pepper
    ¼   cup pitted kalamata olives,
        quartered
    2   Tbsp. thinly sliced fresh mint,
        divided

1. Scrub beets; trim tops to 1 in. Place in a single layer in a large microwave-safe dish. Drizzle with water. Microwave, covered, on high for 14-15 minutes or until easily pierced with a fork, turning once; let stand 5 minutes.
2. When cool enough to handle, peel and cut beets into ¾-in. pieces. In a bowl, whisk vinegar, oil, salt and pepper until blended. Add olives, beets and 1 Tbsp. mint; toss to coat. Refrigerate, covered, at least 1 hour or until cold. Top with the remaining mint.
½ CUP: 123 cal., 6g fat (1g sat. fat), 0 chol., 406mg sod., 16g carb. (12g sugars, 3g fiber), 3g pro.
DIABETIC EXCHANGES: *1 vegetable, 1 fat.*

YORKSHIRE PUDDING WITH BACON & SAGE

These savory treats, topped with crumbled bacon and fresh sage, are more substantial than a souffle and more custardlike than bread—a nice change from dinner rolls. Yorkshire pudding was traditionally cooked alongside the meat to catch the drippings; these are conveniently baked in muffin tins.
—Melissa Jelinek, Apple Valley, MN

PREP: 15 min. • **BAKE:** 20 min.
MAKES: 1 dozen

    5   bacon strips, chopped
    2   Tbsp. butter, melted
    1½   cups all-purpose flour
    3   Tbsp. minced fresh sage, divided
    ½   tsp. salt
    1½   cups 2% milk
    3   large eggs

1. Preheat oven to 450°. In a large skillet, cook bacon over medium heat until crisp. Remove to paper towels with a slotted spoon; drain, reserving drippings.
2. Transfer drippings to a measuring cup; add enough melted butter to measure ¼ cup. Pour into 12 ungreased muffin cups. Place in oven until hot.
3. Meanwhile, in a small bowl, combine the flour, 2 Tbsp. sage and salt; beat in milk and eggs until smooth. Fold in two-thirds of the bacon. Divide batter among prepared muffin cups.
4. Bake for 10 minutes. Reduce heat to 350° (do not open oven door). Bake 10-12 minutes longer or until puddings are puffed and golden brown. Sprinkle with the remaining bacon and sage.
1 PUDDING: 150 cal., 8g fat (3g sat. fat), 67mg chol., 224mg sod., 14g carb. (2g sugars, 0 fiber), 5g pro.

Ham Feast

THE RIGHT HAM FOR THE FEAST

A little confused about ham? Ham comes in three styles: city, country and fresh. Country (dry-cured, uncooked) and fresh hams (uncured, uncooked) are relatively rare in stores, so odds are you'll be buying a city ham, which is usually cured by brining and sold fully cooked.

Then there's the choice between bone-in and boneless. Boneless hams are easier to carve, of course, but the bone gives the meat better flavor and texture, and once the feast is over, the bone is great for making soups and stews. Semi-boneless, where available, will offer a win-win combination of easier carving without loss of flavor. Whichever you choose, check the label and look for the ham with the least water content; the flavor and texture will be better.

Generations of meat carvers struggled with that ham bone. But in the 1940s, Harry Hoenselaar invented the spiral-slicing machine, which holds ham securely while an oscillating blade makes thin cuts into the meat around the bone. A new era in ham had begun! Spiral-cut ham is now a heat-and-serve holiday classic. Many spiral-sliced hams come pre-glazed, so read the label to make sure you're getting an unglazed ham for recipes like this one.

You can swap out the spiral-cut ham in this recipe for another style of city ham, but do check the recommended cooking time of the ham you choose—the bone will make a difference!

ROOT BEER GLAZED HAM

For a distinctly new spin on the traditional glazed ham, try this southern specialty in which the secret ingredient is root beer!
—Taste of Home *Test Kitchen*

- -

PREP: 15 min. • **BAKE:** 2½ hours
MAKES: 15 servings

- 1 bone-in fully cooked spiral-sliced ham (7 to 9 lbs.)
- 3 cups root beer
- ¾ cup packed brown sugar
- ½ cup ketchup
- ¼ cup white wine vinegar
- 3 Tbsp. steak sauce
- 1 Tbsp. Dijon mustard
- ½ tsp. crushed red pepper flakes
- ¼ tsp. ground cloves

1. Preheat oven to 325°. Place ham on a rack in a shallow roasting pan. Score the surface of the ham, making diamond shapes ½ in. deep. Bake for 2 hours.
2. In a large saucepan, combine the remaining ingredients. Bring to a boil; cook until the liquid is reduced by half, about 30 minutes.
3. Brush ham with some of the glaze; bake 30-60 minutes longer or until a thermometer reads 140°, brushing occasionally with the remaining glaze.
6 OZ. COOKED HAM: *338 cal., 5g fat (1g sat. fat), 47mg chol., 2097mg sod., 36g carb. (19g sugars, 0 fiber), 38g pro.*

BABY SWISS CHRISTMAS CHEESECAKE

This beautiful cheesecake appetizer can be refrigerated for up to 24 hours before serving, so it's the perfect make-ahead recipe for special occasions.
—Marilyn Edelman, Sabetha, KS

- -

PREP: 35 min. + cooling
BAKE: 35 min. + chilling • **MAKES:** 24 servings

- 1½ cups crushed Ritz crackers (about 36 crackers)
- 3 Tbsp. butter, melted
- 3 pkg. (8 oz. each) cream cheese, softened
- ¼ cup heavy whipping cream
- 1 Tbsp. oil from sun-dried tomatoes
- 3 large eggs, room temperature, lightly beaten
- 6 oz. baby Swiss cheese, shredded
- ½ cup oil-packed sun-dried tomatoes, patted dry and thinly sliced
- 4 green onions, chopped
  Crackers

1. Preheat oven to 375°. In a small bowl, mix cracker crumbs and butter. Press onto bottom of a greased 9-in. springform pan. Place pan on a baking sheet. Bake until golden brown, about 10 minutes. Cool on a wire rack. Reduce oven setting to 325°.
2. In a large bowl, beat the cream cheese until smooth. Beat in cream and oil. Add eggs; beat on low speed just until blended. Fold in the cheese, tomatoes and green onions. Pour over the crust. Return pan to baking sheet.
3. Bake until center is almost set, 35-40 minutes. Cool on a wire rack 10 minutes, then loosen sides from pan with a knife. Cool 1 hour longer. Refrigerate overnight, covering when completely cooled.
4. Remove rim from the pan. Serve cheesecake with crackers.
1 SLICE: *197 cal., 17g fat (9g sat. fat), 65mg chol., 176mg sod., 6g carb. (2g sugars, 0 fiber), 5g pro.*

Holiday Helper

Looking to make this a few weeks ahead of time? After baking, let the cheesecake cool, wrap it tightly with plastic wrap and freeze. To use, thaw overnight in the refrigerator.

SWEET POTATO & CHIPOTLE CASSEROLE

Sweet potato marshmallow casserole is old-school—my sweet potatoes with a streusel topping is a blockbuster! Everyone who tries it gives it a big thumbs-up.
—Diana Malach, Vancouver, WA

- -

PREP: 45 min. • **BAKE:** 35 min.
MAKES: 18 servings

- 6 lbs. sweet potatoes, peeled and cubed (about 20 cups)
- 1 to 2 chipotle peppers in adobo sauce, finely chopped
- 1 cup heavy whipping cream
- 4 large eggs, beaten
- 1 tsp. salt

TOPPING
- 1 cup packed brown sugar
- ¾ cup all-purpose flour
- ¾ tsp. ground ginger
- ¾ tsp. ground cumin
- ½ tsp. ground cloves
- ¼ tsp. cayenne pepper
- ⅓ cup cold butter
- 1½ cups chopped pecans

1. Preheat oven to 350°. Place sweet potatoes in a large stockpot; cover with water. Bring to a boil. Reduce heat; cook, uncovered, 15-20 minutes or until the potatoes are tender.

2. Drain; return potatoes to pot. Mash potatoes with chipotle pepper to reach desired consistency. Cool slightly. Stir in cream, eggs and salt. Transfer to a greased 13x9-in. baking dish (dish will be full).

3. For the topping, in a large bowl, mix brown sugar, flour and spices; cut in butter until crumbly. Stir in pecans. Sprinkle over the casserole. Bake, uncovered, for 35-40 minutes or until a thermometer reads 160°.

¾ **CUP:** *377 cal., 16g fat (6g sat. fat), 69mg chol., 204mg sod., 55g carb. (28g sugars, 6g fiber), 6g pro.*

RED PEPPER CORNMEAL SOUFFLE

I use vegetables from our garden in all my cooking. Doing so adds from-scratch flavor that just can't be beat. Dotted with parsley and red pepper, this souffle is a favorite.
—Janet Eckhoff, Woodland, CA

PREP: 20 min. • **BAKE:** 35 min.
MAKES: 10 servings

- 1 large onion, chopped
- 1 cup chopped sweet red pepper
- ¼ cup butter
- 3 cups whole milk
- ⅔ cup cornmeal
- 1 cup shredded sharp cheddar cheese
- 2 Tbsp. minced fresh parsley
- 1 tsp. salt, divided
- ½ tsp. white pepper
- 2 large egg yolks, beaten
- 7 large egg whites
- ½ tsp. cream of tartar

1. Preheat the oven to 375°. In a large saucepan, saute the onion and red pepper in butter until tender. Add milk. Bring to a boil. Gradually whisk in cornmeal; whisk constantly until thickened, about 5 minutes. Add the cheese, parsley, ½ tsp. salt and pepper. Add 1 cup of the cornmeal mixture to the egg yolks; mix well. Return all to saucepan.

2. In a large bowl, beat the egg whites, cream of tartar and remaining salt until stiff peaks form. Fold into the cornmeal mixture. Transfer to a greased 2-qt. souffle dish.

3. Bake until golden brown, 35-40 minutes.
1 SERVING: *193 cal., 11g fat (7g sat. fat), 77mg chol., 427mg sod., 14g carb. (5g sugars, 1g fiber), 9g pro.*

ONION MUSTARD BUNS

As an avid bread baker, I was thrilled to find this recipe. It makes delectably different rolls that are a hit wherever I take them. The onion and mustard flavors go so well with ham or hamburgers and are special enough to serve alongside an elaborate main dish.
—Melodie Shumaker, Elizabethtown, PA

PREP: 25 min. + rising
BAKE: 20 min. • **MAKES:** 2 dozen

- 1 pkg. (¼ oz.) active dry yeast
- ¼ cup warm water (110° to 115°)
- 2 cups warm 2% milk (110° to 115°)
- 3 Tbsp. dried minced onion
- 3 Tbsp. prepared mustard
- 2 Tbsp. canola oil
- 2 Tbsp. sugar
- 1½ tsp. salt
- 6 to 6½ cups all-purpose flour
   Optional: Beaten egg, poppy seeds, and additional dried minced onion

1. In a large bowl, dissolve the yeast in water. Add the milk, onion, mustard, oil, sugar, salt and 4 cups flour; beat until smooth. Add enough remaining flour to form a soft dough.

2. Turn out onto a floured surface; knead until dough is smooth and elastic, 6-8 minutes. Place in a greased bowl, turning once to grease top. Cover and let rise in a warm place until doubled, about 1 hour.

3. Punch the dough down; divide into 24 pieces. Flatten each piece into a 3-in. circle. Place 1 in. apart on greased baking sheets. Cover and let rise until doubled, about 45 minutes. If desired, brush with beaten egg and sprinkle with poppy seeds or dried minced onion.

4. Bake at 350° for 20-25 minutes or until golden brown. Cool on wire racks.
1 BUN: *138 cal., 2g fat (0 sat. fat), 0 chol., 181mg sod., 26g carb. (0 sugars, 0 fiber), 4g pro.*
DIABETIC EXCHANGES: *1½ starch, ½ fat.*

TRIPLE CHOCOLATE RICOTTA ICE CREAM

You're going to fall in love with this thick, rich ice cream made from ricotta cheese. It has a creamy texture that can't be beaten.
—Colleen Delawder, Herndon, VA

PREP: 20 min. • **PROCESS:** 20 min. + freezing
MAKES: 1½ qt.

- 1 carton (15 oz.) whole-milk ricotta cheese
- 1¼ cups whole milk
- 1 cup sugar
- 4 oz. cream cheese, softened
- ½ cup baking cocoa
- ½ tsp. instant espresso powder
- ¼ tsp. salt
- 1 cup heavy whipping cream
- 3½ oz. milk chocolate, melted and cooled
- 3½ oz. dark chocolate candy bar, chopped

1. Place the first 7 ingredients in a blender; cover and process until combined, about 1 minute. Add cream and cooled melted chocolate; cover and process until slightly thickened, 30 seconds.

2. Fill cylinder of ice cream maker no more than two-thirds full; freeze according to manufacturer's directions, adding dark chocolate during the last 5 minutes of processing in proportion to the amount of mixture in the ice cream maker. Refrigerate any remaining mixture until ready to freeze.

3. Transfer ice cream to freezer containers, allowing headspace for expansion. Freeze until firm, 2-4 hours.

½ CUP: 321 cal., 20g fat (12g sat. fat), 53mg chol., 141mg sod., 33g carb. (30g sugars, 2g fiber), 8g pro.

BRUSSELS SPROUTS & KALE SAUTE

This colorful side dish is filled with healthy greens. It pairs well with turkey, ham, potatoes and other holiday staples. Crispy salami—my kid's favorite ingredient—makes it over-the-top delicious.
—Jennifer McNabb, Brentwood, TN

TAKES: 30 min. • **MAKES:** 12 servings

- ¼ lb. thinly sliced hard salami, cut into ¼-in. strips
- 1½ tsp. olive oil
- 2 Tbsp. butter
- 2 lbs. fresh Brussels sprouts, thinly sliced
- 2 cups shredded fresh kale
- 1 large onion, finely chopped
- ½ tsp. kosher salt
- ⅛ tsp. cayenne pepper
- ¼ tsp. coarsely ground pepper
- 1 garlic clove, minced
- ½ cup chicken broth
- ½ cup chopped walnuts
- 1 Tbsp. balsamic vinegar

1. In a Dutch oven, cook and stir salami in oil over medium-high heat until crisp, 3-5 minutes. Remove to paper towels with a slotted spoon; reserve drippings in pan.

2. Add butter to drippings over medium-high heat. Add Brussels sprouts, kale, onion, salt, cayenne and black pepper; cook and stir until the vegetables are crisp-tender. Add the garlic; cook for 1 minute longer.

3. Stir in the broth; bring to a boil. Reduce heat; cover and cook until the Brussels sprouts are tender, 4-5 minutes. Stir in walnuts and vinegar. Top with salami strips to serve.

½ CUP: 126 cal., 9g fat (3g sat. fat), 14mg chol., 341mg sod., 9g carb. (3g sugars, 3g fiber), 6g pro.
DIABETIC EXCHANGES: *2 fat, 1 vegetable.*

More Choices for Christmas Menus

With this tantalizing selection of entrees, side dishes, breads and desserts, you can adapt any of the set feasts in this chapter to your family's individual tastes. Swap in a dish or two, or create your own completely new menu!

ROSEMARY ROASTED TURKEY

Perching a turkey on top of onions makes for a tender and flavorful bird. The onions will cook down and caramelize in the pan drippings—if you like, you can serve them alongside the carved turkey, and spread the roasted garlic on bread or rolls. The pairing of white wine and rosemary creates a mouthwatering gravy.
—Taste of Home *Test Kitchen*

PREP: 30 min. • **BAKE:** 3½ hours + standing
MAKES: 14 servings (2½ cups gravy)

- 3   whole garlic bulbs
- 6   large onions, halved
- 5   fresh rosemary sprigs
- 1   turkey (14 to 16 lbs.)
- 2   cups white wine
- 3   Tbsp. olive oil
- 1   Tbsp. minced fresh rosemary
- ¾   tsp. salt
- ¾   tsp. pepper
- ¼   cup butter, cubed
- ¼   cup all-purpose flour

1. Preheat oven to 325°. Remove papery outer skin from garlic (do not peel or separate cloves) and cut tops off the bulbs. Place garlic, onions and rosemary sprigs in a shallow roasting pan. Pat the turkey dry. Tuck wings under turkey; tie drumsticks together. Place breast side up over onion mixture. Pour wine into pan.
2. Brush the turkey with oil and sprinkle with rosemary, salt and pepper. Bake, uncovered, until a thermometer inserted in thickest part of thigh reads 170°-175°, 3½-4 hours, basting occasionally with pan drippings. Cover loosely with foil if turkey browns too quickly. Cover and let stand for 20 minutes before slicing.
3. For gravy, strain drippings into a small bowl. In a small saucepan, melt butter. Stir in flour until smooth; gradually add drippings. Bring to a boil; cook and stir until thickened, 2 minutes. Serve with the turkey.
8 OZ. COOKED TURKEY WITH 2 TBSP. GRAVY: *658 cal., 31g fat (10g sat. fat), 254mg chol., 328mg sod., 12g carb. (3g sugars, 1g fiber), 74g pro.*

MUSHROOM & SPINACH RISOTTO

I had never tried risotto until a trip to Paris a few years ago. Since then, I worked hard to create a recipe that tasted similar, and I finally succeeded with this rich and indulgent version. To serve it as a main dish, I add cubed cooked chicken.
—Sandi Ogden, Clinton, MO

PREP: 25 min. • **COOK:** 45 min.
MAKES: 8 servings

- 5¼ cups reduced-sodium chicken broth
- 2½ cups sliced fresh mushrooms
- 1   medium onion, finely chopped
- 3   Tbsp. butter
- 3   garlic cloves, minced
- ¾   cup white wine or reduced-sodium chicken broth
- 1   cup heavy whipping cream
- 1¾ cups uncooked arborio rice
- 2   Tbsp. olive oil
- 1½ cups frozen chopped spinach, thawed and squeezed dry
- ½   tsp. pepper
- ¼   tsp. salt
- 1   cup grated Parmesan cheese
  Optional: Chopped fresh parsley and shaved Parmesan cheese

1. In a large saucepan, heat broth and keep warm. In a large skillet, saute mushrooms and onion in butter until tender. Add garlic; cook 1 minute longer. Stir in wine. Bring to a boil; cook until liquid is reduced by half. Add cream; cook and stir over medium heat until slightly thickened.
2. In a large saucepan, saute rice in oil for 2-3 minutes or until lightly browned. Stir in ½ cup hot broth. Reduce heat; cook and stir for 20 minutes or until broth is absorbed.
3. Continue adding hot broth, ½ cup at a time, and stirring until all the broth has been absorbed and rice is tender but firm. Add the mushroom mixture, spinach, pepper, salt and grated Parmesan cheese; cook and stir until heated through. If desired, sprinkle with parsley and shaved Parmesan cheese. Serve immediately.
¾ CUP: *409 cal., 22g fat (12g sat. fat), 61mg chol., 667mg sod., 41g carb. (3g sugars, 2g fiber), 11g pro.*

TOMATO & CORN AU GRATIN

Corn is an essential part of any of our family get-togethers, and it's even better when paired with tomatoes in this delicious dish.
—Holly Jones, Kennesaw, GA

- -

PREP: 25 min. • **BAKE:** 30 min.
MAKES: 14 servings

- 2½ cups crushed butter-flavored crackers
- ½ cup butter, melted
- ½ cup grated Parmesan cheese
- 1 can (28 oz.) crushed tomatoes
- 1 can (15¼ oz.) whole kernel corn, drained
- 2 cups shredded sharp cheddar cheese, divided
- 1 medium green pepper, chopped
- 4 green onions, chopped
- 6 bacon strips, cooked and crumbled
- 2 Tbsp. sugar
- 1 tsp. garlic salt
- 1 tsp. pepper
- 1 cup heavy whipping cream

1. Preheat oven to 350°. In a small bowl, mix crushed crackers and butter until blended; press half of the mixture onto the bottom of a greased 13x9-in. baking dish. Stir Parmesan cheese into the remaining cracker mixture; set aside.
2. In a large bowl, mix tomatoes, corn, 1 cup cheddar cheese, green pepper, green onions, bacon, sugar, garlic salt and pepper; carefully spoon over crust. Sprinkle with the remaining cheddar cheese; drizzle with cream. Top with the reserved cracker mixture.
3. Bake, uncovered, for 30 minutes, then broil on high for 5 minutes until the top is bubbly and golden brown.
¾ **CUP:** 339 cal., 25g fat (13g sat. fat), 59mg chol., 745mg sod., 22g carb. (8g sugars, 2g fiber), 9g pro.

GOLDEN TART

This recipe is one I use every year. Squash is not my kids' favorite—except when I fix it this way. The unique presentation and blend of flavors are just right for a holiday meal.
—Theresa Gutsch, Wausau, WI

- -

PREP: 45 min. • **BAKE:** 30 min. + standing
MAKES: 9 servings

- Pastry for single-crust pie
- 1 lb. onions, thinly sliced
- 2 garlic cloves, minced
- ¼ tsp. salt
- ¼ tsp. pepper
- 2 Tbsp. canola oil
- ¼ cup heavy whipping cream
- ¼ tsp. dried thyme
- 1 small tart apple, thinly sliced
- 1 cup mashed cooked butternut squash
- 1 large egg
- 4 slices Swiss cheese, cut into ½-in. strips

1. On a lightly floured surface, roll dough to a ⅛-in.-thick square. Transfer to a greased 8-in. square baking dish. Trim to ½ in. above edge of dish; flute edges.

Line the unpricked crust with a double thickness of heavy-duty foil. Bake at 450° for 8 minutes. Remove foil; bake 5 minutes longer. Cool on a wire rack.
2. Meanwhile, in a large skillet, cook the onions, garlic, salt and pepper in oil over low heat for 25-30 minutes or until onions are golden brown, stirring frequently. Add cream and thyme. Bring to a gentle boil. Reduce heat; simmer for 2-4 minutes or until thickened. Cool slightly.
3. Pour into crust. Top with apple slices. In a small bowl, combine squash and egg; spread over top.
4. Cover and bake at 375° for 15 minutes. Uncover; arrange cheese strips in a lattice pattern over the top. Bake 15-20 minutes longer or until apple is tender. Let stand for 10 minutes before cutting.
1 PIECE: 251 cal., 16g fat (7g sat. fat), 49mg chol., 200mg sod., 22g carb. (6g sugars, 2g fiber), 6g pro.
PASTRY FOR SINGLE-CRUST PIE (9 IN.): Combine 1¼ cups all-purpose flour and ¼ tsp. salt; cut in ½ cup cold butter until crumbly. Gradually add 3-5 Tbsp. ice water, tossing with a fork until dough holds together when pressed. Cover and refrigerate 1 hour.

PUMPKIN WITH WALNUTS & BLUE CHEESE

Don't hold off on serving pumpkin, thinking it can be only the finale to dinner. Bring it to the forefront with this distinctive and lovely side dish that is sure to garner you lots of recipe requests.
—Laurie Bock, Lynden, WA

PREP: 20 min. • **BAKE:** 25 min. • **MAKES:** 12 servings

- 5   lbs. pie pumpkin, seeded, peeled and cut into 1-in. cubes
- ¼   cup olive oil, divided
- 2   tsp. salt
- 1   tsp. pepper
- 2   medium onions, chopped
- ⅔   cup chopped walnuts
- ⅔   cup crumbled blue cheese
- 20 fresh sage leaves, thinly sliced

1. Preheat oven to 375°. Place pumpkin in a greased 15x1x1-in. baking pan; drizzle with 2 Tbsp. oil and sprinkle with salt and pepper. Bake for 30-35 minutes or until tender.
2. In a large skillet, saute onions in the remaining oil until tender. Add walnuts; cook 3-5 minutes longer or until toasted.
3. Place pumpkin on a serving platter. Top with the onion mixture. Sprinkle with blue cheese and sage.
1 SERVING: *154 cal., 11g fat (2g sat. fat), 6mg chol., 500mg sod., 12g carb. (4g sugars, 2g fiber), 4g pro.*
DIABETIC EXCHANGES: *2 fat, 1 starch.*

POMEGRANATE PERSIMMON SALAD

To bring some sunshine to the table, I toss up a bright salad of persimmons and pomegranate seeds, dressed with a puckery vinaigrette. When persimmons are hard to find, I use plums instead.
—Linda Tambunan, Dublin, CA

TAKES: 15 min. • **MAKES:** 12 servings

- ½   cup olive oil
- ½   cup maple syrup
- ¼   cup rice vinegar
- 2   Tbsp. Dijon mustard
- ¼   tsp. salt
- ¼   tsp. pepper

SALAD
- 3   ripe Fuyu persimmons or 3 plums, sliced
- 2   pkg. (10 oz. each) baby kale salad blend
- 1   cup pomegranate seeds

1. Place the first 6 ingredients in a jar with a lid; shake well. Refrigerate until serving.
2. To serve, shake vinaigrette and toss ½ cup with persimmons. Toss the remaining vinaigrette with salad blend. Top with persimmons and pomegranate seeds.
1½ CUPS: *175 cal., 9g fat (2g sat. fat), 0 chol., 220mg sod., 23g carb. (17g sugars, 3g fiber), 2g pro.*
DIABETIC EXCHANGES: *2 vegetable, 2 fat, ½ starch, ½ fruit.*

CARDAMOM BRAIDS

This is an old recipe that I've been making for years. It makes a lovely holiday bread or a not-too-sweet alternative to breakfast pastries. Slices are wonderful for dunking in a cup of coffee!
—Walter Dust, Rapid City, MI

- -

PREP: 25 min. + rising • **BAKE:** 25 min.
MAKES: 2 loaves (16 slices each)

- 1   pkg. (¼ oz.) active dry yeast
- 1½ cups warm whole milk (110° to 115°), divided
- 1   cup sugar, divided
- 3   large eggs yolks, room temperature, lightly beaten
- ½   cup butter, softened
- 1   Tbsp. ground cardamom
- ½   tsp. salt
- 5   to 6 cups all-purpose flour
- 2   Tbsp. whole milk

1. In a large bowl, dissolve yeast in ½ cup warm milk. Add ¾ cup sugar, egg yolks, butter, cardamom, salt, 3 cups flour and the remaining warm milk; beat until smooth. Stir in enough remaining flour to form a soft dough.
2. Turn onto a floured surface; knead until smooth and elastic, 6-8 minutes. Place in a greased bowl, turning once to grease top. Cover and let rise in a warm place until doubled, about 1¼ hours.
3. Punch dough down; divide into 6 pieces. Shape each piece into a 16-in. rope. Place 3 ropes on a greased baking sheet; braid. Pinch ends firmly and tuck under. Repeat with the remaining 3 ropes on another baking sheet. Cover and let rise until doubled, about 45 minutes.
4. Brush braids with milk and sprinkle with the remaining sugar. Bake at 350° until golden brown, 25-30 minutes. Remove to wire racks to cool.
1 SLICE: *135 cal., 4g fat (2g sat. fat), 29mg chol., 73mg sod., 22g carb. (7g sugars, 1g fiber), 3g pro.*

MAPLE CHIPOTLE HASSELBACK BUTTERNUT SQUASH

Butternut squash makes the perfect holiday side dish, especially when it's dressed up like this. The thin slits cut into each squash half allow the butter, maple syrup, brown sugar and ground chipotle mixture to reach all the nooks and crannies. This is one side that everyone at your holiday table will be excited to gobble up!
—Colleen Delawder, Herndon, VA

- -

PREP: 15 min. • **BAKE:** 50 min. + cooling
MAKES: 6 servings

- 1   medium butternut squash (about 4 lbs.)
- 2   Tbsp. olive oil
- ¼   tsp. finely ground sea salt
- 2   Tbsp. butter, melted
- 2   Tbsp. maple syrup
- 1   Tbsp. light brown sugar
- ¼   tsp. ground chipotle pepper
     Fried sage leaves, optional

1. Preheat oven to 400°. Peel squash. Cut lengthwise in half; remove and discard seeds. Place squash cut side down in a 13x9-in. baking pan or shallow roasting pan. Drizzle with oil and sprinkle with salt. Bake, uncovered, 20 minutes. Let cool 15 minutes.
2. Cut squash crosswise into ⅛-in. slices, leaving them intact at the bottom. Combine the remaining ingredients; brush over the squash. Bake until tender, 30-40 minutes longer. If desired, top with fried sage leaves.
1 SERVING: *236 cal., 9g fat (3g sat. fat), 10mg chol., 127mg sod., 42g carb. (14g sugars, 10g fiber), 3g pro.*

Holiday Helper
Fried sage leaves are quick and easy to make, and have a delightfully crispy texture. Fry fresh sage leaves in melted butter over medium-high heat, turning once, until leaves are darkened and crisp; drain on a paper towel and sprinkle with salt.

THE BEST CHEESY SCALLOPED POTATOES

For my tried-and-true scalloped potatoes, I slice them extra thin and toss them in a rich cheese sauce. To make them the best ever, I sprinkle homemade bread crumbs on top, which get nice and crispy in the oven.
—Aria Thornton, Milwaukee, WI

- -

PREP: 40 min. • **BAKE:** 1¼ hours + standing
MAKES: 10 servings

4	Tbsp. butter
½	cup chopped onion
1	tsp. ground mustard
1	tsp. salt
½	tsp. coarsely ground pepper
2	garlic cloves, minced
¼	cup all-purpose flour
2	cups whole milk
3	blocks (4 oz. each) sharp cheddar cheese, shredded and divided
1	block (4 oz.) Monterey Jack cheese, shredded
3	lbs. russet potatoes, peeled and thinly sliced
¾	cup dry bread crumbs
	Minced chives, optional

1. Preheat oven to 350°. In a Dutch oven, melt butter over medium heat. Add onion, mustard, salt and pepper; cook until onion is tender, 6-8 minutes. Add garlic; cook until fragrant. Whisk in flour; continue whisking 3-5 minutes.

2. Whisk in milk; bring to a boil. Reduce heat; simmer, uncovered, until thickened slightly, 8-10 minutes. Gradually stir in 2 cups shredded cheddar cheese; stir in the Monterey Jack cheese. Add potatoes and toss to coat. Simmer for 10 minutes, stirring frequently.

3. Transfer potato mixture to a greased 13x9-in. baking dish. Top with remaining cheddar cheese. Bake, uncovered, for 1 hour. Top with bread crumbs; return to oven until potatoes are tender, 10-15 minutes. Let stand 15 minutes before serving. If desired, sprinkle with chives.

NOTE: *To make dry bread crumbs, tear 3-4 slices of day-old hearty bread into pieces. Pulse, covered, in a food processor or blender until coarse crumbs form. Spread in a single layer over a 15x10x1-in. baking pan. Bake at 350° until lightly browned, 15-20 minutes. Remove from pan to cool until ready for use.*

FREEZE OPTION: *Simmer potatoes in cheese sauce an additional 5-10 minutes, stirring frequently before transferring to greased baking dish. Cool; cover and freeze. To use, partially thaw in the refrigerator overnight. Remove from refrigerator 30 minutes before baking. Bake as directed, increasing initial time to 1¼ hours before topping with bread crumbs.*

SLOW-COOKER OPTION: *Simmer potatoes in cheese sauce on stovetop an additional 5-10 minutes, stirring frequently, then transfer mixture to a greased 6-qt. slow cooker. Place 4 layers of paper towels under the lid; cover and cook on high for 2 hours. Remove lid and paper towels; sprinkle potatoes with bread crumbs. Let stand 15 minutes. If desired, sprinkle with chives.*
¾ CUP: *378 cal., 22g fat (13g sat. fat), 61mg chol., 646mg sod., 31g carb. (5g sugars, 2g fiber), 15g pro.*

Holiday Helper
Russets are the best potatoes for this recipe; their high starch content keeps the cheese sauce smooth. Use a mandoline to get evenly sliced potatoes—the ideal thickness is ⅛ to 3/16 in.

MOLDED CRANBERRY-ORANGE SALAD

I take this dish to potlucks during the holidays, and people always ooh and aah at how beautiful it is. Feel free to top with whipped cream for added appeal.
—Carol Mead, Los Alamos, NM

- -

PREP: 20 min. + chilling • **MAKES:** 12 servings

- 1 tsp. unflavored gelatin
- 1 Tbsp. plus 1 cup cold water, divided
- 1 cup boiling water
- 1 pkg. (3 oz.) raspberry gelatin
- 3 cups (12 oz.) fresh or thawed frozen cranberries, divided
- 2 medium apples, cut into wedges
- 1 medium navel orange, peeled
- 1 cup sugar
- ½ cup chopped walnuts
- ½ cup finely chopped celery

1. Sprinkle unflavored gelatin over 1 Tbsp. cold water; let stand 1 minute. Add boiling water and raspberry gelatin; stir until gelatin is dissolved, about 2 minutes. Stir in remaining cold water. Refrigerate until thickened, about 45 minutes.

2. Pulse 2⅓ cups cranberries, apples and the orange in a food processor until chopped. Transfer to a small bowl; stir in sugar. Stir fruit mixture into thickened gelatin. Fold in walnuts, celery and the remaining whole cranberries.

3. Coat a 10-in. fluted tube pan, an 8-cup ring mold or two 4-cup molds with cooking spray; pour in gelatin mixture. Cover and refrigerate overnight or until firm. Unmold onto a platter.

½ CUP: 154 cal., 3g fat (0 sat. fat), 0 chol., 21mg sod., 32g carb. (28g sugars, 2g fiber), 2g pro.

SPICED EGGNOG PUMPKIN PIE

With its 10-minute prep time and lovely blend of mild eggnog flavor and spices, this is a dream dessert for a busy hostess! It's a staple in our house for Thanksgiving and Christmas. In fact, my grown kids request it whenever they come to visit.
—Patti Leake, Columbia, MO

- -

PREP: 10 min. • **BAKE:** 45 min. + cooling
MAKES: 8 servings

  Pastry for single-crust pie (9 in.)
- 1 can (15 oz.) solid-pack pumpkin
- 1¼ cups eggnog
- ¾ cup sugar
- 2 large eggs
- 1 tsp. ground cinnamon
- ½ tsp. salt
- ½ tsp. ground ginger
- ¼ tsp. ground cloves
- ¼ tsp. ground nutmeg

1. Roll out dough to fit a 9-in. pie plate. Transfer crust to pie plate. Trim crust to ½ in. beyond edge of plate; flute edges.

2. Place the remaining ingredients in a large bowl; beat just until smooth. Pour into crust.

3. Bake at 425° for 15 minutes. Reduce heat to 350°; bake 30-35 minutes longer or until a knife inserted in the center comes out clean. (Cover edges with foil during the last 15 minutes to prevent overbrowning if necessary.) Cool completely on a wire rack. Store in the refrigerator.

1 SLICE: *317 cal., 15g fat (9g sat. fat), 100mg chol., 345mg sod., 42g carb. (24g sugars, 2g fiber), 6g pro.*

PASTRY FOR SINGLE-CRUST PIE (9 IN.):
Combine 1¼ cups all-purpose flour and ¼ tsp. salt; cut in ½ cup cold butter until crumbly. Gradually add 3-5 Tbsp. ice water, tossing with a fork until dough holds together when pressed. Cover and refrigerate 1 hour.

TIMESAVING SIDES

When preparing a holiday meal, the main course tends to grab the attention—but these side dishes more than hold their own, and none take over 20 minutes of prep time!

AIRY & BRIGHT

Even if you're dealing with a packed holiday schedule, your decorations can still be absolute standouts without taking a whole lot of time. Start with a purchased evergreen wreath and weave a couple of air plants into the greens for an unexpected burst of winter white. Air plants have a remarkably long shelf life and don't require soil, which makes them ideal for holiday decorating. The wreath above has two air plants (*Tillandsia tectorum*, to be specific) woven in alongside blue cedar branches and sprigs of berries. You can find air plants at garden stores, many home supply stores, and online.

SCALLOPED CRANBERRIES

This warm cranberry casserole is a nice substitute for traditional cranberry relish. It's been a staple on my holiday table ever since my aunt gave me the recipe many years ago.
—Ellan Streett, Clear Spring, MD

PREP: 20 min. • **BAKE:** 25 min. • **MAKES:** 6 servings

- 4 cups fresh or frozen cranberries (about 1 lb.)
- 1¼ cups sugar
- 1¼ cups water
- 4½ cups cubed bread (about 5 slices)
- ½ cup raisins
- ⅓ cup butter, melted
- 2 tsp. grated lemon zest

1. In a large saucepan, combine the cranberries, sugar and water. Cook over medium heat for 12-15 minutes or until berries pop. Remove from the heat; stir in the remaining ingredients.
2. Transfer to a greased 1½-qt. baking dish. Bake, uncovered, at 350° for 25-30 minutes or until heated through.
½ **CUP:** *388 cal., 11g fat (6g sat. fat), 27mg chol., 246mg sod., 72g carb. (55g sugars, 4g fiber), 3g pro.*

MASHED PEPPERY TURNIPS

I created this recipe as an attempt to use up a great turnip harvest from our garden, and to lighten up one of our favorite dishes. By using turnips in place of potatoes, I made a low-carb side. Now we rarely serve plain mashed potatoes!
—*Courtney Stultz, Weir, KS*

TAKES: 30 min. • **MAKES:** 4 servings

4 medium turnips (about 1 lb.), peeled and cut into 1¼-in. pieces
1 large potato (about ¾ lb.), peeled and cut into 1¼-in. pieces
2 Tbsp. reduced-fat cream cheese
1 Tbsp. butter
1 Tbsp. minced fresh parsley
1 tsp. sea salt
½ tsp. garlic powder
¼ tsp. pepper
⅛ tsp. chili powder
⅛ tsp. ground chipotle pepper

1. Place turnips, potato and enough water to cover in a large saucepan; bring to a boil. Reduce heat; cook, uncovered, until tender, 15-20 minutes. Drain; return to pan.
2. Mash vegetables to desired consistency. Stir in the remaining ingredients.
¾ CUP: *140 cal., 5g fat (3g sat. fat), 13mg chol., 608mg sod., 23g carb. (5g sugars, 3g fiber), 3g pro.*
DIABETIC EXCHANGES: *1½ starch, 1 fat.*

ONION PIE

My grandmother and mother always make this pie during the holidays but it's good anytime. You can serve this savory side dish with most any meat or main course. We think it's especially good with roast beef.
—*Mary West, Marstons Mills, MA*

PREP: 15 min. • **BAKE:** 35 min. • **MAKES:** 8 servings

6 to 8 medium onions, thinly sliced
2 Tbsp. canola oil
6 large eggs
1 cup soft bread crumbs
½ cup grated Parmesan cheese
½ cup minced fresh parsley

1. In a large skillet, saute onions in oil until soft but not browned; drain well. In a large bowl, whisk eggs. Stir in the bread crumbs, cheese, parsley and onions.
2. Place in a greased 10-in. pie plate. Bake at 350° until a knife inserted in the center comes out clean, 35-40 minutes.
1 PIECE: *170 cal., 9g fat (3g sat. fat), 163mg chol., 176mg sod., 14g carb. (8g sugars, 3g fiber), 9g pro.*

MOM'S SWEET POTATO BAKE

Mom loves sweet potatoes and fixed this creamy, comforting casserole often. With its nutty topping, this yummy side dish could almost serve as a dessert!
—Sandi Pichon, Memphis, TN

PREP: 10 min. • **BAKE:** 45 min.
MAKES: 8 servings

3	cups cold mashed sweet potatoes (prepared without milk or butter)
1	cup sugar
3	large eggs
½	cup 2% milk
¼	cup butter, softened
1	tsp. salt
1	tsp. vanilla extract

TOPPING

½	cup packed brown sugar
½	cup chopped pecans
¼	cup all-purpose flour
2	Tbsp. cold butter

1. Preheat oven to 325°. In a large bowl, beat the sweet potatoes, sugar, eggs, milk, butter, salt and vanilla until smooth. Transfer to a greased 2-qt. baking dish.
2. In a small bowl, combine brown sugar, pecans and flour; cut in the butter until crumbly. Sprinkle over the potato mixture. Bake, uncovered, for 45-50 minutes or until a thermometer reads 160°.
½ CUP: *417 cal., 16g fat (7g sat. fat), 94mg chol., 435mg sod., 65g carb. (47g sugars, 4g fiber), 6g pro.*

Holiday Helper
To save time on your feast day, mash the sweet potatoes ahead of time and keep them in the refrigerator. Assembling the casserole takes only 10 minutes!

CAPE COD CORN PUDDING

This delicious dish of corn baked with cheddar and ricotta is a family recipe. Don't skip the fresh basil—it adds a hint of sweet flavor reminiscent of mint and anise.
—Melinda Messer, Benson, NC

PREP: 20 min. • **BAKE:** 30 min. + standing
MAKES: 8 servings

¼	cup butter, cubed
5	cups frozen corn (about 24 oz.)
1	medium onion, finely chopped
4	large eggs, lightly beaten
2	cups whole milk
1	cup whole-milk ricotta cheese
½	cup cornmeal
1	Tbsp. sugar
1	tsp. salt
¾	tsp. pepper
1½	cups shredded cheddar cheese, divided
2	Tbsp. chopped fresh basil, optional

1. Preheat oven to 375°. In a 6-qt. stockpot, heat butter over medium-high heat. Add corn and onion; cook and stir until onion is crisp-tender, 6-8 minutes. Remove from heat.
2. In a large bowl, whisk the eggs, milk, ricotta cheese, cornmeal, sugar, salt and pepper. Stir in ¾ cup cheddar cheese, the corn mixture and, if desired, basil.
3. Transfer mixture to a greased 11x7-in. baking dish. Sprinkle with the remaining cheddar cheese. Bake, uncovered, until set, 30-35 minutes. Let stand 10 minutes before serving.
1 SERVING: *378 cal., 21g fat (12g sat. fat), 148mg chol., 582mg sod., 34g carb. (9g sugars, 2g fiber), 17g pro.*

ROASTED BEET WEDGES

This recipe makes ordinary beets taste tender and delicious with just a few simple ingredients. You can also make the beets a day ahead, then slice them and serve them cold in a salad.
—Wendy Stenman, Germantown, WI

PREP: 15 min. • **BAKE:** 1 hour • **MAKES:** 4 servings

- 1 lb. medium fresh beets, peeled
- 4 tsp. olive oil
- ½ tsp. kosher salt
- 3 to 5 fresh rosemary sprigs

1. Preheat oven to 400°. Cut each beet into 5 wedges; place in a shallow dish. Add olive oil and salt; toss gently to coat.
2. Place a 12-in.-long piece of heavy-duty foil in a 15x10x1-in. baking pan. Arrange beets on foil; top with rosemary. Fold foil around beets and seal tightly.
3. Bake until tender, about 1 hour. Open foil carefully to allow steam to escape. Discard rosemary sprigs.
3 WEDGES: *92 cal., 5g fat (1g sat. fat), 0 chol., 328mg sod., 12g carb. (9g sugars, 3g fiber), 2g pro.*
DIABETIC EXCHANGES: *1 vegetable, 1 fat.*

Holiday Helper
For a milder herb flavor, try using fresh thyme instead of rosemary.

SPINACH SOUFFLE SIDE DISH

You just can't make an easier, more delicious side dish than this. It's great with beef, pork and lamb, and I especially like serving it for a festive meal like Christmas or New Year's Eve.
—Bette Duffy, Kenmore, WA

PREP: 20 min. • **BAKE:** 35 min. • **MAKES:** 6 servings

- 2 pkg. (10 oz. each) frozen chopped spinach, thawed and squeezed dry
- 1 pkg. (8 oz.) cream cheese, cubed
- 1½ cups shredded Monterey Jack cheese
- 4 large eggs, lightly beaten
- ¼ cup butter, melted
- 1 garlic clove, minced
- ½ tsp. salt

Preheat oven to 350°. In a large bowl, combine all ingredients. Transfer to a greased 1½-qt. baking dish. Bake until edges are lightly browned, 35-40 minutes.
½ CUP: *375 cal., 33g fat (20g sat. fat), 228mg chol., 630mg sod., 5g carb. (0 sugars, 3g fiber), 17g pro.*

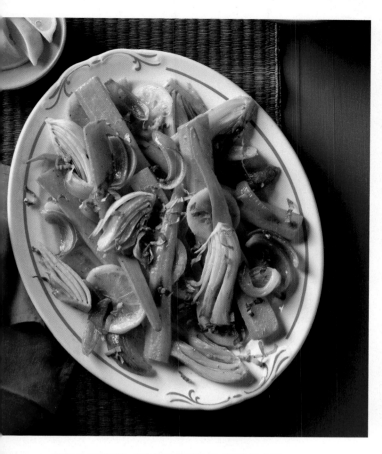

CHIMICHURRI MONKEY BREAD

The herby goodness of my favorite sauce shines in this bread recipe that comes together quickly thanks to refrigerated biscuits. Serve as an appetizer with a tasty dipping sauce, or alongside an entree.
—Eden Dranger, Los Angeles, CA

PREP: 20 min. • **BAKE:** 20 min. • **MAKES:** 12 servings

- ¼ cup minced fresh parsley
- ¼ cup olive oil
- 2 Tbsp. minced fresh oregano
- 1 Tbsp. white wine vinegar
- 2 garlic cloves, minced
- ¾ tsp. kosher salt
- ¼ tsp. ground cumin
- ¼ tsp. pepper
- ⅛ tsp. crushed red pepper flakes
- 2 tubes (12 oz. each) refrigerated buttermilk biscuits

1. Preheat oven to 375°. In a shallow bowl, combine the first 9 ingredients. Cut each biscuit in half and shape into a ball. Roll in herb mixture.
2. Place biscuit pieces in a greased 10-in. fluted tube pan. Bake 18-22 minutes or until golden brown. Cool for 10 minutes before inverting onto a serving plate.
1 SERVING: *209 cal., 11g fat (3g sat. fat), 0 chol., 588mg sod., 25g carb. (3g sugars, 0 fiber), 3g pro.*

ROASTED CARROTS & FENNEL

This addictive combo is a fresh take on one of my mother's beloved wintertime dishes. I usually add more carrots—as many as the pans will hold!
—Lily Julow, Lawrenceville, GA

PREP: 15 min. • **BAKE:** 40 min. • **MAKES:** 8 servings

- 2½ lbs. medium carrots, peeled and cut in half lengthwise
- 1 large fennel bulb, cut into ½-in. wedges
- 1 large red onion, cut into ½-in. wedges
- 1 medium lemon, thinly sliced
- ¼ cup olive oil
- 2 tsp. ground coriander
- 1 tsp. ground cumin
- ½ tsp. salt
- ¼ tsp. pepper
  Thinly sliced fresh basil leaves

1. Preheat oven to 375°. In a large bowl, combine the carrots, fennel, onion and lemon. Mix oil, coriander, cumin, salt and pepper; drizzle over the vegetable mixture and toss to coat. Transfer to 2 foil-lined 15x10x1-in. baking pans.
2. Roast for 40-50 minutes or until the vegetables are tender, stirring occasionally. Sprinkle with basil.
1 SERVING: *139 cal., 7g fat (1g sat. fat), 0 chol., 262mg sod., 18g carb. (9g sugars, 6g fiber), 2g pro.*
DIABETIC EXCHANGES: *2 vegetable, 1½ fat.*

ASPARAGUS & GREEN BEANS WITH TARRAGON LEMON SAUCE

Spicy tarragon balances tangy lemon in the creamy sauce covering colorful asparagus and green beans. If you like, you can serve this as an appetizer—just offer up the sauce on the side as a dip.
—Bonnie Hawkins, Elkhorn, WI

TAKES: 20 min. • **MAKES:** 10 servings

- 1　lb. fresh asparagus, trimmed
- 1　lb. fresh green beans, trimmed
- 1　cup mayonnaise
- ¼　cup lemon juice
- 1　shallot, finely chopped
- 2　Tbsp. minced fresh tarragon or 2 tsp. dried tarragon
- 2　Tbsp. minced fresh parsley or 2 tsp. dried parsley flakes
- 2　tsp. grated lemon zest
　　Dash pepper

1. Place 1 in. of water in a Dutch oven; add asparagus and beans. Bring to a boil. Reduce heat; cover and simmer for 3-5 minutes or until crisp-tender.
2. Meanwhile, in a small bowl, combine the remaining ingredients. Drain the vegetables; transfer to a serving platter. Drizzle with the sauce.
1 SERVING: *183 cal., 18g fat (2g sat. fat), 8mg chol., 126mg sod., 5g carb. (2g sugars, 2g fiber), 1g pro.*

CREAMY POLENTA WITH BALSAMIC GLAZE

This delicious and easy side dish goes incredibly well with braised meat. It makes any meal feel a little more elevated.
—Sarah Vasques, Milford, NH

PREP: 15 min. • **COOK:** 2 hours
MAKES: 4 servings

- 4　Tbsp. butter, divided
- 1½　cups half-and-half cream, divided
- 1　cup 2% milk
- ¼　tsp. salt
- ⅓　cup cornmeal
- 1　cup balsamic vinegar
- 1　Tbsp. sugar
- ½　cup grated Parmesan cheese

1. In a medium saucepan, melt 2 Tbsp. butter over medium heat. Add 1 cup cream, milk and salt. Bring to a low simmer. Gradually whisk in cornmeal. Cook and stir for 3 minutes.
2. Pour the polenta into a 3-qt. slow cooker coated with cooking spray. Cook, covered, on low for 2 hours, stirring every 30 minutes. Meanwhile, in a small saucepan, bring the vinegar and sugar to a boil. Reduce heat; simmer, uncovered, until reduced to ⅓ cup.
3. Just before serving, stir cheese and the remaining cream and butter into the polenta, and drizzle with balsamic glaze.
½ CUP POLENTA WITH 1 TBSP. GLAZE: *415 cal., 25g fat (16g sat. fat), 89mg chol., 494mg sod., 37g carb. (25g sugars, 1g fiber), 9g pro.*

Holiday Helper
Don't try to speed this recipe along by setting your slow cooker on high, or the outer edge is likely to get browned. This recipe makes a generous amount of glaze. If you have any left over, save it to drizzle on pork chops or roasted chicken.

GRANDMA'S POULTRY DRESSING

Every family seems to have its own favorite dressing recipe that becomes their standard, and this is ours. It came from Grandma, who passed it down to my mother. Now our children have carried it on in their kitchens.
—Norma Howland, Joliet, IL

PREP: 20 min. • **BAKE:** 40 min. • **MAKES:** 6 cups

- 1 lb. bulk pork sausage
- 1 cup 2% milk
- 7 cups coarse dry bread crumbs
- 1 cup diced celery
- 2 large eggs
- 2 to 3 Tbsp. minced fresh parsley
- 2 Tbsp. diced onion
- ½ tsp. salt or salt to taste

1. Preheat oven to 350°. In a large skillet, brown sausage. Drain, discarding drippings. Meanwhile, in a small saucepan, heat milk over medium heat until bubbles form around the sides of the pan. In a large bowl, combine the sausage, milk and remaining ingredients.

2. Transfer to a greased 2-qt. baking dish. Cover and bake until lightly browned, about 40 minutes.

½ **CUP:** *352 cal., 12g fat (4g sat. fat), 52mg chol., 826mg sod., 48g carb. (3g sugars, 2g fiber), 12g pro.*

SWISS CHARD WITH ONIONS & GARLIC

This tasty and colorful dish is a favorite with my boys—they ask for it often. Sometimes I'll even serve it over pasta as an entire meal!
—Rebekah Chappel, Portales, NM

TAKES: 25 min. • **MAKES:** 6 servings

- 2 Tbsp. olive oil
- 2 medium onions, chopped
- 6 garlic cloves, sliced
- ½ cup white balsamic vinegar
- 2 bunches Swiss chard, coarsely chopped (about 16 cups)
- ½ cup walnut halves, toasted
- ¼ tsp. salt
- ¼ tsp. pepper

1. In a 6-qt. stockpot, heat oil over medium-high heat. Add the onions; cook and stir until tender. Add garlic; cook for 1 minute longer.

2. Add vinegar, stirring to loosen any browned bits from pot. Add the remaining ingredients; cook 4-6 minutes or until the chard is tender, stirring occasionally.

⅔ **CUP:** *159 cal., 10g fat (1g sat. fat), 0 chol., 381mg sod., 16g carb. (9g sugars, 3g fiber), 4g pro.*
DIABETIC EXCHANGES: *2 fat, 1 starch.*

ACORN SQUASH SLICES

This recipe gets sweet maple flavor from syrup and an appealing nuttiness from pecans. It's easy, too, because you don't have to peel the squash.

—*Richard Lamb, Williamsburg, IN*

PREP: 15 min. • **BAKE:** 40 min. • **MAKES:** 6 servings

> 2   **medium acorn squash (about 1½ lbs. each)**
> ½   **tsp. salt**
> ¾   **cup maple syrup**
> 2   **Tbsp. butter, melted**
> ⅓   **cup chopped pecans, optional**

1. Preheat oven to 350°. Cut squash in half lengthwise; remove and discard seeds and membrane. Cut each half widthwise into ½-in. slices; discard ends.

2. Place squash slices in a greased 13x9-in. baking dish. Sprinkle with salt. Combine syrup and butter; pour over squash. Sprinkle with pecans if desired. Cover and bake for 40-45 minutes or until tender.

3 SLICES: *170 cal., 7g fat (0 sat. fat), 0 chol., 98mg sod., 31g carb. (0 sugars, 0 fiber), 2g pro.*
DIABETIC EXCHANGES: *1 starch, 1 fruit, 1 fat.*

SUPER SIMPLE SCALLOPED POTATOES

I've made many types of scalloped potatoes but I always come back to this rich, creamy, foolproof recipe. The dish gets scraped clean every time I make it.

—*Kallee Krong-McCreery, Escondido, CA*

PREP: 20 min. • **BAKE:** 45 min. + standing • **MAKES:** 10 servings

> 3   **cups heavy whipping cream**
> 1½   **tsp. salt**
> ½   **tsp. pepper**
> 1   **tsp. minced fresh thyme, optional**
> 3   **lbs. russet potatoes, thinly sliced (about 10 cups)**

1. Preheat oven to 350°. In a large bowl, combine cream, salt, pepper and, if desired, thyme. Arrange potatoes in a greased 13x9-in. baking dish. Pour cream mixture over top.

2. Bake, uncovered, until the potatoes are tender and the top is lightly browned, 45-55 minutes. Let stand 10 minutes before serving.

¾ CUP: *353 cal., 27g fat (17g sat. fat), 99mg chol., 390mg sod., 26g carb. (3g sugars, 3g fiber), 4g pro.*

LEMON POPOVERS WITH PECAN HONEY BUTTER

My mom shared this recipe with me many years ago. We love the delicate lemon flavor with the pecan honey butter. The popovers are a lovely addition to dinner or breakfast. Make the butter ahead of time if you like.
—Joan Hallford, N. Richland Hills, TX

PREP: 10 min. • **BAKE:** 25 min.
MAKES: 6 servings

- 2 large eggs, room temperature
- 1 cup 2% milk
- 1 cup all-purpose flour
- ½ tsp. salt
- 5 Tbsp. finely chopped toasted pecans, divided
- ¾ tsp. grated lemon zest
- 2 tsp. lemon juice
- 6 Tbsp. butter, softened
- 6 Tbsp. honey

1. Preheat oven to 450°. In a large bowl, whisk eggs and milk until blended. Whisk in flour and salt just until smooth (do not overbeat). Stir in 3 Tbsp. pecans, the lemon zest and juice.
2. Generously grease a 6-cup popover pan with nonstick spray; fill cups half full with batter. Bake for 15 minutes. Reduce oven setting to 350° (do not open oven door). Bake until deep golden brown, 10-15 minutes longer (do not underbake).
3. Meanwhile, combine butter, honey and remaining 2 Tbsp. pecans. Immediately remove popovers from pan to a wire rack. Pierce side of each popover with a sharp knife to let the steam escape. Serve immediately with pecan honey butter.
1 POPOVER WITH ABOUT 2 TBSP. HONEY BUTTER: *325 cal., 18g fat (9g sat. fat), 96mg chol., 332mg sod., 36g carb. (20g sugars, 1g fiber), 6g pro.*

 Holiday Helper
Traditionally, popover pans are heated in the oven before greasing and filling with batter. Try this trick to give your popovers an extra crisp golden exterior with a higher rise.

NUTTY BARLEY BAKE

When I first brought this dish to holiday dinners, many had never seen barley in anything but soup. They have since dubbed me "the barley lady," and I wouldn't dare bring anything this dish. Even when I double the recipe, I come home with an empty pan!
—Renate Crump, Los Angeles, CA

PREP: 15 min. • **BAKE:** 1¼ hours
MAKES: 6 servings

- 1 medium onion, chopped
- 1 cup medium pearl barley
- ½ cup slivered almonds or pine nuts
- ¼ cup butter, cubed
- ½ cup minced fresh parsley
- ¼ cup thinly sliced green onions
- ¼ tsp. salt
- ⅛ tsp. pepper
- 2 cans (14½ oz. each) beef broth
  Additional parsley and green onions, optional

1. In a large skillet, saute the onion, barley and nuts in butter until the barley is lightly browned. Stir in the parsley, green onions, salt and pepper.
2. Transfer to a greased 2-qt. baking dish. Stir in broth. Bake, uncovered, at 350° for 1¼ hours or until the barley is tender and the liquid is absorbed. If desired, sprinkle with additional parsley and green onions.
¾ CUP: *257 cal., 13g fat (5g sat. fat), 20mg chol., 704mg sod., 30g carb. (2g sugars, 7g fiber), 7g pro.*

SHREDDED GINGERED BRUSSELS SPROUTS

Even people who normally don't care for Brussels sprouts will ask for a second helping of these. This simple technique adapts beautifully to a whole range of flavors, too.
—James Schend, Pleasant Prairie, WI

- -

TAKES: 25 min. • **MAKES:** 6 servings

- 1 lb. fresh Brussels sprouts (about 5½ cups)
- 1 Tbsp. olive oil
- 1 small onion, finely chopped
- 1 Tbsp. minced fresh gingerroot
- 1 garlic clove, minced
- ½ tsp. salt
- 2 Tbsp. water
- ¼ tsp. pepper

1. Trim Brussels sprouts. Cut sprouts lengthwise in half, then cut crosswise into thin slices.
2. Place a large skillet over medium-high heat. Add Brussels sprouts; cook and stir until the sprouts begin to brown lightly, 2-3 minutes. Add oil and toss to coat. Stir in onion, ginger, minced garlic and salt. Add water; reduce heat to medium and cook, covered, until the vegetables are tender, 1-2 minutes. Stir in pepper.
¾ CUP: *56 cal., 2g fat (0 sat. fat), 0 chol., 214mg sod., 8g carb. (2g sugars, 3g fiber), 2g pro.*
DIABETIC EXCHANGES: *1 vegetable, ½ fat.*
MOLASSES-SRIRACHA SPROUTS: Add 1 Tbsp. molasses and 2 tsp. sriracha to the water and cook as directed.
SESAME-GINGER SPROUTS: Substitute toasted sesame oil for the olive oil and proceed as directed. Sprinkle 1 Tbsp. toasted sesame seeds over the cooked sprouts before serving.
CRANBERRY-PECAN SPROUTS: Add ¼ cup dried cranberries with the onion and ginger. Cook as directed; sprinkle with 2 Tbsp. chopped toasted pecans before serving.
CURRY SPROUTS: Add 1 tsp. curry powder with the chopped onion and ginger; cook as directed.

MY MOTHER'S MAC & CHEESE

I remember my mother sending me to the store for 15 cents' worth of cheese. The butcher would cut off a slice from a gigantic wheel covered with a wax-coated cloth. Mother would then blend that cheese into this tasty dish. The memory of her cooking is like food for my soul.
—Phyllis Burkland, Portland, OR

- -

PREP: 10 min. • **BAKE:** 1 hour
MAKES: 4 servings

- 2 cups elbow macaroni, cooked and drained
- 1 can (28 oz.) diced tomatoes, undrained
- ½ tsp. onion salt, optional
- ¼ tsp. pepper
- 2 cups shredded cheddar cheese, divided
- 2 Tbsp. butter

In a bowl, combine macaroni, tomatoes, onion salt, pepper and 1½ cups cheddar cheese. Pour into a greased 2-qt. baking dish. Dot with butter. Bake, uncovered, at 350° for 45 minutes. Sprinkle with the remaining cheese; bake 15 minutes longer.
1 CUP: *373 cal., 22g fat (16g sat. fat), 75mg chol., 759mg sod., 27g carb. (6g sugars, 2g fiber), 16g pro.*

12 DAYS OF CHRISTMAS TREATS

Indulge your craving for treats and snacks with a different flavor for each of the 12 days of Christmas. From sweet breakfast to decadent dessert, these recipes are the perfect way to spoil your family and friends!

3. Gently fold a small amount of the tapioca mixture into egg whites; return all to pan, whisking constantly. Cook and stir 2 minutes. Remove from heat. Cool 15 minutes; stir in vanilla. Transfer to dessert dishes. Press plastic wrap onto surface of pudding. Refrigerate until cold (pudding will thicken upon cooling). If desired, top servings with chocolate-covered espresso beans.

¾ CUP: 156 cal., 3g fat (1g sat. fat), 62mg chol., 182mg sod., 31g carb. (21g sugars, 1g fiber), 3g pro.

ANGEL FOOD CHRISTMAS CANDY

It was my dad who inspired me to try making this candy—he remembered it from when he was a boy. The ultimate compliment was when he told me my version tasted even better than his memories!
—Shelly Matthys, New Richmond, WI

- -

PREP: 20 min. • **COOK:** 25 min.
MAKES: 1½ lbs. (12 servings)

 1 cup sugar
 1 cup dark corn syrup
 1 Tbsp. white vinegar
 1 Tbsp. baking soda
 1 lb. milk chocolate candy coating, melted

1. In a heavy saucepan, combine sugar, corn syrup and vinegar. Cook over medium heat, stirring constantly, until sugar dissolves. Cook without stirring until the temperature reaches 300° (hard-crack stage) on a candy thermometer. Do not overcook.

2. Remove from the heat and quickly stir in baking soda. Pour into a buttered 13x9-in. pan. Do not spread candy; the mixture will not fill the pan.

3. When cool, break into bite-sized pieces. Dip each piece into melted chocolate; place on waxed paper until the chocolate is firm. Store candy tightly covered.

2 OZ.: 337 cal., 11g fat (10g sat. fat), 0 chol., 356mg sod., 63g carb. (61g sugars, 1g fiber), 1g pro.

DARK CHOCOLATE ESPRESSO TAPIOCA PUDDING

I've been experimenting with espresso powder—it really brings out the flavor of chocolate without a strong coffee flavor.
—Shelly Bevington, Hermiston, OR

- -

PREP: 15 min. + standing
COOK: 20 min. + cooling
MAKES: 12 servings

 2 cups water
 ⅔ cup pearl tapioca
 1 carton (32 oz.) unsweetened almond milk
 4 large eggs, separated
 1¼ cups sugar, divided
 1 to 2 Tbsp. instant espresso powder
 ½ tsp. salt
 ¼ cup dark baking cocoa
 1 tsp. vanilla extract
    Chopped chocolate covered espresso beans, optional

1. In a large saucepan, combine water and tapioca; let stand 30 minutes. Whisk in almond milk, egg yolks, ½ cup sugar, the espresso powder and salt. Bring to a boil; reduce heat. Simmer, uncovered, until slightly thickened, 10-15 minutes, stirring frequently. Combine ¼ cup sugar and baking cocoa; stir into pan. Cook and stir 2 minutes longer.

2. In a large bowl, beat egg whites on medium speed until foamy. Gradually add the remaining ½ cup sugar, 1 Tbsp. at a time, beating on high after each addition until sugar is dissolved. Continue beating until soft glossy peaks form.

MOM'S CHOCOLATE BREAD

My mom made this divine chocolaty bread only for holidays or special requests, but it makes any old morning even better. I always think of our family when I smell it baking.
—Rachel Rhodes, Hartsville, SC

PREP: 10 min. • **BAKE:** 30 min. + cooling
MAKES: 1 loaf (12 slices)

- 4 Tbsp. sugar, divided
- 3 Tbsp. all-purpose flour
- 1 Tbsp. cold butter
- 1 to 3 Tbsp. ground cinnamon
- 1 tube (8 oz.) refrigerated crescent rolls
- ⅔ cup semisweet chocolate chips
- 1 Tbsp. butter, melted

1. Preheat oven to 375°. For streusel, in a small bowl, mix 3 Tbsp. sugar and the flour; cut in butter until crumbly. Reserve half the streusel for topping. Stir cinnamon and the remaining sugar into remaining streusel.
2. Unroll crescent dough into a long rectangle; press perforations to seal. Sprinkle with chocolate chips and the cinnamon mixture. Roll up jelly-roll style, starting with a long side; pinch seam to seal. Fold roll in half lengthwise; transfer to a greased 8x4-in. loaf pan. Brush with butter; sprinkle with reserved streusel.
3. Bake until pastry is golden brown, 30-35 minutes. Cool in pan 10 minutes before removing to a wire rack to cool completely.

1 SLICE: *164 cal., 9g fat (4g sat. fat), 5mg chol., 165mg sod., 21g carb. (11g sugars, 2g fiber), 2g pro.*

CHOCOLATE-COVERED CHEESECAKE SQUARES

Satisfy your cheesecake craving with these bite-sized treats. Dipped in chocolate, the sweet, creamy delights are party favorites. But be warned—you won't be able to eat just one!
—Esther Neustaeter, La Crete, AB

PREP: 1½ hours + freezing
MAKES: 49 squares

- 1 cup graham cracker crumbs
- ¼ cup finely chopped pecans
- ¼ cup butter, melted

FILLING
- 2 pkg. (8 oz. each) cream cheese, softened
- ½ cup sugar
- ¼ cup sour cream
- 2 large eggs, room temperature, lightly beaten
- ½ tsp. vanilla extract

COATING
- 24 oz. semisweet chocolate, chopped
- 3 Tbsp. shortening

1. Preheat oven to 325°. Line a 9-in. square baking pan with foil; grease the foil. In a small bowl, combine the graham cracker crumbs, pecans and butter. Press into prepared pan; set aside.
2. In a large bowl, beat the cream cheese, sugar and sour cream until smooth. Add the eggs and vanilla; beat on low speed just until combined. Pour over crust. Bake for 35-40 minutes or until the center is almost set. Cool on a wire rack. Freeze overnight.
3. In a microwave, melt chocolate and shortening; stir until smooth. Cool slightly.
4. Using foil, lift cheesecake out of pan. Gently peel off foil; cut cheesecake into 1¼-in. squares. Work with a few pieces at a time for dipping; keep the remaining squares refrigerated until ready to dip.
5. Using a toothpick, completely dip squares, 1 at a time, into the melted chocolate; allow excess to drip off. Place on waxed paper-lined baking sheets. Spoon additional chocolate over the tops if necessary to coat. (Reheat chocolate if needed to finish dipping.) Let stand for 20 minutes or until set. Store in an airtight container in the refrigerator or freezer.

1 PIECE: *141 cal., 10g fat (6g sat. fat), 22mg chol., 48mg sod., 12g carb. (10g sugars, 1g fiber), 2g pro.*

LEMON-FILLED GINGERBREAD MUFFINS

These seemingly plain gingerbread muffins hide a delicious surprise—a sweet lemon filling! You can add a frosting or glaze if you prefer, but the simple appearance makes the surprise all the sweeter.
—Suzette Jury, Keene, CA

PREP: 25 min. • **BAKE:** 15 min. • **MAKES:** 1½ dozen

- ½ cup butter, softened
- ⅔ cup sugar
- 2 large eggs, room temperature
- ½ cup molasses
- 2 cups all-purpose flour
- 1½ tsp. ground ginger
- 1 tsp. baking soda
- ½ tsp. salt
- ½ tsp. ground allspice
- 1 cup water

FILLING
- 4 oz. cream cheese, softened
- ¼ cup confectioners' sugar
- 1 Tbsp. lemon juice
- 2 tsp. grated lemon zest

1. Preheat oven to 375°. In a large bowl, cream butter and sugar until light and fluffy, 5-7 minutes. Add eggs, 1 at a time, beating well after each addition. Beat in molasses. In another bowl, whisk flour, ginger, baking soda, salt and allspice; add to the creamed mixture alternately with water, beating after each addition just until combined. (Batter may appear curdled.)
2. Fill 18 paper-lined muffin cups one-fourth full. In a small bowl, beat the filling ingredients until blended. Drop filling by rounded teaspoonfuls into center of each muffin; cover with the remaining muffin batter.
3. Bake until a toothpick inserted in the muffin portion comes out clean, 14-18 minutes. Cool 5 minutes before removing from pans to wire racks. Serve warm.
1 MUFFIN: *188 cal., 8g fat (5g sat. fat), 41mg chol., 207mg sod., 27g carb. (16g sugars, 0 fiber), 3g pro.*

LEMONY LIMONCELLO TIRAMISU

Here's a standout citrus twist on a classic Italian dessert. It's always a favorite, whether at winter holiday meals or summer gatherings!
—Deena Resnick, Oregon City, OR

PREP: 25 min. + chilling • **MAKES:** 12 servings

- 2 cartons (8 oz. each) mascarpone cheese
- 6 large egg yolks
- ¾ cup sugar
- ⅔ cup 2% milk
- 1¼ cups heavy whipping cream
- ½ tsp. vanilla extract
- ¼ cup lemon juice
- ½ cup limoncello
- 1 pkg. (7 oz.) crisp ladyfinger cookies
- 1 jar (10 oz.) lemon curd
  Candied lemon slices

1. Stir mascarpone cheese; let stand at room temperature for 30 minutes. Whisk egg yolks, sugar and milk in the top of a double boiler until mixture is thickened (ribbon stage) and a thermometer reads 160°. Remove from heat; cool completely. Whisk in mascarpone cheese until almost smooth.
2. Whip heavy cream and vanilla until soft peaks form.
3. Combine lemon juice and limoncello. Briefly dip 24 ladyfingers into lemon mixture and place in the bottom of a 11x7-in. baking dish. Top with half the mascarpone mixture, half the lemon curd and half the whipped cream. Repeat layers. Refrigerate, covered, 6 hours or overnight. To serve, garnish with candied lemon slices as desired.
1 PIECE: *509 cal., 31g fat (17g sat. fat), 204mg chol., 80mg sod., 47g carb. (40g sugars, 0 fiber), 7g pro.*

CONTEST-WINNING HAZELNUT TOFFEE

This is one of my most-asked-for recipes. It's sweet and buttery with plenty of crunch. You could use dark, milk or even white chocolate and substitute almonds for the hazelnuts if you wish.
—Joanne Simpson, Portland, OR

- -

PREP: 15 min. • **COOK:** 30 min. + standing
MAKES: about 1¾ lbs.

- 2 tsp. plus 1 cup butter, divided
- 1 cup sugar
- 3 Tbsp. water
- 1 Tbsp. light corn syrup
- ⅓ cup chopped hazelnuts

TOPPING
- 2 cups (12 oz. each) semisweet chocolate chips
- ½ cup finely chopped hazelnuts

1. Line a 13x9-in. pan with foil; coat the foil with cooking spray and set aside.
2. Butter the sides of a large heavy saucepan with 2 tsp. butter. Cube the remaining butter; place in pan. Add the sugar, water and corn syrup. Cook and stir until mixture turns golden brown and a candy thermometer reads 300° (hard crack stage).
3. Remove from the heat; stir in hazelnuts. Pour into the prepared pan without scraping; spread evenly. Let stand at room temperature until cool, about 1 hour.
4. For the topping, in a microwave, melt chocolate chips; stir until smooth. Spread evenly over toffee. Sprinkle with hazelnuts, pressing down gently. Let stand for 1 hour.
5. Break into bite-sized pieces. Store in the refrigerator.
ABOUT 1 OZ.: 229 cal., 16g fat (9g sat. fat), 18mg chol., 58mg sod., 24g carb. (21g sugars, 2g fiber), 2g pro.

EASY NUTELLA CHEESECAKE

A creamy chocolate-hazelnut spread tops a crust made of crushed Oreo cookies to make this irresistible baked cheesecake.
—Nick Iverson, Denver, CO

- -

PREP: 35 min. • **BAKE:** 1¼ hours + chilling
MAKES: 16 servings

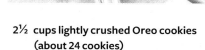

- 2½ cups lightly crushed Oreo cookies (about 24 cookies)
- ¼ cup sugar
- ¼ cup butter, melted

FILLING
- 4 pkg. (8 oz. each) cream cheese, softened
- ½ cup sugar
- 2 jars (26½ oz. each) Nutella
- 1 cup heavy whipping cream
- 1 tsp. salt
- 4 large eggs, room temperature, lightly beaten
- ½ cup chopped hazelnuts, toasted

1. Preheat oven to 325°. Pulse cookies and sugar in a food processor until fine crumbs form. Continue processing while gradually adding melted butter in a steady stream. Press mixture onto bottom of a greased 10x3-in. springform pan. Securely wrap bottom and sides of pan in a double thickness of heavy-duty foil (about 18 in. square).

2. For filling, beat cream cheese and sugar until smooth. Beat in Nutella, cream and salt. Add eggs; beat on low speed just until blended. Pour over crust.
3. Bake until a thermometer inserted in the center reads 160°, about 1¼ hours. Cool for 1¼ hours on a wire rack. Refrigerate overnight, covering when completely cooled.
4. Gently loosen sides from pan with a knife; remove rim. Top cheesecake with chopped hazelnuts.
1 SLICE: 900 cal., 62g fat (22g sat. fat), 129mg chol., 478mg sod., 84g carb. (71g sugars, 4g fiber), 12g pro.

Holiday Helper
Don't overbeat the eggs—mixing too much air into them will make the cheesecake puff up in the oven, then collapse and crack once it's out.

HOLIDAY PISTACHIO DESSERT

For my best festive menu, I make this famous dessert, which my children gobble up immediately. It's a hit at every gathering!
—Edie DeSpain, Logan, UT

PREP: 30 min. + chilling
MAKES: 15 servings

- 1¼ cups biscuit/baking mix
- ½ cup chopped walnuts
- 1 Tbsp. brown sugar
- 6 Tbsp. cold butter
- 1 pkg. (8 oz.) cream cheese, softened
- 1 cup plus 1 Tbsp. confectioners' sugar, divided
- 1 cup heavy whipping cream, whipped, divided
- 2½ cups cold milk
- 2 pkg. (3.4 oz. each) instant pistachio pudding mix
  Chocolate curls, optional

1. Preheat oven to 375°. In a small bowl, combine the biscuit mix, walnuts and brown sugar. Cut in butter until mixture resembles coarse crumbs.
2. Press into an ungreased 13x9-in. baking pan. Bake for 10-12 minutes or until lightly browned. Cool on a wire rack.
3. In a small bowl, beat cream cheese and 1 cup confectioners' sugar until fluffy. Fold in half of the whipped cream; spread over crust. Stir the remaining confectioners' sugar into the remaining whipped cream; refrigerate until serving.
4. In another bowl, whisk milk and pudding mixes for 2 minutes. Let stand for 2 minutes or until soft-set. Spread over the cream cheese layer. Cover and refrigerate for at least 4 hours before serving.
5. Garnish with the sweetened whipped cream and, if desired, chocolate curls.
1 PIECE: *279 cal., 16g fat (8g sat. fat), 38mg chol., 392mg sod., 30g carb. (20g sugars, 0 fiber), 4g pro.*

RICH PISTACHIO BRITTLE

Here's a fun twist on traditional brittle. Pistachios not only add wonderful taste to the rich, buttery candy, but also delicious texture.
—Valonda Seward, Coarsegold, CA

PREP: 10 min. • **COOK:** 30 min. + cooling
MAKES: about 1½ lbs.

- 1¼ cups sugar
- ⅓ cup water
- ⅓ cup light corn syrup
- 1 tsp. salt
- ½ cup butter, cubed
- 2 cups pistachios, toasted
- ½ tsp. baking soda
- ½ tsp. vanilla extract

1. Butter a 15x10x1-in. pan; set aside. In a large saucepan, combine sugar, water, corn syrup and salt. Cook over medium heat until a candy thermometer reads 240° (soft-ball stage). Carefully add butter and pistachios; cook and stir until mixture reaches 284° (soft-crack stage).
2. Remove from the heat; stir in baking soda and vanilla. Immediately pour into prepared pan. Spread to ¼-in. thickness. Cool before breaking into pieces. Store in an airtight container.
1 OZ.: *161 cal., 9g fat (3g sat. fat), 11mg chol., 215mg sod., 18g carb. (14g sugars, 1g fiber), 3g pro.*

GLAZED CRANBERRY SWIRL LOAF

This is one of my favorite recipes to serve during the holidays. If you leave out the filling, it makes a great soft, chewy bread for any regular day!
—Chris Carattini, Chadron, NE

- -

PREP: 30 min. + rising
BAKE: 25 min. + cooling
MAKES: 1 loaf (16 slices)

  2½ **to 3 cups all-purpose flour**
   2 **Tbsp. sugar**
   1 **pkg. (¼ oz.) active dry yeast**
   ½ **tsp. salt**
   ½ **cup 2 % milk**
   ¼ **cup water**
   2 **Tbsp. butter**
   1 **large egg, room temperature**
FILLING
   ½ **cup chopped fresh or frozen cranberries, thawed**
   ½ **cup packed brown sugar**
   2 **Tbsp. chopped pecans**
   ½ **tsp. grated orange zest**
   ¼ **tsp. ground nutmeg**
GLAZE
   ¾ **cup confectioners' sugar**
   2 **to 3 Tbsp. orange juice**

1. In a large bowl, combine 1 cup flour, sugar, yeast and salt. In a small saucepan, heat the milk, water and butter to 120°-130°. Add to dry ingredients; beat until moistened. Add the egg. Beat on medium speed for 2 minutes. Add 1 cup flour. Beat until smooth. Stir in enough remaining flour to form a soft dough.
2. Turn onto a lightly floured surface; knead until smooth and elastic, 6-8 minutes. Place in a greased bowl, turning once to grease top. Cover and let rise in a warm place until doubled, about 1 hour. Meanwhile, combine filling ingredients.
3. Punch dough down. Divide in half. Roll each portion into a 12x9-in. rectangle. Spread filling over each rectangle to within ½ in. of edges. Roll up jelly-roll style, starting with a long side; pinch seams to seal. Twist the 2 rolls together; pinch ends to seal. Place in a greased 9x5-in. loaf pan. Cover and let rise until doubled, about 30 minutes.
4. Bake at 375° for 25-30 minutes or until golden brown. Cool for 10 minutes before removing from pan to a wire rack.
5. Combine the glaze ingredients; drizzle over bread.

1 SLICE: *157 cal., 3g fat (1g sat. fat), 18mg chol., 95mg sod., 30g carb. (14g sugars, 1g fiber), 3g pro.*
DIABETIC EXCHANGES: *2 starch.*

CRANBERRY DARK CHOCOLATE TRAIL MIX

A close friend once gave me a jar of absolutely delicious trail mix. My re-creation comes pretty close to the original and is truly one of my favorite snacks—and now I give to my friends!
—Nancy Johnson, Laverne, OK

TAKES: 5 min. • **MAKES:** 6 cups

- 1 pkg. (10 oz.) dark chocolate chips
- 1½ cups dried cranberries (about 8 oz.)
- 1½ cups sliced almonds
- 1 cup raisins
- 1 cup coarsely chopped walnuts
- ½ cup pistachios

Toss together all ingredients. Store in airtight containers.

¼ CUP: *176 cal., 11g fat (3g sat. fat), 0 chol., 16mg sod., 21g carb. (15g sugars, 3g fiber), 3g pro.*

CRANBERRY WHITE CHOCOLATE CHUNK CHEESECAKE

My New York-style cheesecake has tart cranberries, white chocolate chunks and a smidge of yuletide red. It's an impressive addition to holiday dessert tables.
—Angela Spengler, Niceville, FL

PREP: 30 min. • **BAKE:** 1 hour + chilling
MAKES: 16 servings

- 15 Oreo cookies, finely crushed (about 1½ cups)
- ⅓ cup butter, melted

CHEESECAKE
- 5 pkg. (8 oz. each) cream cheese, softened
- 1½ cups sugar
- 1 Tbsp. cranberry juice or 2% milk
- 1 Tbsp. vanilla extract
- 3 large eggs, room temperature, lightly beaten
- 12 oz. white baking chocolate, cut into ½-in. pieces
- 1 cup dried cranberries

1. Preheat oven to 325°. Place a greased 10-in. springform pan on a double thickness of heavy-duty foil (about 18 in. square). Wrap foil securely around pan.

2. In a small bowl, mix crushed cookies and melted butter. Press mixture onto bottom of prepared pan.

3. In a large bowl, beat cream cheese and sugar until smooth. Beat in cranberry juice and vanilla. Add the eggs; beat on low speed just until blended. Fold in white chocolate and cranberries. Pour over crust. Place the springform pan in a larger baking pan; add 1 in. of hot water to the larger pan.

4. Bake 60-70 minutes or until center is just set and top appears dull. Remove springform pan from water bath. Cool on a wire rack 10 minutes. Loosen sides from pan with a knife; remove foil. Cool 1 hour longer. Refrigerate overnight, covering when completely cooled. Remove rim from pan before serving.

1 SLICE: *545 cal., 37g fat (22g sat. fat), 123mg chol., 362mg sod., 50g carb. (44g sugars, 1g fiber), 7g pro.*

DAY 6: CARAMEL

CARAMEL PRETZEL BITES

I created this recipe when I wanted to make my own version of a candy-coated pretzel log from a popular candy store. Mine are smothered with homemade caramel.
—Michilene Klaver, Grand Rapids, MI

TAKES: 45 min. + cooling • **MAKES:** 6 dozen

- 2 tsp. butter, softened
- 4 cups pretzel sticks
- 2½ cups pecan halves, toasted
- 2¼ cups packed brown sugar
- 1 cup butter, cubed
- 1 cup corn syrup
- 1 can (14 oz.) sweetened condensed milk
- ⅛ tsp. salt
- 1 tsp. vanilla extract
- 1 pkg. (11½ oz.) milk chocolate chips
- 1 Tbsp. plus 1 tsp. shortening, divided
- ⅓ cup white baking chips

1. Line a 13x9-in. pan with foil; grease foil with softened butter. Spread pretzels and pecans on bottom of prepared pan.
2. In a large heavy saucepan, combine brown sugar, cubed butter, corn syrup, condensed milk and the salt; cook and stir over medium heat until a candy thermometer reads 240° (soft-ball stage). Remove from heat. Stir in vanilla. Pour over the pretzel mixture.
3. In a microwave, melt chocolate chips and 1 Tbsp. shortening; stir until smooth. Spread over the caramel layer. In a small bowl in a microwave, melt white baking chips and the remaining shortening; stir until smooth. Drizzle over top. Let stand until set.
4. Using foil, lift candy out of pan; remove foil. Using a buttered knife, cut candy into 72 bite-sized pieces.
1 PIECE: *146 cal., 8g fat (3g sat. fat), 10mg chol., 76mg sod., 19g carb. (14g sugars, 1g fiber), 1g pro.*

CINNAMON-CARAMEL PEANUT BUTTER TART

Peanut butter, cinnamon and caramel create a unique, upscale flavor combination. This rich and creamy creation is one of my daughter's favorites. Keep copies of the recipe handy—everyone wants it.
—Mary Hawkes, Prescott, AZ

TAKES: 30 min. + chilling
MAKES: 12 servings

- 2½ cups crushed peanut butter-filled sandwich cookies (about 27 cookies)
- ¼ cup butter, melted

FILLING
- ⅔ cup peanut butter chips
- ½ cup creamy peanut butter
- ⅔ cup fat-free caramel ice cream topping
- ½ tsp. ground cinnamon
- 1¼ cups heavy whipping cream
  Sweetened whipped cream and chopped peanuts

1. Preheat oven to 325°. In a small bowl, mix crushed cookies and butter. Press mixture onto bottom and up sides of an ungreased 9-in. fluted tart pan with removable bottom. Bake 7-9 minutes or until edges are lightly browned. Cool on a wire rack.
2. In a small saucepan over medium-low heat, melt the peanut butter chips with the peanut butter, caramel topping and cinnamon; stir until smooth. Transfer to a large bowl; cool to lukewarm (90°), about 25-30 minutes.
3. In a small bowl, beat heavy cream until stiff peaks form. Fold a third of the plain whipped cream into the peanut butter mixture, then fold in the remainder; spread over crust. Refrigerate, covered, at least 4 hours or overnight.
4. Serve with sweetened whipped cream; sprinkle with peanuts.
1 SLICE: *411 cal., 28g fat (12g sat. fat), 39mg chol., 289mg sod., 36g carb. (22g sugars, 3g fiber), 7g pro.*

BILTMORE'S BREAD PUDDING

This is a comforting and very special dessert from the historic Biltmore Estate. The caramel sauce makes it so good.
—Biltmore Estate, Asheville, NC

PREP: 30 min. • **BAKE:** 40 min.
MAKES: 12 servings

8	cups cubed day-old bread
9	large eggs
2¼	cups milk
1¾	cups heavy whipping cream
1	cup sugar
¾	cup butter, melted
3	tsp. vanilla extract
1½	tsp. ground cinnamon

CARAMEL SAUCE

1	cup sugar
¼	cup water
1	Tbsp. lemon juice
2	Tbsp. butter
1	cup heavy whipping cream

1. Preheat oven to 350°. Place bread cubes in a greased 13x9-in. baking dish. In a large bowl, whisk the eggs, milk, cream, sugar, butter, vanilla and cinnamon. Pour evenly over bread.

2. Bake, uncovered, for 40-45 minutes or until a knife inserted in the center comes out clean. Let stand for 5 minutes before cutting.

3. Meanwhile, in a small saucepan, bring the sugar, water and lemon juice to a boil. Reduce heat to medium; cook until the sugar is dissolved and mixture turns a golden amber color. Stir in butter until melted. Gradually stir in cream. Serve warm with bread pudding.

1 PIECE: *581 cal., 39g fat (23g sat. fat), 273mg chol., 345mg sod., 49g carb. (37g sugars, 1g fiber), 9g pro.*

CHOCOLATE PECAN PAVLOVA TORTE

This will definitely capture your taste buds! Although it may take a little longer to make and assemble, it is truly worth the work. It's a rich-tasting yet light dessert that everyone will enjoy. I usually use pecans, but you can substitute walnuts, hazelnuts or other nuts.
—Nancy Preussner, Delhi, IA

PREP: 1 hour + chilling
BAKE: 45 min. + standing
MAKES: 8 servings

- 4 large egg whites
- 1 tsp. vanilla extract
- ¼ tsp. cream of tartar
- 1⅔ cups sugar, divided
- 2 Tbsp. baking cocoa
- 1 cup ground pecans
- 4 oz. cream cheese, softened
- 2 Tbsp. butter, softened
- 1 cup heavy whipping cream
- 3 Tbsp. coffee liqueur
- ½ cup hot fudge ice cream topping, divided
- ¼ cup coarsely chopped pecans

1. Place egg whites in a large bowl; let stand at room temperature 30 minutes. Meanwhile, line a baking sheet with parchment paper. Trace two 8-in. circles 1 in. apart on parchment; invert parchment.
2. Preheat oven to 300°. Add vanilla and cream of tartar to the egg whites; beat on medium speed until foamy. Sift 1⅓ cups sugar and cocoa together twice. Gradually add sugar mixture to the egg whites, 1 Tbsp. at a time, beating on high after each addition until the sugar is dissolved. Continue beating until stiff glossy peaks form, about 7 minutes. Gently fold in ground pecans. Spread mixture evenly over the circles on prepared pan.
3. Bake until meringue is set and dry, 45-55 minutes. Turn off oven (do not open oven door); leave meringues in the oven for 1 hour. Remove from oven; cool completely on baking sheet. Carefully remove 1 meringue to a serving plate.
4. In a large bowl, beat cream cheese, butter and the remaining ⅓ cup sugar until smooth. In a small bowl, beat cream until soft peaks form; fold into the cream cheese mixture. Stir in liqueur.

5. Spread ⅓ cup fudge ice cream topping over the meringue. Top with half of the cream cheese filling. Layer with the remaining meringue and remaining filling. Sprinkle with chopped pecans. Warm remaining fudge ice cream topping; drizzle over top. Refrigerate at least 2 hours before serving.
1 PIECE: *553 cal., 33g fat (13g sat. fat), 56mg chol., 129mg sod., 61g carb. (55g sugars, 2g fiber), 6g pro.*

VANILLA MERINGUE COOKIES

These sweet little swirls are light as can be. They're all you need after a big, special dinner, or as an eye-catching addition to a tray of holiday sweets.
—Jenni Sharp, Milwaukee, WI

PREP: 20 min. • **BAKE:** 40 min. + standing
MAKES: about 5 dozen

- 3 large egg whites
- 1½ tsp. clear or regular vanilla extract
- ¼ tsp. cream of tartar
-   Dash salt
- ⅔ cup sugar

1. Place egg whites in a small bowl; let stand at room temperature 30 minutes.
2. Preheat oven to 250°. Add vanilla, cream of tartar and salt to egg whites; beat on medium speed until foamy. Gradually add sugar, 1 Tbsp. at a time, beating on high after each addition until sugar is dissolved. Continue beating until stiff glossy peaks form, about 7 minutes.
3. Cut a small hole in the tip of a pastry bag or in a corner of a food-safe plastic bag; insert a #32 star tip. Transfer meringue to bag. Pipe 1¼-in.-diameter cookies 2 in. apart onto parchment paper-lined baking sheets.
4. Bake 40-45 minutes or until firm to the touch. Turn off oven; leave meringues in oven 1 hour (leave oven door closed). Remove from oven; cool completely on baking sheets. Remove meringues from paper; store in an airtight container at room temperature.
1 COOKIE: *10 cal., 0 fat (0 sat. fat), 0 chol., 5mg sod., 2g carb. (2g sugars, 0 fiber), 0 pro.*

Holiday Helper
Room-temperature, older eggs produce better meringues. Their whites can be beaten to loftier heights!

style, starting with a long slide; pinch seam to seal. Place ropes on a parchment-lined baking sheet. Using a sharp knife, make a ½-in.-deep cut lengthwise down the center of each rope, stopping ½ in. from ends. Keeping cut surfaces facing up, braid ropes. Pinch ends to seal; tuck ends under. Cover with a kitchen towel; let rise in a warm place until almost doubled, about 30 minutes.

4. Preheat oven to 375°. Bake until golden brown, 30-35 minutes. Remove to a wire rack to cool. Combine glaze ingredients to the desired consistency; drizzle over warm stollen.

1 SLICE: *270 cal., 10g fat (4g sat. fat), 13mg chol., 73mg sod., 41g carb. (16g sugars, 2g fiber), 5g pro.*

CINNAMON TOASTED ALMONDS

Crunchy, cinnamon almonds are a spectacular treat to bring to a party or gathering. They taste just like the cinnamon roasted almonds you get at the fair.
—*Janice Thompson, Stacy, MN*

PREP: 15 min. • **BAKE:** 25 min. + cooling
MAKES: about 4 cups

2 large egg whites
6 tsp. vanilla extract
4 cups unblanched almonds
⅓ cup sugar
⅓ cup packed brown sugar
1 tsp. salt
½ tsp. ground cinnamon

1. Preheat oven to 300°. In a large bowl, beat egg whites until frothy; beat in vanilla. Add almonds; stir gently to coat. Combine the sugars, salt and cinnamon; add to the nut mixture and stir gently to coat.
2. Spread nut mixture evenly into 2 greased 15x10x1-in. baking pans. Bake 25-30 minutes or until the almonds are crisp, stirring once. Cool. Store in an airtight container.

¼ CUP: *250 cal., 18g fat (1g sat. fat), 0 chol., 166mg sod., 16g carb. (10g sugars, 4g fiber), 8g pro.*

OMA'S MARZIPAN STOLLEN

My German grandma made this stollen recipe for us when we were young, and I love it. The sweet bread tastes incredible, reminding me of her and the German food she made. I often freeze the dough once it's shaped into a braid. Then I can pull it out the night before, let it rise on the counter overnight and bake it in the morning.
—*Abigail Leszczynski, Beaufort, SC*

PREP: 30 min. + rising • **BAKE:** 30 min.
MAKES: 1 loaf (16 slices)

3 to 3½ cups all-purpose flour
⅓ cup sugar
1 pkg. (¼ oz.) active dry yeast
1¼ cups 2% milk
6 Tbsp. butter, cubed
2 tsp. grated lemon zest
FILLING
1 can (12½ oz.) almond cake and pastry filling
1 cup finely ground almonds
1 Tbsp. 2% milk
1 tsp. rum extract
GLAZE
¼ cup confectioners' sugar
½ to 1 tsp. 2% milk

1. In a large bowl, combine 2 cups flour, the sugar and yeast. In a small saucepan, heat milk and butter to 120°-130°. Add to dry ingredients; beat just until moistened. Add lemon zest; beat until smooth. Stir in enough remaining flour to form a soft dough (dough will be sticky).
2. Turn onto a floured surface; knead until smooth and elastic, 6-8 minutes. Place in a greased bowl, turning once to grease the top. Cover and let rise in a warm place until doubled, about 1 hour.
3. For filling, in a large bowl, beat almond pastry filling, almonds, milk and extract. Punch dough down; turn onto a floured surface. Divide into thirds. Roll each portion into a 15x6-in. rectangle. Spread each portion with a third of the filling to within ¼ in. of edges. Roll up jelly-roll

CHOCOLATE LEBKUCHEN CHERRY BALLS

Here's my twist on the traditional holiday lebkuchen—with a surprise inside. Maraschino cherries add a sweet, unexpected punch to the holiday spice of gingersnaps.
—Arlene Erlbach, Morton Grove, IL

PREP: 45 min. + chilling • **MAKES:** 5 dozen

- 40 gingersnap cookies
- 1 pkg. (8 oz.) cream cheese, softened
- 1½ cups semisweet chocolate chips, divided
- 1¼ cups sliced almonds, divided
- 2 Tbsp. chopped candied orange peel
- 1 tsp. almond extract
- 60 maraschino cherries, stems removed

1. Place gingersnaps, cream cheese, ½ cup chocolate chips, ½ cup almonds, orange peel and extract in a food processor; process until combined. Refrigerate until firm enough to form into balls. Pat cherries dry with paper towels. Wrap each cherry with a rounded tablespoonful of cream cheese mixture; shape into a ball. Freeze until firm, about 20 minutes.
2. Chop the remaining sliced almonds; set aside. In a double boiler, melt the remaining chocolate chips; stir until smooth. Dip cherry balls in chocolate; allow excess to drip off. Sprinkle balls with almonds. Place on waxed paper. Refrigerate until set, about 1 hour.
1 BALL: *76 cal., 4g fat (2g sat. fat), 4mg chol., 37mg sod., 10g carb. (7g sugars, 1g fiber), 1g pro.*

ALMOND SPRITZ COOKIES

These almond spritz cookies can be left plain or decorated with colored sugar and frosting. In our house, it just wouldn't be Christmas without some cookie press recipes!
—Tanya Hart, Muncie, IN

PREP: 15 min. • **BAKE:** 10 min./batch • **MAKES:** about 7 dozen

- 1 cup butter, softened
- ½ cup sugar
- ½ cup packed brown sugar
- 1 large egg, room temperature
- ½ tsp. almond extract
- ½ tsp. vanilla extract
- 2½ cups all-purpose flour
- ¼ tsp. baking soda
- ¼ tsp. salt
  Pink and red colored sugar, optional

1. In a large bowl, cream butter and sugars for 5-7 minutes. Beat in egg and extracts. Combine the flour, baking soda and salt; gradually add to the creamed mixture and mix well.
2. Using a cookie press fitted with the disk of your choice, press dough 2 in. apart onto ungreased baking sheets. If desired, sprinkle with colored sugar.
3. Bake at 375° for 7-9 minutes or until edges just begin to brown. Cool on wire racks.
1 COOKIE: *44 cal., 2g fat (1g sat. fat), 8mg chol., 29mg sod., 5g carb. (2g sugars, 0 fiber), 0 pro.*

ITALIAN CREAM CHEESE CAKE

Buttermilk makes every bite of this awesome Italian cream cheese cake recipe moist and flavorful. It's impressive, too.
—Joyce Lutz, Centerview, MO

PREP: 40 min. • **BAKE:** 20 min. + cooling
MAKES: 16 servings

- ½ cup butter, softened
- ½ cup shortening
- 2 cups sugar
- 5 large eggs, separated, room temperature
- 1 tsp. vanilla extract
- 2 cups all-purpose flour
- 1 tsp. baking soda
- 1 cup buttermilk
- 1½ cups sweetened shredded coconut
- 1 cup chopped pecans

CREAM CHEESE FROSTING

- 11 oz. cream cheese, softened
- ¾ cup butter, softened
- 6 cups confectioners' sugar
- 1½ tsp. vanilla extract
- ¾ cup chopped pecans

1. Preheat oven to 350°. Grease and flour three 9-in. round baking pans. In a large bowl, cream butter, shortening and granulated sugar until light and fluffy, 5-7 minutes. Beat in egg yolks and vanilla. Combine flour and baking soda; add to the creamed mixture alternately with buttermilk. Beat until just combined. Stir in coconut and pecans.

2. In another bowl, beat egg whites with clean beaters until stiff but not dry. Fold one-fourth of the egg whites into the batter, then fold in remaining whites. Pour into prepared pans.

3. Bake until a toothpick inserted in center comes out clean, 20-25 minutes. Cool 10 minutes before removing from pans to wire racks to cool completely.

4. For frosting, beat cream cheese and butter until smooth. Beat in confectioners' sugar and vanilla until fluffy. Stir in pecans. Spread frosting between layers and over top and sides of cake. Refrigerate.

1 SLICE: *736 cal., 41g fat (19g sat. fat), 117mg chol., 330mg sod., 90g carb. (75g sugars, 2g fiber), 7g pro.*

ALOHA BRITTLE

A vacation to Hawaii inspired me to create this mouthwatering brittle. Coconuts, macadamia nuts and pecans make my tropical-tasting recipe deliciously different.
—Marylyn Richardson, Windermere, BC

PREP: 20 min. + cooling
MAKES: 1 lb. (16 servings)

- 2 tsp. butter, divided
- ½ cup sweetened shredded coconut
- 1 cup sugar
- ½ cup light corn syrup
- 1 jar (3 oz.) macadamia nuts
- ½ cup chopped pecans
- 1 tsp. baking soda
- 1 tsp. water
- 1 tsp. vanilla extract

1. Grease a large baking sheet with 1 tsp. butter. Sprinkle coconut in a 12-in. circle on the prepared pan. In a large heavy saucepan, combine sugar and corn syrup. Cook over medium heat until a candy thermometer reads 240° (soft-ball stage), stirring constantly. Stir in the macadamia nuts, pecans and remaining 1 tsp. butter; cook and stir until the mixture reads 300° (hard-crack stage).

2. Combine the baking soda, water and vanilla. Remove saucepan from the heat; stir in the baking soda mixture. Quickly pour over the coconut. Cool before breaking into pieces. Store in an airtight container with waxed paper between the layers.

1 OZ.: *164 cal., 9g fat (2g sat. fat), 1mg chol., 119mg sod., 23g carb. (19g sugars, 1g fiber), 1g pro.*

DAY 9: COCONUT

CHOCOLATE COCONUT CANDIES

(PICTURED ON P. 194)

These candies always disappear just as fast as I put them out. Fortunately, they are a snap to whip up. I mound them high on a serving platter, sprinkle with coconut— then watch them vanish!
—Mary Ann Marino, West Pittsburgh, PA

- -

TAKES: 30 min. + chilling • **MAKES:** 5 dozen

- 1¾ cups confectioners' sugar
- 1¾ cups sweetened shredded coconut
- 1 cup chopped almonds
- ½ cup sweetened condensed milk
- 2 cups semisweet chocolate chips
- 2 Tbsp. shortening
  Optional ingredients: Chopped almonds, sliced almonds, sprinkles and additional coconut

1. In a large bowl, combine the confectioners' sugar, coconut, almonds and condensed milk. Shape into 1-in. balls. Refrigerate until firm, about 20 minutes.
2. In a microwave, melt semisweet chips and shortening on high for about 1 minute; stir. Microwave at additional 10- to 20-second intervals, stirring until smooth.
3. Dip balls in chocolate; allow excess to drip off. Coat or garnish with optional ingredients of your choice. Place on waxed paper; let stand until set. Store in an airtight container.

1 CANDY: *157 cal., 9g fat (4g sat. fat), 2mg chol., 22mg sod., 20g carb. (18g sugars, 1g fiber), 2g pro.*

MACADAMIA NUT MINI LOAVES

These loaves may be small, but they have a big rich flavor. The macadamia nuts make them a special treat with tropical flair. Plus, they're so pretty with the toasted coconut topping.
—Kim Gilliland, Simi Valley, CA

- -

PREP: 20 min. • **BAKE:** 40 min. + cooling
MAKES: 5 loaves (6 slices each)

- 1 jar (3½ oz.) macadamia nuts, divided
- ⅓ cup sweetened shredded coconut
- 1½ cups sugar, divided
- ¾ cup butter, softened
- 2 large eggs, room temperature
- 3 cups all-purpose flour
- 1 tsp. baking powder
- ½ cup 2% milk
- 3 Tbsp. lemon juice
- 2 tsp. grated lemon zest
- 1½ tsp. vanilla extract

1. Finely chop enough macadamia nuts to measure ⅓ cup; set aside. Coarsely chop the remaining nuts; toss with coconut and 1 Tbsp. sugar. Set aside.
2. In a large bowl, cream butter and the remaining sugar until light and fluffy, 5-7 minutes. Beat in eggs. Combine flour and baking powder; gradually add to creamed mixture alternately with milk, beating well after each addition. Stir in the lemon juice, lemon zest, vanilla and reserved finely chopped nuts.
3. Spoon into 5 greased 5¾x3x2-in. loaf pans. Sprinkle with the reserved coconut mixture. Bake at 325° for 40-45 minutes or until a toothpick inserted in the center comes out clean (cover loosely with foil if top browns too quickly). Cool for 10 minutes before removing from pans to wire racks to cool completely.

1 SLICE: *162 cal., 8g fat (4g sat. fat), 27mg chol., 78mg sod., 21g carb. (11g sugars, 1g fiber), 2g pro.*

PEPPERMINT FUDGE

Three of the season's best flavors—nuts, chocolate and peppermint—combine in a delightful manner in this scrumptious fudge. The two distinct layers are eye-catching—another reason this candy makes a holiday gift that's sure to please.
—Connie Denmark, St. Joseph, IL

- -

PREP: 20 min. + chilling
MAKES: 1¼ lbs. (32 pieces)

- 1½ tsp. butter, softened
- 2 oz. cream cheese, softened
- 2 cups sifted confectioners' sugar
- 3 Tbsp. baking cocoa
- 1 to 2 tsp. 2% milk
- ½ tsp. vanilla extract
- ¼ cup chopped nuts

PEPPERMINT LAYER

- 2 oz. cream cheese, softened
- 2 cups sifted confectioners' sugar
- 1½ to 2½ tsp. 2% milk
- ½ tsp. peppermint extract
- ¼ cup crushed peppermint candy

1. Line the bottom and sides of an 8x4-in. loaf pan with foil. Grease foil with 1½ tsp. butter; set aside.
2. In a small bowl, beat cream cheese until creamy. Gradually beat in the confectioners' sugar, cocoa, milk and vanilla until smooth. Stir in nuts. Spread into prepared pan. Chill until firm, about 1 hour.
3. For peppermint layer, beat cream cheese in a small bowl until creamy. Gradually beat in the confectioners' sugar, milk and extract until smooth. Stir in peppermint candy. Spread evenly over the chocolate layer. Chill until firm, about 1 hour.
4. Using foil, lift fudge from pan. Gently peel off foil. Cut into squares.
1 PIECE: *83 cal., 2g fat (1g sat. fat), 4mg chol., 13mg sod., 16g carb. (14g sugars, 0 fiber), 1g pro.*

PEPPERMINT STICK DESSERT

With every spoonful of this cool, creamy concoction, my family goes back in time to when our Grandma Dagmar made it each Christmas. The minty, refreshing flavor can't be topped.
—Dianne Oertel, Racine, WI

- -

PREP: 20 min. + chilling
MAKES: 12 servings

- 8 oz. peppermint candy, crushed
- ½ cup half-and-half cream
- 1¼ tsp. unflavored gelatin
- 1 Tbsp. cold water
- 1½ cups heavy whipping cream, whipped
- 27 chocolate wafers

1. In a small saucepan, combine crushed candy and cream. Cook over low heat until candy is melted, stirring occasionally.
2. In a small bowl, sprinkle gelatin over water; let stand for 1 minute. Stir into hot peppermint mixture until dissolved. Refrigerate until mixture begins to set, about 20 minutes. Fold in whipped cream.
3. Crush 3 chocolate wafers; set aside for garnish. Line a 1½-qt. serving bowl with 12 wafers. Top with half the peppermint mixture. Repeat layers. Sprinkle with chocolate crumbs. Refrigerate for at least 8 hours. If desired, sprinkle with additional crushed peppermint candy just before serving.
1 PIECE: *250 cal., 14g fat (8g sat. fat), 46mg chol., 103mg sod., 29g carb. (13g sugars, 0 fiber), 2g pro.*

PUMPKIN COFFEE RING

I make this delicious coffee cake with its creamy pumpkin filling every year for the holidays, and everyone loves it. It's a great way to start a special brunch!
—Carol McCartney, Danville, OH

PREP: 25 min. + rising • **BAKE:** 20 min.
MAKES: 1 ring

- 2¼ cups all-purpose flour
- ¾ cup sugar, divided
- 1 pkg. (¼ oz.) active dry yeast
- ½ tsp. salt
- ¼ cup water
- ¼ cup whole milk
- 3 Tbsp. butter
- 1 large egg, room temperature
- 3 oz. cream cheese, softened
- ½ cup canned pumpkin
- 1 tsp. ground cinnamon
- ½ tsp. salt
- ½ tsp. ground ginger
- ½ tsp. ground nutmeg
- ½ cup chopped walnuts
- ½ cup raisins
- 1 large egg yolk, beaten

GLAZE
- ½ cup confectioners' sugar
- ⅛ tsp. vanilla extract
- 1 to 2 Tbsp. whole milk
- ¼ cup finely chopped walnuts

1. In a bowl, combine 1½ cups flour, ¼ cup sugar, the yeast and salt. In a saucepan, heat water, milk and butter to 120°-130°. Add to the dry ingredients; beat just until moistened. Beat in egg. Stir in enough remaining flour to form a soft dough.

2. Turn onto a floured surface; knead until smooth and elastic, 6-8 minutes. Place in a greased bowl, turning once to grease top. Cover and let rise in a warm place until doubled, about 1 hour.

3. In a small bowl, beat cream cheese and remaining sugar until smooth. Add the pumpkin, cinnamon, salt, ginger and nutmeg. Punch dough down; turn onto a floured surface. Roll into a 20x10-in. rectangle; spread pumpkin mixture to within ½ in. of edges. Sprinkle with nuts and raisins. Roll up jelly-roll style, starting with a long side; pinch ends together to form a ring. Place on a greased baking sheet. Cover and let rise until doubled, about 1 hour.

4. Brush dough with egg yolk. Bake at 350° for 20-25 minutes or until golden brown. Remove from pan to a wire rack. For glaze, combine the confectioners' sugar, vanilla and enough milk to achieve drizzling consistency. Drizzle over warm ring. Sprinkle with nuts.

1 SLICE: *217 cal., 8g fat (3g sat. fat), 39mg chol., 193mg sod., 32g carb. (16g sugars, 1g fiber), 5g pro.*

DAY 11: PUMPKIN

PUMPKIN FUDGE

A lot of delicious flavor is packed into these bite-sized morsels. Each one of the creamy, heartwarming treats is like a miniature pumpkin pie!
—Kathleen Henne, Camp Hill, PA

PREP: 20 min. + cooling • **MAKES:** 3 lbs. (117 pieces)

- 1 tsp. plus ¾ cup butter or margarine, divided
- 3 cups sugar
- 1 can (5 oz.) evaporated milk
- ½ cup canned pumpkin
- 1 to 2 tsp. pumpkin pie spice
- 1 pkg. (11 oz.) butterscotch chips
- 1 jar (7 oz.) marshmallow creme
- 1 tsp. vanilla extract
- 1 cup chopped almonds or pecans, toasted

1. Line a 13x9-in. pan with foil. Butter foil with 1 tsp. butter; set aside. In a saucepan, combine sugar, milk, pumpkin, pumpkin pie spice and remaining butter. Cook over medium heat until candy thermometer reads 238° (soft-ball stage), stirring constantly.
2. Remove from the heat. Stir in the chips, marshmallow creme and vanilla until smooth. Stir in nuts. Pour into prepared pan. Cool completely.
3. Using foil, lift fudge out of pan. Discard foil; cut fudge into 1-in. squares. Store in an airtight container.
1 PIECE: *60 cal., 3g fat (2g sat. fat), 4mg chol., 14mg sod., 8g carb. (8g sugars, 0 fiber), 1g pro.*

CHOCOLATE CHIP PUMPKIN BREAD

The aroma of this bread is mouthwatering and the taste is divine!
—Vicki Raboine, Kansasville, WI

PREP: 15 min. • **BAKE:** 45 min. • **MAKES:** 4 mini loaves (6 slices each)

- 1 cup packed brown sugar
- 1 cup sugar
- ⅔ cup butter, softened
- 3 large eggs, room temperature
- 2⅓ cups all-purpose flour
- 1½ cups canned pumpkin
- ½ cup water
- 2 tsp. baking soda
- 1 tsp. ground cinnamon
- 1 tsp. salt
- ½ tsp. ground cloves
- 2 cups semisweet chocolate chips

1. Preheat oven to 350°. In a bowl, cream sugars, butter and eggs. Add flour, pumpkin, water, baking soda, cinnamon, salt and cloves. Mix thoroughly. Fold in chocolate chips.
2. Pour into 4 greased and floured 5¾x3x2-in. loaf pans. Bake for 45 minutes or until breads test done.
1 SLICE: *239 cal., 10g fat (6g sat. fat), 37mg chol., 258mg sod., 37g carb. (26g sugars, 2g fiber), 3g pro.*

MAPLE PECAN TARTS

I absolutely love pecans and use them whenever a recipe doesn't specify the kind of nuts. Here, I combine pecans with maple and vanilla to create the ultimate single-serving tart. Make it even richer by adding a scoop of vanilla ice cream on top!
—Redawna Kalynchuk, Rochester, AB

PREP: 25 min. + chilling
BAKE: 25 min. + cooling • **MAKES:** 1 dozen

- 1 cup butter, softened
- 6 oz. cream cheese, softened
- 2 cups all-purpose flour

FILLING
- 4 large eggs
- 1 cup packed brown sugar
- ¾ cup maple syrup
- ⅔ cup butter, melted
- 2 tsp. vanilla extract
  Dash salt
- 3 cups pecan halves
  Vanilla ice cream, optional

1. In a large bowl, cream butter and cream cheese until smooth. Gradually beat flour into the creamed mixture. Shape into a disk; wrap and refrigerate 1 hour or until firm enough to handle.

2. Divide dough into 12 portions. Roll each portion into a 5-in. circle; transfer to 12 ungreased 4-in. fluted tart pans with removable bottoms. Trim crust even with edges. Refrigerate 20 minutes. Preheat oven to 375°.

3. Meanwhile, in a large bowl, whisk the first 6 filling ingredients. Pour into tart shells; arrange pecans over top. Bake 25-30 minutes or until the centers are just set (mixture will jiggle). Cool on wire racks. If desired, serve with ice cream. Refrigerate leftovers.

1 TART: *669 cal., 50g fat (21g sat. fat), 145mg chol., 299mg sod., 52g carb. (32g sugars, 3g fiber), 8g pro.*

DAY 12: MAPLE

MAPLE CRUNCH POPCORN

For a snack that's sure to bring smiles, try this medley of popcorn and pecans covered in a sweet, buttery maple coating.
—Elmira Trombetti, Paducah, KY

TAKES: 25 min. • **MAKES:** 3½ qt.

- 10 cups popped popcorn
- 1½ cups pecan halves, toasted
- 1⅓ cups sugar
- 1 cup butter, cubed
- ¼ cup maple syrup
- ¼ cup corn syrup
- ½ tsp. salt
- 1 tsp. maple flavoring

1. Place popcorn and pecans in a large bowl; set aside. In a large heavy saucepan, combine sugar, butter, maple syrup, corn syrup and salt. Cook and stir over medium heat until a candy thermometer reads 300° (hard-crack stage). Remove from the heat; stir in maple flavoring. Quickly pour over popcorn mixture and mix well.

2. Transfer to baking sheets lined with waxed paper to cool. Break into clusters. Store in airtight containers.

¾ CUP: *270 cal., 19g fat (7g sat. fat), 27mg chol., 205mg sod., 25g carb. (19g sugars, 1g fiber), 1g pro.*

MAPLE BUTTER TWISTS

My stepmother shared her recipe for this delicious yeast coffee cake that's shaped into pretty rings. The maple flavor and beautiful appearance make it a perfect match for holiday breakfasts. When I make it for friends, they always ask for seconds.
—June Gilliland, Hope, IN

- -

PREP: 35 min. + rising
BAKE: 25 min. + cooling
MAKES: 2 coffee cakes (16 slices each)

3¼ to 3½ cups all-purpose flour
3 Tbsp. sugar
1½ tsp. salt
1 pkg. (¼ oz.) active dry yeast
¾ cup 2% milk
¼ cup butter
2 large eggs, room temperature
FILLING
⅓ cup packed brown sugar
¼ cup sugar
3 Tbsp. butter, softened
3 Tbsp. maple syrup
4½ tsp. all-purpose flour
¾ tsp. ground cinnamon
¾ tsp. maple flavoring
⅓ cup chopped walnuts
GLAZE
½ cup confectioners' sugar
¼ tsp. maple flavoring
2 to 3 tsp. 2% milk

1. In a large bowl, combine 1½ cups flour, sugar, salt and yeast. In a saucepan, heat milk and butter to 120°-130°. Add to dry ingredients; beat just until moistened. Add eggs; beat on medium for 2 minutes. Stir in enough remaining flour to form a firm dough. Turn onto a floured surface; knead until smooth and elastic, 5-7 minutes. Place in a greased bowl, turning once to grease top. Cover and let rise in a warm place until doubled, about 70 minutes.
2. In a small bowl, combine the first 7 filling ingredients; beat for 2 minutes. Punch dough down; turn onto a lightly floured surface. Divide in half; roll each into a 16x8-in. rectangle. Spread filling to within ½ in. of edges. Sprinkle with nuts. Roll up jelly-roll style, starting with a long side.
3. With a sharp knife, cut a roll in half lengthwise. Open halves so cut side is up; gently twist ropes together. Repeat with the second roll. Transfer to 2 greased 9-in. round baking pans. Coil into a circle. Tuck ends under; pinch to seal. Cover and let rise in a warm place until doubled, about 45 minutes.
4. Bake at 350° for 25-30 minutes or until golden brown. Cool for 10 minutes; remove from pans to wire racks. Combine the confectioners' sugar, maple flavoring and enough milk to reach desired consistency; drizzle over warm cakes.
1 SLICE: *119 cal., 4g fat (2g sat. fat), 21mg chol., 144mg sod., 19g carb. (8g sugars, 0 fiber), 2g pro.*

SNOW DAY!

*Children love snow days—and you can make them
a joy for everyone with a special breakfast, a hot lunch,
or the perfect hot chocolate after playing in the snow...
all without a special shopping trip.*

GRILLED CHEESE & PEPPERONI SANDWICH

Who doesn't love a good grilled cheese sandwich? This super decadent version comes fully loaded with pepperoni and five types of cheese!
—*Josh Rink, Milwaukee, WI*

TAKES: 25 min. • **MAKES:** 4 servings

- 6   Tbsp. butter, softened, divided
- 3   Tbsp. mayonnaise
- 3   Tbsp. finely shredded Manchego or Parmesan cheese
- ⅛   tsp. onion powder
- 8   slices sourdough bread
- 4   oz. Brie cheese, rind removed and sliced
- ½   cup shredded sharp white cheddar cheese
- ½   cup shredded Monterey Jack cheese
- ½   cup shredded Gruyere cheese
- 24 slices slices pepperoni

1. Spread 3 Tbsp. butter on 1 side of each slice of bread. Place bread, butter side down, in a large cast-iron skillet or electric griddle over medium-low heat until golden brown, 2-3 minutes; remove. In a small bowl, combine the cheddar, Monterey Jack and Gruyere cheeses. In another bowl, mix together remaining 3 Tbsp. butter, mayonnaise, Manchego cheese and onion powder.

2. To assemble sandwiches, top toasted side of 4 bread slices with pepperoni; add sliced Brie. Sprinkle cheddar cheese mixture evenly over Brie. Top with remaining bread slices, toasted side facing inward. Spread the butter-mayonnaise mixture on the outsides of each sandwich. Place in same skillet and cook until golden brown and cheese is melted, 5-6 minutes on each side. Serve immediately.

1 SANDWICH: *719 cal., 55g fat (29g sat. fat), 134mg chol., 1207mg sod., 30g carb. (3g sugars, 1g fiber), 27g pro.*

MEXICAN HOT CHOCOLATE

This delicious, not-too-sweet hot chocolate is richly flavored with cocoa and delicately seasoned with warm spices. The blend of cinnamon and chocolate is wonderful—just the thing for a special treat on a cold day!
—*Kathy Young, Weatherford, TX*

TAKES: 10 min. • **MAKES:** 4 servings

- ¼   cup baking cocoa
- 2   Tbsp. brown sugar
- 1   cup boiling water
- ¼   tsp. ground cinnamon
      Dash ground cloves or nutmeg
- 3   cups whole milk
- 1   tsp. vanilla extract
      Whipped cream
      Whole cinnamon sticks

1. In a small saucepan, mix cocoa and sugar; stir in water. Bring to a boil. Reduce heat; cook 2 minutes, stirring constantly.

2. Add cinnamon and cloves; stir in milk. Simmer for 5 minutes (do not boil). Whisk in vanilla. Pour hot chocolate into mugs; top with whipped cream. Use cinnamon sticks for stirrers.

1 CUP: *156 cal., 7g fat (4g sat. fat), 25mg chol., 92mg sod., 18g carb. (15g sugars, 1g fiber), 7g pro.*

CHOCOLATE OAT BARS

These are one of my favorite go-to snack bars. I love that I usually have all the items on hand and can whip them up quickly.
—John Kleckner, Muscoda, WI

PREP: 20 min. • **BAKE:** 30 min. • **MAKES:** 2 dozen

- 1   cup plus 2 Tbsp. butter, softened, divided
- 2   cups packed brown sugar
- 2   large eggs, room temperature
- 4   tsp. vanilla extract, divided
- 3   cups old-fashioned oats
- 2½ cups all-purpose flour
- ¾   tsp. baking soda
- ¾   tsp. salt, divided
- 1   can (14 oz.) sweetened condensed milk
- 2   cups (12 oz.) semisweet chocolate chips
- 1   cup chopped pecans

1. In a large bowl, cream together 1 cup butter and brown sugar until light and fluffy, 5-7 minutes. Beat in eggs and 2 tsp. vanilla. Combine the oats, flour, baking soda and ½ tsp. salt; gradually add to the creamed mixture and mix well. Set aside.

2. In a large heavy saucepan over low heat, combine the condensed milk, chips and remaining butter and salt. Cook and stir until smooth. Add the nuts and remaining vanilla. Press 4 cups of the oat mixture into an ungreased 13x9-in. baking pan; spread with the chocolate mixture. Sprinkle with the remaining oat mixture.

3. Bake at 350° for 30-35 minutes. Cool completely on a wire rack. Cut into bars.

1 BAR: *391 cal., 19g fat (9g sat. fat), 46mg chol., 210mg sod., 53g carb., 3g fiber, 6g pro.*

SNOW DAY PROJECT: MAKE A SNOWMAN PIN

For a fun snow day arts and crafts project your kids will love, turn battery-operated tealights into adorable snowman pins. Draw the face with marker and use a hot glue gun to attach decorations—a length of pipe cleaner with two puff balls glued at the end make earmuffs, and black cardstock cut into a top hat, with a red or green hatband. Colorful ribbon glued to the back of the light, wrapped around and knotted, makes a jaunty scarf. Glue a pin back to the underside of the light, and you're done!

QUICK CHICKEN MINESTRONE

You'll love this flavorful soup that comes together with pantry ingredients. Dress it up by serving with garlic bread.
—Patricia Harmon, Baden, PA

PREP: 20 min. • **COOK:** 20 min.
MAKES: 8 servings (3 qt.)

  1 lb. boneless skinless chicken breasts, cubed
  1 large onion, chopped
  1 celery rib, chopped
  1 Tbsp. olive oil
  1 garlic clove, minced
  3 cups reduced-sodium chicken broth
2½ cups water
  1 can (15 oz.) white kidney or cannellini beans, rinsed and drained
  1 can (14½ oz.) diced tomatoes, undrained
  1 pkg. (5.9 oz.) chicken and garlic-flavored rice and vermicelli mix
1½ cups frozen vegetable blend (broccoli, red pepper, onion)
  ½ cup chopped pepperoni
  ½ tsp. dried basil
  ½ tsp. dried oregano
  ⅔ cup shredded Parmesan cheese
    Crushed red pepper flakes, optional

1. In a Dutch oven over medium heat, cook the chicken, onion and celery in oil until the chicken is no longer pink. Add garlic; cook 1 minute longer. Add broth, water, beans, tomatoes, rice and vermicelli mix, vegetables, pepperoni, basil and oregano. Bring to a boil.
2. Reduce heat; simmer, uncovered, until rice is tender, 18-20 minutes. Sprinkle each serving with cheese and, if desired, pepper flakes.
1½ CUPS: 299 cal., 10g fat (3g sat. fat), 44mg chol., 932mg sod., 31g carb. (5g sugars, 5g fiber), 22g pro.

TURKEY & SWISS FRITTATA

Tangy sweet apricots, Swiss cheese, green onions and other veggies make a winning combination in this lovely frittata. You can use different spices and veggies to suit your personal taste.
—Aysha Schurman, Ammon, ID

PREP: 25 min. • **BAKE:** 15 min.
MAKES: 4 servings

  8 large eggs
  ¾ cup shredded Swiss cheese, divided
  2 Tbsp. grated Parmesan cheese
  2 Tbsp. 2% milk
  1 garlic clove, minced
  1 tsp. minced fresh parsley
  ½ tsp. salt
  ½ tsp. pepper
  1 Tbsp. olive oil
  1 cup fresh baby spinach
  ⅓ cup finely chopped dried apricots
  2 green onions, chopped
  6 oz. thick-sliced deli smoked turkey, chopped
  ¼ cup chopped marinated quartered artichoke hearts
    Additional green onions, optional

1. In a large bowl, whisk eggs, ¼ cup Swiss cheese, the Parmesan cheese, milk, garlic, parsley, salt and pepper.
2. In a 10-in. ovenproof skillet, heat oil over medium heat. Add spinach, apricots and green onions; cook and stir until spinach is wilted, 1 minute. Reduce heat; stir in turkey and egg mixture. Sprinkle with the remaining Swiss cheese and the artichoke hearts.
3. Bake at 350° until eggs are completely set, 15-20 minutes. Let stand 5 minutes. Cut into wedges. Garnish with additional green onions if desired.
1 WEDGE: 373 cal., 23g fat (8g sat. fat), 409mg chol., 964mg sod., 12g carb. (6g sugars, 3g fiber), 29g pro.

PB&J TO GO!

These peanut butter and jelly bites are fun to make and fun to eat! The easy, no-bake recipe lets kids get in on the fun of mixing, wrapping and rolling. For a change of pace, replace the jam with Nutella and the rolled oats with sugar or crushed puffed rice cereal.
—Kelly Ward, Stratford, ON

PREP: 20 min. • **MAKES:** 1 dozen

1½ cups quick-cooking oats, divided
1 cup creamy peanut butter
½ cup confectioners' sugar
6 tsp. favorite jam

Combine 1 cup oats, peanut butter and confectioners' sugar until well blended. Shape dough into 1¼-in. balls; flatten into ¼-in.-thick circles. Place ½ tsp. of jam in center of each circle; wrap peanut butter mixture around jam. Pinch the edges to seal; shape into ball. Repeat with remaining jam and dough. Roll the balls in the remaining oats. Refrigerate on parchment-lined baking sheet for 30 minutes.
1 COOKIE: *186 cal., 12g fat (2g sat. fat), 0 chol., 91mg sod., 18g carb. (9g sugars, 2g fiber), 6g pro.*

CHEESY ITALIAN ROLL-UPS

This quick and tasty recipe goes over well at my house as a snack or appetizer. Each bite has gooey melted cheese and real pizza flavor. Try serving them with pizza sauce for dipping.
—Debra Purcell, Safford, AZ

TAKES: 20 min. • **MAKES:** 8 appetizers

1 tube (8 oz.) refrigerated crescent rolls
16 slices pepperoni, cut into quarters
2 pieces string cheese (1 oz. each), cut into quarters
¾ tsp. Italian seasoning, divided
¼ tsp. garlic salt

1. Preheat oven to 350°. Unroll crescent dough; separate into 8 triangles. Place 8 pepperoni pieces on each. Place a piece of cheese on the short side of each triangle; sprinkle with ½ tsp. Italian seasoning. Roll up each, starting with the short side; pinch seams to seal. Sprinkle with garlic salt and the remaining Italian seasoning.
2. Place 2 in. apart on a greased baking sheet. Bake 10-12 minutes or until golden brown. Serve warm.
2 ROLL-UPS: *282 cal., 17g fat (5g sat. fat), 12mg chol., 766mg sod., 22g carb. (4g sugars, 0 fiber), 7g pro.*

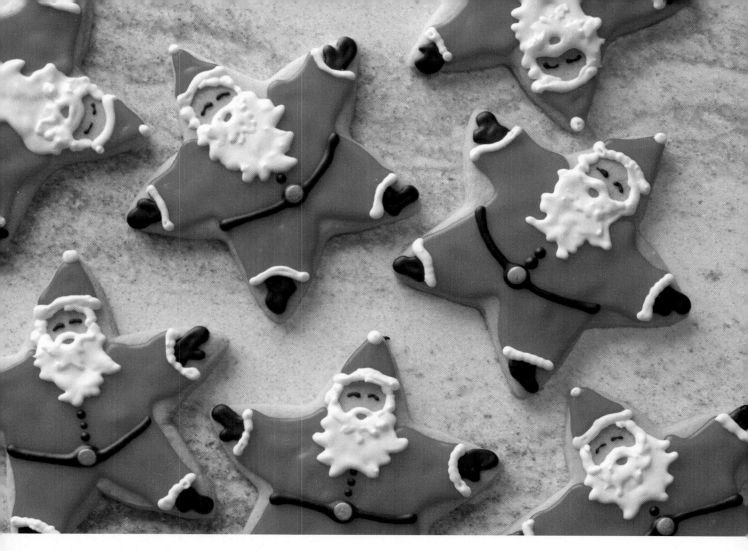

SANTA STAR COOKIES

Cookie baking can't get any more fun than when you are making—and decorating—these adorable Santa cookies. They are also really good to eat.
—Taste of Home *Test Kitchen*

- -

PREP: 1½ hours + chilling • **BAKE:** 10 min./batch + standing • **MAKES:** about 6 dozen

1½ cups butter, softened
½ cup shortening
1 cup sugar
1 cup packed brown sugar
2 large eggs, room temperature
¼ cup thawed orange juice concentrate
1 tsp. vanilla extract
5 cups all-purpose flour
1 tsp. baking soda
1 tsp. salt
FROSTING
2 cups confectioners' sugar
2 Tbsp. plus 2 tsp. water
4½ tsp. meringue powder
¼ tsp. cream of tartar
Red and black paste food coloring
Decorating sprinkles, optional

1. In a large bowl, cream the butter, shortening and sugars together until light and fluffy, 5-7 minutes. Add eggs, 1 at a time, beating well after each addition. Beat in the orange juice concentrate and vanilla.

2. Combine the flour, baking soda and salt; gradually add to the creamed mixture and mix well. Cover and refrigerate until easy to handle, about 2 hours.

3. Preheat oven to 350°. On a lightly floured surface, roll out the dough to ¼-in. thickness. Cut with a floured 4-in. star-shaped cookie cutter. Place the cutouts 1 in. apart on ungreased baking sheets. Bake until the edges are firm, 7-8 minutes. Remove to wire racks to let cool completely.

4. In a small bowl, combine confectioners' sugar, water, meringue powder and cream of tartar; beat on low speed just until combined. Beat on high until stiff peaks form, 4-5 minutes. In separate bowls, tint 9 Tbsp. of the icing red and 2 Tbsp. of the icing black; leave the remaining icing white. Keep any unused icing covered at all times with a damp cloth. If necessary, beat again on high speed to restore texture and consistency.

5. Place red icing in a pastry bag. With a #3 round pastry tip, pipe Santa's hats and suits. Once the red icing is dry, use black icing with a #1 round tip for eyes, mittens, belts and boots. With white frosting and a #2 round tip, add the trim for hats and suits. Use the same tip for mustaches and beards. If desired, use sprinkles for belt buckles and mouth.

1 COOKIE: *117 cal., 5g fat (3g sat. fat), 15mg chol., 85mg sod., 16g carb. (9g sugars, 0 fiber), 1g pro.*

RASPBERRY WHITE CHOCOLATE PANCAKES

I created these pancakes on a whim, and my husband—who's not a big fan of raspberries—thought they were great! Semisweet chocolate chips can easily be substituted for the white baking chips.
—Sue Gronholz, Beaver Dam, WI

TAKES: 30 min. • **MAKES:** 4 servings

- 1½ cups all-purpose flour
- 2 Tbsp. sugar
- 1½ tsp. baking powder
- ½ tsp. salt
- ⅛ tsp. ground nutmeg
- 2 large eggs, room temperature
- ¾ cup 2% milk
- ¾ cup plain Greek yogurt
- 2 Tbsp. canola oil
- ¼ tsp. almond extract
- 1 cup fresh or frozen raspberries
- ¼ cup white baking chips
  Additional raspberries and baking chips

1. Preheat griddle over medium heat. In a large bowl, combine flour, sugar, baking powder, salt and nutmeg. In a small bowl, combine eggs, milk, yogurt, oil and extract; stir into the dry ingredients just until moistened. Fold in raspberries and baking chips.

2. Lightly grease griddle. Pour batter by ¼ cupfuls onto griddle; cook until bubbles on top begin to pop and the bottoms are golden brown. Turn; cook until second sides are golden brown. If desired, serve pancakes with additional raspberries and baking chips.

FREEZE OPTION: *Freeze cooled pancakes between layers of waxed paper in freezer containers. To use, place pancakes on an ungreased baking sheet, cover with foil and reheat in a preheated 375° oven until heated through, 5-10 minutes. Or, place a stack of 3 pancakes on a microwave-safe plate and microwave on high until heated through, 45-90 seconds.*

3 PANCAKES: *439 cal., 19g fat (7g sat. fat), 110mg chol., 569mg sod., 56g carb. (18g sugars, 3g fiber), 12g pro.*

OLD-FASHIONED CHOCOLATE PUDDING

One of the nicest things about this easy pudding is you don't have to stand and stir it. This is a must for us year-round! I also make it into a pie with a graham cracker crust that our grandchildren love.
—Amber Sampson, Somonauk, IL

PREP: 10 min. • **COOK:** 30 min. + chilling
MAKES: 4 servings

- 2 cups whole milk
- 2 Tbsp. butter
- 2 oz. unsweetened chocolate, chopped
- ⅔ cup sugar
- ⅓ cup all-purpose flour
- ¼ tsp. salt
- 2 large egg yolks, beaten
- ½ tsp. vanilla extract
  Whipped cream, optional

1. In a double boiler or metal bowl over simmering water, heat the milk, butter and chocolate until chocolate is melted (chocolate may appear curdled).

2. Combine sugar, flour and salt. Sprinkle over chocolate mixture (do not stir). Cover and continue to cook in a double boiler over medium-low heat, 20 minutes. With a wooden spoon, stir until smooth. Remove from the heat.

3. Stir a small amount of hot mixture into egg yolks; return all to the pan, stirring constantly. Cook and stir until mixture is thickened and a thermometer reads 160°. Remove from heat; stir in vanilla. Cool for 15 minutes, stirring occasionally. Transfer to dessert dishes.

4. Cover and refrigerate for 1 hour. If desired, top with whipped cream.

⅔ CUP: *413 cal., 20g fat (11g sat. fat), 120mg chol., 254mg sod., 52g carb. (40g sugars, 3g fiber), 8g pro.*

MAGIC BROWNIE BARS

One of my all-time favorite treats as a kid was magic cookie bars (also called Hello Dolly bars). This recipe combines all the same classic flavors in a brownie!
—Mandy Rivers, Lexington, SC

PREP: 15 min. • **BAKE:** 35 min. + cooling • **MAKES:** 3 dozen

- 1 pkg. (17½ oz.) brownie mix
- 1 pkg. (11 oz.) butterscotch chips
- 2 cups sweetened shredded coconut
- 1 cup chopped pecans, optional
- 1 can (14 oz.) sweetened condensed milk

1. Preheat oven to 350°. Line a 13x9-in. baking pan with foil, letting the ends extend up the sides of the pan; grease foil.
2. Prepare brownie mix batter according to package directions. Transfer to prepared pan. Top with butterscotch chips, coconut and, if desired, pecans. Drizzle with milk. Bake until topping is light golden, 35-40 minutes.
3. Cool completely in pan on a wire rack. Lifting with foil, remove brownies from pan. Cut into bars. Store in an airtight container.
1 BAR: *200 cal., 10g fat (5g sat. fat), 14mg chol., 91mg sod., 25g carb. (21g sugars, 1g fiber), 3g pro.*

MINI CARAMEL ROLLS

Here's the perfect warm treat for pajama-clad family mornings. These ooey-gooey baked rolls come together in moments thanks to a tube of refrigerated crescent rolls—and disappear just as fast.
—Kayla Wiegand, Congerville, IL

PREP: 20 min. • **BAKE:** 15 min. • **MAKES:** 12 servings

- ⅓ cup packed brown sugar
- ⅓ cup butter, cubed
- 2 Tbsp. light corn syrup
- 1½ tsp. 2% milk
- 1 tube (8 oz.) refrigerated crescent rolls
- 2 tsp. sugar
- ½ tsp. ground cinnamon

1. Preheat oven to 375°. In a small saucepan, combine brown sugar, butter, corn syrup and milk; cook and stir over medium heat until blended. Pour into a greased 9-in. pie plate.
2. Separate crescent dough into 4 rectangles; gently press perforations to seal. In a small bowl, mix sugar and cinnamon; sprinkle evenly over rectangles. Roll up jelly-roll style, starting with a long side; pinch seams to seal.
3. Cut each roll into 9 slices; place in prepared dish, cut side down. Bake 15-18 minutes or until golden brown. Cool 1 minute before inverting onto a serving plate.
3 ROLLS: *155 cal., 9g fat (4g sat. fat), 13mg chol., 189mg sod., 17g carb. (9g sugars, 0 fiber), 1g pro.*

SLOPPY JOE MEATBALL SUBS

A mashup of two favorite recipes, these meatball subs are their own thing because of the sloppy joe-flavored sauce. I love to make them on a lazy afternoon and freeze leftovers for an easy weeknight meal.
—Susan Seymour, Valatie, NY

PREP: 1 hour • **BAKE:** 20 min./batch
MAKES: 12 servings

- 2 large eggs, lightly beaten
- ¼ cup canola oil, divided
- 2 medium onions, finely chopped, divided
- ½ cup dry bread crumbs
- 1 tsp. dried oregano
- 2 lbs. ground beef
- 1 medium green pepper, chopped
- 2 cans (15 oz. each) tomato sauce
- ¼ cup packed brown sugar
- 2 Tbsp. prepared mustard
- 2½ tsp. chili powder
- ¾ tsp. salt
- ¾ tsp. garlic powder
- ½ tsp. pepper
  Dash Louisiana-style hot sauce

ADDITIONAL INGREDIENTS (PER SERVING)
- 1 hoagie bun, split and toasted
- 2 Tbsp. shredded cheddar cheese

1. Preheat oven to 400°. In a large bowl, combine the eggs, 2 Tbsp. oil, ½ cup onion, bread crumbs and oregano. Crumble beef over mixture and mix well. With wet hands, shape into 1½-in. balls.
2. Place meatballs on greased racks in shallow baking pans. Bake, uncovered, until no longer pink, 20-25 minutes; remove meatballs from pan and drain on paper towels.
3. Meanwhile, in a Dutch oven, saute green peppers and the remaining onion in remaining oil until tender. Stir in the tomato sauce, brown sugar, mustard, chili powder, salt, garlic powder, pepper and hot sauce. Bring to a boil. Reduce heat; simmer, uncovered, for 5 minutes. Add meatballs to sauce and stir to coat.
4. For each sandwich, place 4 meatballs on a bun and sprinkle with cheese.
FREEZE OPTION: *Cool meatballs; transfer to freezer containers. Cover and freeze for up to 3 months. To use, thaw meatballs in the refrigerator. Place in an ungreased shallow*

microwave-safe dish. Cover and microwave on high until heated through. Prepare sandwiches as directed above.
1 SANDWICH: *649 cal., 31g fat (10g sat. fat), 138mg chol., 1369mg sod., 58g carb. (17g sugars, 4g fiber), 36g pro.*
DIABETIC EXCHANGES: *1 lean meat.*

BACON BREAKFAST PIZZA

Pizza for breakfast? Yes, please! I used to make this rise-and-shine recipe for my morning drivers when I worked at a pizza delivery place. It's a quick, easy eye-opener that became quite a hit!
—Cathy Shortall, Easton, MD

TAKES: 30 min. • **MAKES:** 8 servings

- 1 tube (13.8 oz.) refrigerated pizza crust
- 2 Tbsp. olive oil, divided
- 6 large eggs
- 2 Tbsp. water
- 1 pkg. (3 oz.) bacon bits
- 1 cup shredded Monterey Jack cheese
- 1 cup shredded cheddar cheese

1. Unroll and press dough onto bottom and ½ in. up sides of a greased 15x10x1-in. pan. Prick thoroughly with a fork; brush with 1 Tbsp. oil. Bake at 400° until lightly browned, 7-8 minutes.
2. Meanwhile, whisk together eggs and water. In a nonstick skillet, heat remaining oil over medium heat. Add the eggs; cook and stir just until thickened and no liquid egg remains.
3. Spoon eggs over crust. Sprinkle with bacon bits and cheeses. Bake until cheese is melted, 5-7 minutes.
1 PIECE: *352 cal., 20g fat (8g sat. fat), 169mg chol., 842mg sod., 24g carb. (3g sugars, 1g fiber), 20g pro.*

HAM & BISCUIT BREAKFAST BITES

I love using my grandfather's homemade horseradish in dishes. This breakfast recipe is distinctive because it calls for rosemary. I love making these on the weekend and often share with my neighbors. These little bites also freeze nicely.
—Danielle Lee, Sewickley, PA

PREP: 20 min. • **BAKE:** 20 min.
MAKES: 1 dozen

- 3½ cups biscuit/baking mix
- 1 cup 2% milk
- ⅔ cup shredded cheddar cheese
- ½ cup chopped green pepper
- ⅔ cup cubed fully cooked ham or 3½ oz. Canadian bacon, cubed
- 4 large eggs or 1 cup egg substitute
- 2 to 3 Tbsp. prepared horseradish
- ½ tsp. salt
- ½ tsp. pepper
- 1½ tsp. minced fresh rosemary or ½ tsp. dried rosemary, crushed

1. Preheat oven to 375°. Stir together biscuit mix and milk to form a soft dough. On a lightly floured surface, pat dough to ¼-in. thickness; use floured 3½-in. round cutter to cut out 12 biscuits. Press each biscuit onto the bottom and up the sides of a greased muffin cup.
2. Divide cheese, green pepper and ham among the cups. Whisk together eggs, horseradish, salt and pepper; pour into cups. Sprinkle with rosemary.
3. Bake until eggs are set, 20-25 minutes. Let stand for 5 minutes before removing from pan.

1 BREAKFAST BITE: *204 cal., 8g fat (3g sat. fat), 74mg chol., 640mg sod., 26g carb. (2g sugars, 1g fiber), 9g pro.*

CREAMY RANCH PASTA

I came up with this dish after making some recipes for a bridal shower. It was party day and I needed some shortcuts! Everyone loves the simple Parmesan ranch white sauce, and it's easy to throw in veggies you have on hand.
—Merry Graham, Newhall, CA

PREP: 25 min. • **BAKE:** 30 min.
MAKES: 8 servings

- 2½ cups uncooked bow tie pasta
- 2 cups shredded Italian cheese blend
- 1¼ cups grated Parmesan cheese, divided
- 1 cup sour cream
- 1 cup ranch salad dressing
- 1 pkg. (10 oz.) frozen chopped spinach, thawed and squeezed dry or 2 cups chopped fresh spinach
- 2 slices day-old French bread (½ in. thick)
- 1 Tbsp. olive oil
- 1 tsp. grated lemon zest
- 1 tsp. dried parsley flakes
- ¼ tsp. garlic salt

1. Preheat oven to 350°. Cook pasta according to the package directions.
2. In a large bowl, mix Italian cheese blend, 1 cup Parmesan cheese, sour cream and salad dressing. Drain pasta; add to the cheese mixture. Fold in spinach. Transfer to a greased 13x9-in. baking dish.
3. Tear French bread into pieces; place in a food processor. Cover and pulse until crumbs form. Toss bread crumbs with olive oil, lemon zest, parsley, garlic salt and the remaining Parmesan cheese. Sprinkle over the pasta mixture.
4. Bake, covered, 25 minutes. Uncover; bake until golden brown and bubbly, 5-10 minutes.

¾ CUP: *436 cal., 30g fat (12g sat. fat), 40mg chol., 841mg sod., 25g carb. (3g sugars, 2g fiber), 15g pro.*

Holiday Helper
You can use either refrigerated or bottled ranch dressing in this recipe, depending on your personal preference.

SEASONAL GET-TOGETHERS

*An off-the-wall party with the gaudiest in seasonal attire,
a comforting night of companionship, or a heartwarming
celebration of a Christmas tradition—this season,
treat visitors to these amazing party spreads!*

Crazy Sock Party

In the time-honored tradition of the Ugly Sweater Party, it's time for the Crazy Sock Party! Exchange socks as presents, award prizes for the gaudiest footwear and offer up treats in holiday-themed stockings. And of course, pull out the stops with a spectacular spread of colorful and downright fun food!

SOCK MONKEY COOKIES

Try these classic cookies on for size. The first thing you'll notice about them is how cute they are—the second is how delicious they are!
—Christy Thelen, Kellogg, IA

PREP: 1 hour + chilling
BAKE: 10 min./batch + cooling
MAKES: about 4 dozen

- ¾ cup butter, softened
- 1 cup packed brown sugar
- 1 large egg, room temperature
- ¾ cup molasses
- 4 cups all-purpose flour
- 1½ tsp. baking soda
- ¼ tsp. salt
- 2 tsp. ground ginger
- 1½ tsp. ground cinnamon
- ¾ tsp. ground cloves

ROYAL ICING
- 4½ cups confectioners' sugar
- ⅓ cup water
- 4 tsp. meringue powder
- ¼ tsp. cream of tartar
- ⅛ tsp. salt
- 1 to 3 Tbsp. heavy whipping cream
  Food coloring and assorted sprinkles, optional

1. In a large bowl, cream butter and brown sugar until light and fluffy, 5-7 minutes. Beat in egg and molasses. In another bowl, whisk flour, baking soda, salt and spices; gradually beat into the creamed mixture. Divide dough in half; shape each half into a disk. Wrap each disk individually and refrigerate, covered, until firm enough to roll, 4 hours or overnight.

2. On a lightly floured surface, roll each portion of dough to ⅛-in. thickness. Cut with a floured 3½-in. monkey-shaped cookie cutter. Place cutouts 2 in. apart on ungreased baking sheets.

3. Bake at 350° until the edges are firm, 8-10 minutes. Remove from pans to wire racks; cool completely.

4. Place the first 5 icing ingredients in a small bowl; beat on low speed just until blended. Beat on high until stiff peaks form, 4-5 minutes. Thin with cream to desired consistency. Divide icing into thirds. Tint 1 portion red and 1 portion gray; leave the remaining portion white.

5. Pipe icing onto cookies and decorate with black sprinkles as desired. (Keep unused icing covered at all times with a damp cloth. If necessary, beat again on high speed to restore texture.) Let cookies stand at room temperature several hours or until frosting is dry and firm. Store in an airtight container.

1 COOKIE: *143 cal., 3g fat (2g sat. fat), 12mg chol., 88mg sod., 28g carb. (19g sugars, 0 fiber), 1g pro.*

TROUBLESHOOTING ROYAL ICING

That colorful coating might look pretty, but royal icing can be, well, a royal pain. Here are the most common frosting faux pas—and how to avoid them.

- **Don't overmix.** Use the lowest speed on your mixer. Whipping too much air into the mix will produce frosting that looks more like a sponge than a smooth finish.

- **Don't skimp on the sugar.** If the frosting isn't stiff enough, add a little more powdered sugar until it reaches a creamier consistency.

- **Completely mix the colors.** Tinting your own icing instead of buying pricey pre-blended tubes isn't hard, but be sure to thoroughly stir the coloring into the base icing, or you'll end up with sloppy streaks.

- **Don't ignore air bubbles.** A tiny air bubble can quickly become a huge dent in the frosting. Lightly tap the cookies on a flat surface after you ice them to bring the air bubbles to the surface. Then, use a toothpick to carefully pop each bubble and blend it into the rest of the frosting.

- **Don't leave it white.** Royal icing base might look like fresh snow when it's wet, but it'll dry as more of an off-white, cream shade. For a pure white tint, mix in a couple of drops of blue color.

- **Outline before flooding.** The key to flawless flooding is to pipe a border of slightly thicker icing around the edge of the area you want to fill in. If you skip this step, the different colors of royal icing will run together.

- **Sift the powdered sugar.** If you don't sift powdered sugar when you're mixing it into the royal icing, you'll wind up with clumps, which will clog the piping tips, make decorating difficult and make the final result look sloppy.

- **Give it time to dry.** Allow at least 24 hours of uninterrupted air drying before moving the cookies. To speed the process, place the cookies under a fan on the lowest setting while they set.

BACON CHEESE WREATH

My grandmother makes this smoky bacon and Parmesan spread for parties and holiday get-togethers. For a pretty yuletide presentation, accent the cream cheese wreath with green parsley and bright red pimientos.
—Lisa Carter, Warren, IN

PREP: 10 min. + chilling • **MAKES:** about 3 cups

- 2 pkg. (8 oz. each) cream cheese, softened
- ½ cup mayonnaise
- ⅓ cup grated Parmesan cheese
- ¼ cup sliced green onions, optional
- 10 bacon strips, cooked and crumbled
  Italian parsley sprigs and diced pimientos, optional
  Assorted crackers

1. In a small bowl, beat the cream cheese, mayonnaise, Parmesan cheese and, if desired, onions. Stir in bacon. Cover; refrigerate for 1-2 hours.
2. Invert a small bowl in the center of a serving platter. Drop the cream cheese mixture by rounded tablespoonfuls around the edge of bowl. Remove bowl and smooth the cream cheese mixture, forming a wreath. Garnish with parsley and pimientos if desired. Serve with crackers.
2 TBSP.: 87 cal., 9g fat (3g sat. fat), 15mg chol., 116mg sod., 0 carb. (0 sugars, 0 fiber), 2g pro.

BROKEN GLASS DESSERT

This decidedly vintage dessert may sound dangerous, but it's fun to make and to eat. When it's cut, it looks like stained glass windows!
—Kathy Crow, Cordova, AK

PREP: 30 min. + chilling • **MAKES:** 15 servings

- 1 pkg. (3 oz.) lime gelatin
- 4½ cups boiling water, divided
- 1 pkg. (3 oz.) strawberry gelatin
- 1 pkg. (3 oz.) orange gelatin
- 1½ cups graham cracker crumbs
- ½ cup sugar
- ½ cup butter, melted
- 1 envelope unflavored gelatin
- ¼ cup cold water
- 1 cup pineapple juice
- 1 carton (8 oz.) frozen whipped topping, thawed

1. Combine the lime gelatin and 1½ cups boiling water; stir until gelatin is dissolved. Pour into a lightly greased 8x4-in. loaf pan; chill until very firm. Repeat to make the strawberry and orange gelatins in separate pans. Combine the crumbs, sugar and butter; press into a greased 13x9-in. dish. Chill.
2. Meanwhile, in a small bowl, soften unflavored gelatin in cold water for 5 minutes. In a small saucepan, bring pineapple juice to a boil. Stir in unflavored gelatin until dissolved. Transfer to a large bowl; set aside until room temperature, 20-30 minutes.
3. When flavored gelatins are firm, cut into ½-in. cubes. In a large bowl, whisk whipped topping into pineapple juice mixture. Gently fold ⅔ of the gelatin cubes into whipped topping mixture. Spoon over crust; top with remaining cubes. Chill for at least 2 hours.
1 PIECE: 183 cal., 4g fat (3g sat. fat), 0 chol., 86mg sod., 35g carb. (29g sugars, 0 fiber), 3g pro.

CAPRESE SALAD KABOBS

Trade in the usual veggie party platter for these lively kabobs. I often make them for my family to snack on—and the kids like to help with the recipe!
—*Christine Mitchell, Glendora, CA*

TAKES: 10 min. • **MAKES:** 12 kabobs

- 24 grape tomatoes
- 12 cherry-size fresh mozzarella cheese balls
- 24 fresh basil leaves
- 2 Tbsp. olive oil
- 2 tsp. balsamic vinegar

On each of 12 appetizer skewers, alternately thread 2 tomatoes, 1 cheese ball and 2 basil leaves. To serve, whisk together oil and vinegar; drizzle over kabobs.
1 KABOB: *44 cal., 4g fat (1g sat. fat), 5mg chol., 10mg sod., 2g carb. (1g sugars, 0 fiber), 1g pro.*
DIABETIC EXCHANGES: *1 fat.*

WARM CHRISTMAS PUNCH

Red Hot candies add rich color and spiciness to this festive punch, and the cranberry juice gives it a little tang. Our children always request it for December brunches.
—*Julie Sterchi, Campbellsville, KY*

PREP: 5 min. • **COOK:** 2 hours • **MAKES:** 8 servings (2 qt.)

- 1 bottle (32 oz.) cranberry juice
- 5 cans (6 oz. each) unsweetened pineapple juice
- ⅓ cup Red Hots
- 1 cinnamon stick (3½ in.)
   Additional cinnamon sticks or sugared cranberries, optional

1. In a 3-qt. slow cooker, combine cranberry and pineapple juices, Red Hots and cinnamon stick. Cover and cook on low for 2-4 hours or until heated through and candies are dissolved.
2. Discard cinnamon stick before serving. Serve with additional cinnamon sticks or sugared cranberries if desired.
1 CUP: *161 cal., 0 fat (0 sat. fat), 0 chol., 5mg sod., 41g carb. (34g sugars, 0 fiber), 1g pro.*

SWISS CHEESE CHICKEN PUFFS

My neighborhood has a progressive dinner before Christmas each year, and every house provides a course. These delightful puffs were served one year to everyone's enjoyment. The cheesy flavor and creamy texture of the chicken salad mixture is wonderful inside the tender puffs.
—Donna Kittredge, Westborough, MA

- -

PREP: 35 min. • **BAKE:** 20 min./batch
MAKES: 3 dozen

- 1¼ cups water
- ¼ cup butter, cubed
- ½ tsp. salt
- 1 cup all-purpose flour
- 4 large eggs, room temperature
- 1 cup shredded Swiss cheese

FILLING
- 2 cups finely chopped cooked chicken
- 1 cup shredded Swiss cheese
- ¾ cup chopped celery
- ½ cup mayonnaise
- ½ tsp. salt
- ½ tsp. prepared yellow mustard
- ⅛ tsp. pepper
  Minced chives, optional

1. Preheat the oven to 400°. In a large saucepan, bring the water, butter and salt to a boil. Add flour all at once and stir until a smooth ball forms. Remove from the heat; let stand for 5 minutes. Add the eggs, 1 at a time, beating well after each addition. Continue beating until the mixture is smooth and shiny. Stir in the Swiss cheese.
2. Drop by tablespoonfuls 2 in. apart onto greased baking sheets. Bake until golden brown, 20-25 minutes. Remove to wire racks. Immediately split puffs open; remove tops and set aside. Discard soft dough from inside. Cool puffs.
3. Meanwhile, in a large bowl, combine the filling ingredients. Spoon into the puffs and, if desired, sprinkle with chives; replace tops. Serve immediately.
1 PUFF: *92 cal., 7g fat (3g sat. fat), 40mg chol., 124mg sod., 3g carb. (0 sugars, 0 fiber), 5g pro.*

ARGYLE CAKE

This wacky cake will be the star of your retro Christmas party. Have fun with the decorations and coloring, choosing the colors and sock patterns you like best.
—Taste of Home *Test Kitchen*

- -

PREP: 1 hour • **BAKE:** 40 min. + cooling
MAKES: about 50 servings

- 2¼ cups butter, softened
- 12 oz. cream cheese, softened
- 4½ cups sugar
- 12 large eggs, room temperature
- 1½ tsp. vanilla extract
- 4½ cups cake flour

FROSTING
- 1½ cups butter, softened
- 8 cups confectioners' sugar
- 3 tsp. vanilla extract
- 8 to 10 Tbsp. whole milk
- 1 cup seedless raspberry jam
- 1 pkg. (24 oz.) ready-to-use rolled blue fondant
- 1 pkg. (24 oz.) ready-to-use rolled green fondant
  Red gel food coloring

1. Preheat oven to 325°. Line two 13x9-in. baking pans with parchment and grease the paper; set aside.
2. In a large bowl, beat butter, cream cheese and sugar until light and fluffy, 5-7 minutes. Add the eggs, 1 at a time, beating well after each addition. Beat in vanilla. Add flour; mix well. Transfer to prepared pans. Bake until a toothpick inserted in the center comes out clean, 40-45 minutes. Cool completely on a wire rack; remove parchment.
3. In a large bowl, beat butter until light and fluffy. Beat in the confectioners' sugar and vanilla. Add enough milk to achieve the desired consistency.
4. Using a serrated knife, level tops of cakes if necessary. Place 1 cake layer on a cake board. Frost top with frosting; spread raspberry jam to within ½ in. of edges. Top with the remaining layer. Frost top and sides of cake with the remaining frosting, reserving 1 cup frosting for decoration.
5. For fondant argyle: On a work surface dusted with confectioners' sugar, roll out green fondant into an ⅛-in.-thick rectangle. Using a 4-in. diamond cutter, cut out 10 diamonds. Repeat with blue fondant. Place fondant diamonds in alternating colors on the top and sides of cake, cutting in half to fit the ends.
6. Color the reserved frosting with red gel food coloring and place in a piping bag fitted with a #2 piping tip. Pipe dashed lines diagonally across the fondant diamonds to create an argyle pattern.
1 PIECE: *426 cal., 18g fat (11g sat. fat), 88mg chol., 150mg sod., 63g carb. (53g sugars, 0 fiber), 3g pro.*

Holiday Soup Party

When the winter winds blow, welcome friends to your home with a selection of savory soups and stews, paired with delicious homemade breads. It's the ultimate in cold-weather comfort and ideal for a casual and relaxed gathering with people you love.

PORK & GREEN CHILE STEW

This easily adaptable stew is ready in four hours if cooked on high in a slow cooker, or in eight hours if cooked low and slow.
—Paul Sedillo, Plainfield, IL

PREP: 40 min. • **COOK:** 7 hours
MAKES: 8 servings (2 qt.)

- 2 lbs. boneless pork shoulder butt roast, cut into ¾-in. cubes
- 1 large onion, cut into ½-in. pieces
- 2 Tbsp. canola oil
- 1 tsp. salt
- 1 tsp. coarsely ground pepper
- 4 large potatoes, peeled and cut into ¾-in. cubes
- 3 cups water
- 1 can (16 oz.) hominy, rinsed and drained
- 2 cans (4 oz. each) chopped green chiles
- 2 Tbsp. quick-cooking tapioca
- 2 garlic cloves, minced
- ½ tsp. dried oregano
- ½ tsp. ground cumin
- 1 cup minced fresh cilantro
  Sour cream, optional

1. In a large skillet, brown pork and onion in oil in batches. Sprinkle with salt and pepper. Transfer to a 5-qt. slow cooker.
2. Stir in potatoes, water, hominy, chiles, tapioca, garlic, oregano and cumin. Cover and cook on low until meat is tender, 7-9 hours. Stir in cilantro during the last 30 minutes of cooking. If desired, serve with sour cream and additional cilantro.
1 CUP: *322 cal., 15g fat (4g sat. fat), 67mg chol., 723mg sod., 25g carb. (3g sugars, 3g fiber), 21g pro.*
DIABETIC EXCHANGES: *3 medium-fat meat, 1½ starch, ½ fat.*

BAY LEAF WREATH

A bay leaf is a regular addition to any great soup stock, so why not deck the halls with a wreath of the fragrant herb for your soup party? You can buy plain bay wreaths online or from culinary or craft stores and add ribbons, berries or ornaments for a touch of color. Or, order bay branches from a garden supplier and build your own around a foam core.

GOUDA & ROASTED POTATO BREAD

Our family tried roasted potato bread at a bakery on a road trip, and I came up with my own recipe when we realized we lived much too far away to have it regularly. It makes for a really fantastic roast beef sandwich and also goes well with soups.
—Elisabeth Larsen, Pleasant Grove, UT

PREP: 45 min. + rising • **BAKE:** 40 min.
MAKES: 1 loaf (16 slices)

- ½ lb. Yukon Gold potatoes, chopped (about ¾ cup)
- 1½ tsp. olive oil
- 1½ tsp. salt, divided
- 1 pkg. (¼ oz.) active dry yeast
- 2½ to 3 cups all-purpose flour
- 1 cup warm water (120° to 130°)
- ½ cup shredded smoked Gouda cheese

1. Arrange 1 oven rack at lowest rack setting; place a second rack in the middle of the oven. Preheat oven to 425°. Place potatoes in a greased 15x10x1-in. baking pan. Drizzle with oil; sprinkle with ½ tsp. salt. Toss to coat. Roast until tender, 20-25 minutes, stirring occasionally.
2. In a large bowl, mix yeast, remaining 1 tsp. salt and 2 cups flour. Add warm water; beat on medium until smooth.

Stir in enough remaining flour to form a soft dough (dough will be sticky). Turn dough onto a floured surface; knead until smooth and elastic, 6-8 minutes. Gently knead in the roasted potatoes and cheese. Place in a greased bowl, turning once to grease the top. Cover and let rise in a warm place until doubled, about 1 hour.
3. Punch down dough. Shape into a 7-in. round loaf. Place on a parchment-lined baking sheet. Cover with a kitchen towel; let rise in a warm place until the dough expands to a 9-in. loaf, about 45 minutes.
4. Place an oven-safe skillet on the bottom oven rack. Meanwhile, in a teakettle, bring 2 cups water to a boil. Using a sharp knife, make a slash (¼ in. deep) across the top of the loaf. Place bread on top rack. Pull bottom rack out by 6-8 in.; add boiling water to the skillet. (Work quickly and carefully, pouring water away from you. Don't worry if some water is left in the kettle.) Carefully slide bottom rack back into place; quickly close door to trap steam in oven.
5. Bake 10 minutes at 425°, then reduce oven setting to 375°. Bake until deep golden brown, 30-35 minutes longer. Remove loaf to a wire rack to cool.
1 SLICE: *101 cal., 2g fat (1g sat. fat), 4mg chol., 253mg sod., 18g carb. (0 sugars, 1g fiber), 3g pro.*

BUTTERY CORNBREAD

A friend gave me this recipe several years ago, and it's my favorite. I love to serve the melt-in-your-mouth cornbread hot from the oven with butter and syrup. It gets rave reviews on holidays and at potluck dinners.
—Nicole Callen, Auburn, CA

PREP: 15 min. • **BAKE:** 25 min. • **MAKES:** 15 servings

  ⅔ cup butter, softened
  1 cup sugar
  3 large eggs, room temperature
1⅔ cups 2% milk
2⅓ cups all-purpose flour
  1 cup cornmeal
4½ tsp. baking powder
  1 tsp. salt

1. Preheat oven to 400°. In a large bowl, cream butter and sugar until light and fluffy, 5-7 minutes. Combine eggs and milk. Combine flour, cornmeal, baking powder and salt; add to the creamed mixture alternately with the egg mixture.
2. Pour into a greased 13x9-in. baking pan. Bake 22-27 minutes or until a toothpick inserted in center comes out clean. Cut into squares; serve warm.
1 SQUARE: *259 cal., 10g fat (6g sat. fat), 68mg chol., 386mg sod., 37g carb. (15g sugars, 1g fiber), 5g pro.*

WHITE CHILI WITH A KICK

Store-bought rotisserie chicken makes this spicy chili easy, but you could also cook your own. We like it with various combinations of sour cream, green onions, cheese and salsa on top.
—Emmajean Anderson, Mendota Heights, MN

PREP: 20 min. • **COOK:** 15 min. • **MAKES:** 9 servings (2¼ qt.)

  1 large onion, chopped
  6 Tbsp. butter, cubed
  2 Tbsp. all-purpose flour
  2 cups chicken broth
  ¾ cup half-and-half cream
  1 rotisserie chicken, cut into bite-sized pieces
  2 cans (15 oz. each) cannellini beans, rinsed and drained
  1 can (11 oz.) white corn, drained
  2 cans (4 oz. each) chopped green chiles
  2 tsp. ground cumin
  1 tsp. chili powder
  ½ tsp. salt
  ½ tsp. white pepper
  ½ tsp. hot pepper sauce
1½ cups shredded pepper jack cheese
    Optional: Salsa and chopped green onions

1. In a Dutch oven, saute onion in butter. Stir in flour until blended; cook and stir until golden brown, about 3 minutes. Gradually add broth and cream. Bring to a boil; cook and stir until thickened, about 2 minutes.
2. Add the chicken, beans, corn, chiles, cumin, chili powder, salt, pepper and pepper sauce; heat through. Stir in cheese until melted. If desired, garnish individual servings with salsa and green onions.
1 CUP: *424 cal., 21g fat (11g sat. fat), 113mg chol., 896mg sod., 26g carb. (3g sugars, 5g fiber), 31g pro.*

AUTUMN PUMPKIN CHILI

We serve this chili often because everyone loves it, even our finicky grandchildren. It's also earned a thumbs-up rating with family and friends who've tried it in other states. It's a definite keeper in my book!
—Kimberly Nagy, Port Hadlock, WA

- -

PREP: 20 min. • **COOK:** 7 hours
MAKES: 4 servings (1¼ qt.)

- 1 medium onion, chopped
- 1 small green pepper, chopped
- 1 small sweet yellow pepper, chopped
- 1 Tbsp. canola oil
- 1 garlic clove, minced
- 1 lb. ground turkey
- 1 can (15 oz.) solid-pack pumpkin
- 1 can (14½ oz.) diced tomatoes, undrained
- 4½ tsp. chili powder
- ¼ tsp. salt
- ¼ tsp. pepper
  Optional toppings: Shredded cheddar cheese, sour cream, corn chips and sliced green onions

1. In a large skillet, saute the onion and green and yellow peppers in oil until tender. Add garlic; cook 1 minute longer. Crumble turkey into skillet. Cook over medium heat until meat is no longer pink.
2. Transfer to a 3-qt. slow cooker. Stir in the pumpkin, tomatoes, chili powder, salt and pepper. Cover and cook on low for 7-9 hours. If desired, serve with toppings.
1¼ CUPS: *281 cal., 13g fat (3g sat. fat), 75mg chol., 468mg sod., 20g carb. (9g sugars, 7g fiber), 25g pro.*
DIABETIC EXCHANGES: *3 lean meat, 1 starch, 1 vegetable, 1 fat.*

GARLIC ROSEMARY PULL-APART BREAD

This recipe is a different type of pull-apart bread. It can be eaten by itself dipped in marinara or as part of a meal. You could add sun-dried tomatoes, pesto or an onion soup mix packet instead of the rosemary-garlic blend for a different flavor.
—Christina Trikoris, Clarksville, TN

- -

PREP: 25 min. + rising
BAKE: 55 min. + cooling
MAKES: 16 servings

- 3 tsp. active dry yeast
- 1 tsp. salt
- 5¼ to 6 cups all-purpose flour
- 1 cup water
- 1 cup butter, cubed
- ½ cup whole milk
- 2 large eggs, room temperature
FLAVORING
- ½ cup butter, melted
- 6 garlic cloves, minced
- 2 Tbsp. minced fresh rosemary or 2 tsp. dried rosemary, crushed
- 1 tsp. salt
- 1 cup grated Parmesan cheese

1. In a large bowl, mix yeast, salt and 2 cups flour. In a small saucepan, heat water, cubed butter and milk to 120°-130°. Add to dry ingredients; beat on medium speed 2 minutes. Add eggs; beat on high 2 minutes. Stir in enough of the remaining flour to form a soft dough (dough will be sticky).

2. Turn onto a floured surface; knead until smooth and elastic, 6-8 minutes. Place in a greased bowl, turning once to grease the top. Cover and let rise in a warm place until doubled, about 1 hour.
3. Punch dough down. Turn onto a lightly floured surface; shape into 1½-in. balls. Combine melted butter, garlic, rosemary and salt. Dip 10 dough balls into butter mixture. Place in a greased 10-in. fluted tube pan; sprinkle with a scant ¼ cup Parmesan cheese. Repeat with remaining balls and Parmesan cheese. Drizzle with any remaining butter mixture. Cover and let rise until doubled, about 45 minutes.
4. Bake at 350° until golden brown, 55-70 minutes or until a thermometer inserted into bread reads 200°. Cool for 10 minutes before inverting onto a serving plate. Serve warm.
1 SERVING: *341 cal., 20g fat (12g sat. fat), 74mg chol., 536mg sod., 33g carb. (1g sugars, 1g fiber), 7g pro.*

CHUNKY VEGETARIAN CHILI

This robust chili teams rice and two kinds of beans with a variety of colorful vegetables for a hearty meatless meal that's great tasting and good for you.
—Taste of Home *Test Kitchen*

PREP: 20 min. • **COOK:** 25 min.
MAKES: 11 servings (2¾ qt.)

- 1 medium green pepper, chopped
- 1 medium onion, chopped
- 3 garlic cloves, minced
- 1 Tbsp. canola oil
- 2 cans (14½ oz. each) Mexican-style stewed tomatoes, undrained
- 1 can (16 oz.) kidney beans, rinsed and drained
- 1 can (15 oz.) pinto beans, rinsed and drained
- 1 can (11 oz.) whole kernel corn, drained
- 2½ cups water
- 1 cup uncooked long grain rice
- 1 to 2 Tbsp. chili powder
- 1½ tsp. ground cumin

In a Dutch oven, saute green pepper, onion and garlic in oil until tender. Stir in all remaining ingredients; bring to a boil. Reduce heat; cover and simmer until the rice is cooked, stirring occasionally, 25-30 minutes. If thinner chili is desired, add more water.

1 CUP: *196 cal., 2g fat (0 sat. fat), 0 chol., 424mg sod., 37g carb. (6g sugars, 6g fiber), 7g pro.*
DIABETIC EXCHANGES: *2½ starch.*

BEEFY SWEET POTATO CHILI

This recipe was created with friends when we lived in rainy Seattle. There's nothing better than a bowl of chili on a cold day. The sweet potatoes make this one fabulous, but you can leave them out—the recipe will still give you a delicious basic chili!
—Jonell Tempero, Omaha, NE

PREP: 45 min. • **COOK:** 40 min.
MAKES: 6 servings (2¼ qt.)

- 2 medium sweet potatoes, peeled and cubed
- 2 lbs. ground beef
- 2 celery ribs, chopped
- 1 large onion, chopped
- 1 medium green pepper, chopped
- 4 garlic cloves, minced
- 1 jalapeno pepper, seeded and minced
- 2 cans (14½ oz. each) reduced-sodium chicken broth
- 1 can (14½ oz.) diced tomatoes, undrained
- 2 Tbsp. chili powder
- 2 Tbsp. tomato paste
- ¾ tsp. ground cumin
- ½ tsp. salt
- ½ tsp. pepper
- ¼ tsp. cayenne pepper
- 1 can (16 oz.) kidney beans, rinsed and drained
- 2 Tbsp. butter

1. Place potatoes in a greased 15x10x1-in. baking pan. Bake, uncovered, at 400° until tender, stirring once, 20-25 minutes.
2. Meanwhile, in a Dutch oven, cook the beef, celery, onion, green pepper, garlic and jalapeno over medium heat until the meat is no longer pink and the vegetables are tender; drain.
3. Stir in the broth, tomatoes, chili powder, tomato paste and seasonings. Bring to a boil. Reduce heat; cover and simmer for 30 minutes. Add the sweet potatoes, beans and butter; heat through.

1½ CUPS: *471 cal., 22g fat (9g sat. fat), 104mg chol., 956mg sod., 32g carb. (10g sugars, 8g fiber), 36g pro.*

Tree-Lighting Party

Whether cheering the lighting of your community's tree or the one in your living room, gather friends and family for a heartwarming celebration. As the lights go on, dish up a savory spread of pure holiday comfort food.

CURRY-RUBBED ROAST CHICKEN

There is just something so right about serving a roasted chicken to loved ones! This recipe is simple—yet it's packed with spicy showoff flavors suitable for any special occasion.
—Merry Graham, Newhall, CA

- -

PREP: 20 min. • **COOK:** 1½ hours + standing
MAKES: 6 servings

- 4 Tbsp. coconut oil, divided
- 2½ tsp. salt, divided
- 2 tsp. Madras curry powder
- ½ tsp. granulated garlic
- 1 roasting chicken (5 to 6 lbs.)
- ¼ tsp. pepper
- 1 cup chopped leeks (white portion only)
- 1 celery rib, coarsely chopped
- 3 green onions, chopped
- 1 medium lemon, quartered
- 1 cup reduced-sodium chicken broth

GRAVY
- 1 Tbsp. unsalted butter
- 1 Tbsp. all-purpose flour
- 1 cup reduced-sodium chicken broth
- ½ cup white wine
  Optional: Lemon slices, minced fresh parsley and minced chives

1. Preheat the oven to 350°. Mix 2 Tbsp. coconut oil and 2 tsp. salt with the curry powder and garlic. With fingers, carefully loosen skin from chicken breast and upper legs; rub coconut oil mixture under skin. Remove giblets from cavity and save for another use. Sprinkle cavity with pepper and remaining salt; rub inside and outside of chicken with remaining coconut oil.
2. Combine leeks, celery, green onions and lemon and toss lightly; loosely stuff cavity. Tuck wings under chicken; tie drumsticks together. Place breast side up on a rack in a shallow roasting pan.
3. Roast 45 minutes; add broth to pan. Continue roasting until a thermometer reads 165° when inserted in center of stuffing and at least 170° in the thigh, another 45-60 minutes. (Cover loosely with foil if chicken browns too quickly.)
4. Pour juices from cavity into the pan. Remove chicken to a serving platter; tent with foil. Let stand 15-20 minutes before removing stuffing and slicing.
5. For gravy, pour pan juices into a large saucepan; skim off fat. Bring to a boil over medium heat. Add butter and flour; cook and stir until slightly thickened. Add broth and wine; cook and stir until thickened, 2-3 minutes. Serve with chicken and, if desired, lemon slices, parsley and chives.
1 SERVING: *580 cal., 38g fat (17g sat. fat), 154mg chol., 1328mg sod., 6g carb. (2g sugars, 1g fiber), 49g pro.*

HONEY GARLIC GREEN BEANS

Green beans are an ever-popular standby, but they can seem ordinary on their own. It takes just a few extra ingredients to give them sweet and salty attitude.
—Shannon Dobos, Calgary, AB

- -

TAKES: 20 min. • **MAKES:** 8 servings

- 4 Tbsp. honey
- 2 Tbsp. reduced-sodium soy sauce
- 4 garlic cloves, minced
- ¼ tsp. salt
- ¼ tsp. crushed red pepper flakes
- 2 lbs. fresh green beans, trimmed

1. Whisk together the first 5 ingredients; set aside. In a 6-qt. stockpot, bring 10 cups water to a boil. Add beans in batches; cook, uncovered, just until crisp-tender, 2-3 minutes. Remove beans and immediately drop into ice water. Drain and pat dry.
2. Coat stockpot with cooking spray. Add beans; cook, stirring constantly, over high heat until slightly blistered, 2-3 minutes. Add sauce; continue stirring until beans are coated and sauce starts to evaporate slightly, 2-3 minutes. Remove from heat.
¾ CUP: *72 cal., 0 fat (0 sat. fat), 0 chol., 225mg sod., 18g carb. (12g sugars, 4g fiber), 2g pro.*
DIABETIC EXCHANGES: *1 vegetable, ½ starch.*

TINY TREES

Use pine cones to mimic full-grown trees in these sweet tabletop designs that are perfect as decorations for your tree-lighting party. Spray-paint the pine cones with green paint and let dry completely. Then fill flower pots or candleholders with crumpled tissue paper and set the pine cones in place, securing them with hot glue if you like. Add stars and other holiday decorations and a quick dash of silver spray paint to give them an elegant look. (Just be sure to let the paint dry completely before gluing the decorations in place on the trees.)

APPLE BREAD PUDDING WITH CARAMEL SAUCE

This recipe has been in my life for a long time. It's one of those old recipes that you can't remember where you found it, but you're sure glad you did! It's always on my buffet when I put together a party.
—Cleo Gonske, Redding, CA

- -

PREP: 50 min. • **BAKE:** 40 min.
MAKES: 16 servings (1¾ cups sauce)

- ¾ cup butter, cubed
- 4 cups chopped peeled tart apples (about 4 medium)
- 2 cups sugar
- ½ cup raisins
- ½ cup chopped walnuts
- 3 tsp. ground cinnamon
- 2 tsp. vanilla extract

BREAD PUDDING

- 6 large eggs
- 2½ cups 2% milk
- 1½ cups plus 2 Tbsp. sugar, divided
- 1 cup heavy whipping cream
- 1½ tsp. vanilla extract
  Dash ground nutmeg
- 1 loaf (1 lb.) French bread, cut into 1-in. cubes

CARAMEL SAUCE

- 1 cup sugar
- ¼ cup water
- 1 cup heavy whipping cream
- 2 Tbsp. butter

1. Preheat oven to 350°. In a large skillet, heat butter over medium heat. Add apples, sugar, raisins, walnuts and cinnamon; bring just to a boil, stirring constantly. Reduce heat; simmer, uncovered, stirring occasionally, until the apples are tender. Remove from heat; stir in vanilla.

2. In a large bowl, whisk the eggs, milk, 1½ cups sugar, cream, vanilla and nutmeg until blended. Stir in bread cubes and the apple mixture. Transfer to a greased 13x9-in. baking dish. Sprinkle with remaining sugar. Bake, uncovered, for 40-45 minutes or until a knife inserted in the center comes out clean.

3. For caramel sauce, in a small heavy saucepan, combine sugar and water; stir gently to moisten all the sugar. Cook over medium-low heat, gently swirling pan occasionally, until sugar is dissolved. Cover; bring to a boil over medium-high heat. Cook 1 minute.

4. Uncover pan; continue to boil until syrup turns a medium amber color. Immediately remove from heat and carefully stir in cream and butter. Serve with warm bread pudding.

1 SERVING: 606 cal., 27g fat (15g sat. fat), 149mg chol., 312mg sod., 87g carb. (68g sugars, 2g fiber), 8g pro.

SPINACH SALAD WITH WARM BACON DRESSING

My spinach salad with a comforting bacon dressing is a recipe I turn to again and again in winter. It's quick, elegant and so delicious. I can always count on compliments.
—Sandy Davis, Prescott, AZ

- -

TAKES: 30 min. • **MAKES:** 4 servings

- 3 bacon strips, chopped
- 2 Tbsp. red wine vinegar
- 1 small garlic clove, minced
- ½ tsp. packed brown sugar
- ½ tsp. Dijon mustard
- ¼ tsp. salt
- ⅛ tsp. coarsely ground pepper
  Dash ground nutmeg
  Dash crushed red pepper flakes
- ¼ cup olive oil
- 6 oz. fresh baby spinach (about 8 cups)
- ⅓ cup thinly sliced red onion
- 4 hard-boiled large eggs, chopped

1. In a skillet, cook bacon over medium heat until crisp, stirring occasionally. Using a slotted spoon, remove bacon to paper towels. Discard all but 1 Tbsp. of the drippings.

2. Add the vinegar, garlic, brown sugar, mustard and seasonings to the drippings; heat through, stirring to blend. Transfer to a small bowl; gradually whisk in oil. Stir in half the bacon.

3. Place spinach, onion and eggs in a large bowl; toss with warm dressing. Sprinkle with remaining bacon; serve immediately.

1¾ CUPS: 280 cal., 25g fat (6g sat. fat), 196mg chol., 373mg sod., 5g carb. (2g sugars, 1g fiber), 10g pro.

MUSHROOM SHEPHERD'S PIE

It sounds silly, but the one thing I miss most about meatless meals is, well, the meat! That is, except for this one. Hearty and satisfying, this shepherd's pie works as a meatless entree or in smaller portions as a side dish.

—Glen Warren, Keswick, ON

PREP: 45 min. • **BAKE:** 15 min.
MAKES: 6 servings

- 2 Tbsp. butter
- 3 Tbsp. olive oil, divided
- 1 lb. sliced fresh button mushrooms
- ½ lb. coarsely chopped fresh oyster mushrooms
- ½ lb. coarsely chopped fresh chantrelle mushrooms
- 1 large onion, thinly sliced
- 3 garlic cloves, minced
- ½ cup dry red wine or vegetable stock
- ½ cup vegetable stock
- 2 Tbsp. minced fresh parsley
- 2 Tbsp. minced fresh thyme
- ¼ tsp. salt
- ¼ tsp. pepper
- 1 Tbsp. all-purpose flour
- 1 Tbsp. butter, softened

TOPPING

- 6 medium red potatoes, cubed
- ¼ cup 2% milk
- 2 to 4 Tbsp. butter
- 1 tsp. garlic powder
- ¾ tsp. salt
- ¼ tsp. pepper
- ¾ cup shredded cheddar cheese

1. Preheat oven to 425°. In a Dutch oven, heat butter and 2 Tbsp. oil over medium-high heat. Add mushrooms; cook and stir 4-6 minutes or until browned. Remove and set aside.

2. In the same pan, heat remaining oil. Add onion; cook and stir 3-4 minutes or until tender. Add garlic; cook 1 minute longer. Add wine, stirring to loosen browned bits from pan. Bring to a boil; cook 2-3 minutes or until wine has almost evaporated. Stir in stock, parsley, thyme, salt, pepper and mushrooms. Bring to a boil; cook until liquid is reduced by half, 3-4 minutes.

3. In a small bowl, mix flour and softened butter until blended; stir into mushroom mixture until thickened. Transfer to a greased 11x7-in. baking dish.

4. Meanwhile, place potatoes in a large saucepan; add water to cover. Bring to a boil. Reduce heat; cook, uncovered, 10-15 minutes or until tender. Drain; return to pan. Mash potatoes, gradually adding milk, butter, garlic powder, salt and pepper.

5. Spread potatoes over the mushroom mixture; sprinkle with cheese. Bake for 15-20 minutes or until heated through. If desired, top with additional thyme or parsley.

1½ CUPS: 354 cal., 22g fat (10g sat. fat), 40mg chol., 636mg sod., 30g carb. (6g sugars, 5g fiber), 11g pro.

¼ cup mayonnaise
2 Tbsp. snipped fresh dill
¾ tsp. seasoned salt
¼ tsp. pepper
15 sheets phyllo dough (14x9-in. size)
½ cup butter, melted
Optional: Tzatziki sauce, lemon wedges and fresh dill sprigs

1. Preheat oven to 425°. In a large bowl, mix the first 9 ingredients. Place 1 sheet of phyllo dough on a work surface; brush with butter. Layer with 2 additional phyllo sheets, brushing each layer. (Keep the remaining phyllo covered with plastic wrap and a damp towel to prevent it from drying out.)

2. Arrange ¾ cup of the spinach mixture in a narrow strip along the long end of phyllo to within 1 in. of edges. Fold the bottom edge of phyllo over filling, then roll up. Brush the end of phyllo dough with butter and press to seal. Repeat 4 times with phyllo sheets, butter and the spinach mixture. Place rolls on a parchment-lined 15x10x1-in. baking pan, seam side down.

3. Cut rolls diagonally into 2-in. pieces (do not separate). Brush tops with the remaining butter. Bake until golden brown, 12-15 minutes. If desired, serve with tzatziki sauce, lemon wedges and dill sprigs.

FREEZE OPTION: *Cover and freeze unbaked rolls on a parchment-lined baking sheet until firm. Transfer to a freezer container; return to freezer. To use, bake rolls on a parchment-lined 15x10x1-in. baking pan in a preheated 375° oven until heated through and golden brown, about 25 minutes.*

1 APPETIZER: *96 cal., 8g fat (4g sat. fat), 29mg chol., 155mg sod., 5g carb. (1g sugars, 1g fiber), 2g pro.*

COZY-UP HOT CHOCOLATE

My mom created this recipe to serve large groups of carolers and frozen sledders. For parties, I use a slow cooker to keep it warm for serving—I'll often add flavor extracts, too.
—Mary Nine, Indianapolis, IN

- -

TAKES: 15 min. • **MAKES:** 6 servings

2 cups confectioners' sugar
¾ cup sugar
½ cup baking cocoa
½ tsp. salt
5½ cups water
Large marshmallows, optional

In a large saucepan, mix the sugars, cocoa and salt; gradually stir in water. Bring to a boil over medium heat, stirring constantly. Cook and stir for 2 minutes. Ladle into mugs. If desired, top with marshmallows.

1 CUP: 273 cal., 1g fat (0 sat. fat), 0 chol., 198mg sod., 69g carb. (64g sugars, 1g fiber), 1g pro.

MAKE-AHEAD SPINACH PHYLLO APPETIZERS

I love having appetizers on hand in the freezer, especially when the holiday season is fast approaching. This easy recipe is one of my all-time favorites. Everyone loves them, they're easy to prep and they bake up in about 20 minutes!
—Shannon Dobos, Calgary, AB

- -

PREP: 45 min. • **BAKE:** 15 min.
MAKES: 2½ dozen

2 pkg. (10 oz. each) frozen chopped spinach, thawed and squeezed dry
1 pkg. (8 oz.) cream cheese, softened
½ cup crumbled feta cheese
2 large eggs, lightly beaten
¼ cup finely chopped onion

RED & WHITE CHRISTMAS

Red and white are the colors of peppermint sticks,
of holly berries and snowflakes—and all these delicious
Christmastime treats! Make your sweets table
a sight to behold with this dazzling display.

CINNAMON CANDY POPCORN

This crisp bright-colored snack is more festive than traditional caramel corn. My family just loves it! A friend shared the recipe, and I've given it to several people myself. Set out in pretty bowls, it makes a tasty table decoration. I also put it in sandwich bags for a children's party snack.
—Kaye Kemper, Windfall, IN

PREP: 30 min. • **BAKE:** 1 hour + cooling • **MAKES:** 8 qt.

- 8 qt. popped popcorn
- 1 cup butter, cubed
- ½ cup light corn syrup
- 1 pkg. (9 oz.) Red Hot candies

1. Preheat oven to 250°. Place popcorn in a large bowl; set aside. In a large saucepan, combine butter, corn syrup and candies; bring to a boil over medium heat, stirring constantly. Boil for 5 minutes, stirring occasionally. Pour over popcorn and toss to coat.
2. Transfer to 2 greased 15x10x1-in. baking pans. Bake for 1 hour, stirring every 15 minutes. Remove from pans and place on waxed paper to cool. Break apart; store in airtight containers.
1 CUP: *152 cal., 9g fat (4g sat. fat), 15mg chol., 161mg sod., 18g carb. (9g sugars, 1g fiber), 1g pro.*

STRAWBERRY PANZANELLA SALAD

Always a crowd-pleaser, this salad never disappoints. This version is sweet and offers the opportunity to use fruit in a creative way. For a fun twist, use margarita glasses when serving and rim the glass with sugar and a strawberry garnish.
—Careema Bell, Trenton, NJ

PREP: 15 min. • **BAKE:** 10 min. • **MAKES:** 8 servings

- 1 loaf day-old sourdough or Italian bread (1 lb.), cubed
- 3 cups fresh strawberries, sliced
- ¼ cup sugar
- 2 Tbsp. balsamic vinegar
- ½ cup packed brown sugar
- ¼ tsp. salt
- ⅓ cup butter, melted
- 2 cups plain Greek yogurt
  Mint sprigs

1. Preheat oven to 400°. Mix berries, ¼ cup granulated sugar and vinegar; set aside.
2. Mix brown sugar and salt. Toss bread cubes in melted butter, then brown sugar mixture. On a baking sheet, bake cubes until golden brown, 8-10 minutes. Cool. Meanwhile, strain sliced strawberries, reserving juice.
3. Layer yogurt, bread, and strawberries in 8 small bowls. Top with reserved strawberry juice to taste and mint sprigs. Serve immediately, or refrigerate up to 1 hour.
1 SERVING: *385 cal., 15g fat (9g sat. fat), 35mg chol., 515mg sod., 57g carb. (28g sugars, 2g fiber), 9g pro.*

TRIPLE-CHOCOLATE PEPPERMINT TREATS

Santa is sure to stop by your house if you leave these minty chocolate cookies waiting for him! They're quick and easy for the whole family to make together.
—Teresa Ralston, New Albany, OH

PREP: 40 min.
BAKE: 10 min./batch + cooling
MAKES: about 6½ dozen

- 1   cup butter, softened
- 1   cup packed brown sugar
- ½   cup sugar
- 2   large eggs, room temperature
- 2   tsp. vanilla extract
- 2½ cups all-purpose flour
- ¾   cup baking cocoa
- 1   tsp. salt
- 1   tsp. baking soda
- 1   cup semisweet chocolate chips
- ½   cup 60% cacao bittersweet chocolate baking chips

WHITE CHOCOLATE FROSTING
- ½   cup white baking chips
- 4   oz. cream cheese, softened
- 3   cups confectioners' sugar
- 2   to 3 Tbsp. 2% milk
- ⅓   to ½ cup crushed peppermint candies

1. Preheat oven to 375°. Cream together butter and sugars until light and fluffy, 5-7 minutes. Beat in eggs and vanilla. In a separate bowl, whisk flour, cocoa, salt and baking soda; gradually beat into creamed mixture. Stir in the semisweet and bittersweet chocolate chips.
2. Drop by rounded teaspoonfuls 2 in. apart onto ungreased baking sheets. Bake until set, 8-10 minutes. Cool 2 minutes before removing from pans to wire racks to cool completely.
3. For frosting, melt white baking chips in a microwave; stir until smooth. In another bowl, beat cream cheese and confectioners' sugar until smooth. Beat in the melted chips. Add enough milk to reach desired consistency. Frost cookies; sprinkle with peppermint candies.
1 COOKIE: *99 cal., 4g fat (3g sat. fat), 12mg chol., 72mg sod., 15g carb. (11g sugars, 0 fiber), 1g pro.*

WHY ARE POINSETTIAS THE CHRISTMAS FLOWER?

The bright red splash of poinsettias in stores and public spaces is a sure sign that Christmas is coming. The plants, native to Central America, have distinctive red bracts that have made them a holiday tradition. According to a Mexican folktale, a young girl was distressed that she didn't have a gift to leave for the Baby Jesus at Christmas Eve services. With no money, she picked a humble bouquet of weeds on her way to the church. She left them at the bottom of the Nativity scene, where they were transformed into a beautiful red plant. Known in Mexico as the *flores de noche buena* (flowers of the holy night), the plants came north with Joel Roberts Poinsett after he became the first U.S. minister to Mexico in 1825. In the 1920s, floral entrepreneur Paul Ecke Jr. started marketing the plant by sending free poinsettias to TV studios across the country, as well as *The Tonight Show Starring Johnny Carson* and Bob Hope's holiday specials. As a result, the poinsettia became forever linked with the season. Today, more than 34 million poinsettias are sold every year in the United States, representing almost one-quarter of all flowering potted plants sold.

HEAVENLY ORANGE CRANBERRY BARS

These cranberry cookie bars combine two beloved holiday flavors and top a delicious soft crust with cream cheese icing. We enjoy these every year during the holidays.
—Jennifer Blakely, Visalia, CA

PREP: 30 min. + chilling
BAKE: 20 min. + cooling • **MAKES:** 8 dozen

- 1½ cups packed brown sugar
- 1 cup butter, melted
- 2 large eggs, room temperature
- 2 tsp. vanilla extract
- 2¼ cups all-purpose flour
- 1 tsp. baking powder
- 1 tsp. salt
- 1 cup white baking chips
- 1 cup dried cranberries, coarsely chopped
- 1 cup chopped pecans, toasted
- ¼ cup grated orange zest

FROSTING
- 1 pkg. (8 oz.) cream cheese, softened
- 1 cup confectioners' sugar
- ½ cup butter, softened
- 3 Tbsp. grated orange zest, divided
- 2 tsp. vanilla extract
- ⅓ cup dried cranberries, coarsely chopped

1. Preheat oven to 350°. In a large bowl, beat brown sugar, melted butter, eggs and vanilla until well blended. In another bowl, whisk flour, baking powder and salt; gradually beat into sugar mixture. Stir in baking chips, cranberries, pecans and orange zest.
2. Spread into a greased 15x10x1-in. baking pan. Bake until a toothpick inserted in center comes out clean, 18-22 minutes. Cool completely in pan on a wire rack.
3. For frosting, in a large bowl, combine cream cheese, confectioners' sugar, butter, 1 Tbsp. zest and vanilla; beat until smooth. Spread over bars. Combine dried cranberries and remaining 2 Tbsp. zest; sprinkle over frosting. Refrigerate at least 2 hours. Cut into triangles. Store in the refrigerator.
1 BAR: *89 cal., 5g fat (3g sat. fat), 14mg chol., 64mg sod., 10g carb. (7g sugars, 0 fiber), 1g pro.*

RUSTIC ORANGE-RHUBARB TART

This sweet and tangy tart is the perfect light dessert. We love it with fresh rhubarb in the spring, but it also tastes great with frozen fruit during the winter.
—Taste of Home *Test Kitchen*

PREP: 20 min. + standing • **BAKE:** 30 min.
MAKES: 6 servings

- 1 sheet refrigerated pie pastry
- 2 Tbsp. apricot preserves
- 1 cup sliced fresh or frozen rhubarb, thawed
- 1 can (15 oz.) mandarin oranges, drained
- ½ cup plus 2 Tbsp. sugar, divided
- 3 Tbsp. quick-cooking tapioca
- ½ tsp. ground cinnamon
- ¼ cup slivered almonds
- 1 large egg white
- 1 Tbsp. water
- ½ cup white baking chips
- 1 Tbsp. shortening

1. Preheat oven to 375°. On a lightly floured surface, roll out pastry into a 14-in. circle. Spread preserves to within 2 in. of the edges. Transfer to a parchment-lined baking sheet; set aside.
2. In a large bowl, combine the rhubarb, oranges, ½ cup sugar, the tapioca and cinnamon; let stand for 15 minutes. Spoon over pastry to within 2 in. of the edges; sprinkle with almonds. Fold edges of pastry over the filling, leaving the center uncovered.
3. Beat egg white and water; brush over folded pastry. Sprinkle with the remaining sugar. Bake for 30-35 minutes or until crust is golden and filling is bubbly. Using parchment, slide the tart onto a wire rack to cool.
4. In a microwave, melt white chips and shortening; stir until smooth. Drizzle over tart.
1 PIECE: *432 cal., 18g fat (7g sat. fat), 10mg chol., 163mg sod., 65g carb. (40g sugars, 2g fiber), 4g pro.*

BLACK CHERRY SWIRL FUDGE

This colorful treat is sure to satisfy the sweetest tooth in any family! It's always been a favorite with my nine kids, eight grandkids and my Bible study group. I even vary the soft drink mix flavors to get colors that suit other holidays during the year.
—Pauletta Bushnell, Lebanon, OR

TAKES: 30 min. + chilling • **MAKES:** about 3 lbs. (117 pieces)

- 1½ tsp. plus ¾ cup butter, divided
- 3 cups sugar
- ¾ cup heavy whipping cream
- 1 pkg. (10 to 12 oz.) vanilla or white chips
- 1 jar (7 oz.) marshmallow creme
- 2 envelopes unsweetened black cherry soft drink mix

1. Line a 13x9-in. pan with foil and grease the foil with 1½ tsp. butter; set aside. In a heavy saucepan, combine the sugar, cream and the remaining butter. Bring to a boil over medium heat, stirring constantly. Cook and stir for 4 minutes.
2. Remove from heat; stir in vanilla chips and marshmallow creme. Pour 1 cup into a bowl; set aside. Stir black cherry drink mix into the remaining marshmallow mixture. Pour into the prepared pan. Spoon the reserved marshmallow mixture over top; cut through mixture with a knife to swirl.
3. Refrigerate for 1 hour or until firm. Using foil, lift fudge out of pan. Discard foil; cut into 1-in. squares. Store in an airtight container in the refrigerator.
1 PIECE: *55 cal., 3g fat (2g sat. fat), 6mg chol., 14mg sod., 8g carb. (8g sugars, 0 fiber), 0 pro.*

NANTUCKET CRANBERRY TART

While everyone is enjoying a bountiful meal, this eye-catching tart can be baking to perfection in the oven. The pretty holiday dessert calls for very few ingredients, and it's a snap to assemble.
—Jackie Zack, Riverside, CT

PREP: 15 min. • **BAKE:** 40 min. + cooling • **MAKES:** 12 servings

- 1 pkg. (12 oz.) fresh or frozen cranberries, thawed
- 1 cup sugar, divided
- ½ cup sliced almonds
- 2 large eggs, room temperature
- ¾ cup butter, melted
- 1 tsp. almond extract
- 1 cup all-purpose flour
- 1 Tbsp. confectioners' sugar

1. Preheat oven to 325°. In a small bowl, combine the cranberries, ½ cup sugar and the almonds. Transfer to a greased 11-in. fluted tart pan with a removable bottom. Place on a baking sheet.
2. In a small bowl, beat the eggs, butter, extract and the remaining sugar. Beat in flour just until moistened (the batter will be thick). Spread evenly over berries.
3. Bake for 40-45 minutes or until a toothpick inserted in the center comes out clean. Cool in pan on a wire rack. Dust with confectioners' sugar. Refrigerate leftovers.
1 PIECE: *255 cal., 14g fat (8g sat. fat), 65mg chol., 93mg sod., 30g carb. (19g sugars, 2g fiber), 3g pro.*

Holiday Helper
The tart may ooze from your tart pan a little bit as it bakes. If you'd like, try baking yours on a 15x10x1-in. baking sheet.

SNOWY RASPBERRY GELATIN MOLD

This sweet treat is always on our holiday table. The raspberry layer makes an eye-catching base for the cream cheese.
—Lily Julow, Lawrenceville, GA

TAKES: 30 min. + chilling • **MAKES:** 8 servings

- 1 envelope unflavored gelatin
- ½ cup cold water
- 1 cup half-and-half cream
- ½ cup sugar
- 1 pkg. (8 oz.) cream cheese, softened
- 1 tsp. vanilla extract
- 1 pkg. (3 oz.) raspberry gelatin
- 1 cup boiling water
- 1 pkg. (10 oz.) frozen sweetened raspberries, thawed
  Fresh raspberries, optional

1. In a small bowl, sprinkle unflavored gelatin over cold water; let stand for 1 minute. In a small saucepan, combine half-and-half and sugar. Cook and stir just until mixture comes to a simmer. Remove from heat; stir into gelatin until dissolved.
2. In a large bowl, beat cream cheese until smooth. Fold in the gelatin mixture. Stir in vanilla. Pour into a 6-cup mold coated with cooking spray. Refrigerate until set but not firm, about 45 minutes.
3. In a small bowl, dissolve the raspberry gelatin in boiling water. Stir in raspberries until blended. Carefully spoon over cream cheese layer. Cover and refrigerate for at least 4 hours.
4. Unmold onto a serving plate; garnish with fresh berries if desired.
¾ CUP: 267 cal., 13g fat (8g sat. fat), 46mg chol., 125mg sod., 33g carb. (30g sugars, 2g fiber), 5g pro.

RED VELVET POUND CAKE

This tasty cake is the perfect combination of flavors. Make sure the cake has cooled before icing it, and for extra crunch sprinkle some roasted pecans on top.
—Robin Smith, Old Fort, NC

PREP: 30 min. • **BAKE:** 70 min. + cooling
MAKES: 16 servings

- 1 cup butter, softened
- ½ cup shortening

- 3 cups sugar
- 6 large eggs, room temperature
- 2 bottles (1 oz. each) red food coloring
- 1 tsp. lemon extract
- 1 tsp. vanilla extract
- 3¼ cups all-purpose flour
- 1 Tbsp. baking cocoa
- ½ tsp. baking powder
- ½ tsp. salt
- ¾ cup 2% milk

ICING

- 1 pkg. (8 oz.) cream cheese, softened
- ¼ cup butter or margarine, softened
- ½ tsp. vanilla extract
- 3¾ cups confectioners' sugar
- ½ cup chopped pecans, toasted

1. Preheat oven to 325°. Grease and flour a 10-in. fluted tube pan; set aside.
2. In a large bowl, cream butter and sugar until light and fluffy, 5-7 minutes. Add eggs, 1 at a time, beating well after each addition. Beat in food coloring and extracts (mixture may appear curdled).
3. In another bowl, whisk flour, baking cocoa, baking powder and salt; add to the creamed mixture alternately with milk, beating after each addition just until combined.
4. Transfer batter to prepared pan. Bake until a toothpick inserted in center comes out clean, 70-75 minutes. Cool in pan for 15 minutes before removing to a wire rack to cool completely.
5. For icing, in a large bowl, beat cream cheese and butter until creamy. Beat in vanilla. Gradually beat in confectioners' sugar until smooth. Spread over cake; sprinkle with pecans. Store in the refrigerator.
1 SLICE: 639 cal., 30g fat (14g sat. fat), 123mg chol., 281mg sod., 87g carb. (67g sugars, 1g fiber), 7g pro.

1 SLICE: *176 cal., 5g fat (3g sat. fat), 19mg chol., 161mg sod., 30g carb. (14g sugars, 1g fiber), 3g pro.*

SOUR CREAM BAVARIAN

While the holidays are a time for indulgence, this sweet treat is perfect if you're looking for something lighter. It's sinfully creamy and so pretty with the tart raspberry sauce—no one would guess it's fat-free!
—Judi Janczewski, Berwyn, IL

- -

PREP: 10 min. + chilling • **COOK:** 5 min.
MAKES: 8 servings (1¼ cups sauce)

1	envelope unflavored gelatin
¾	cup cold water
⅔	cup sugar
1	cup fat-free sour cream
1	tsp. vanilla extract
2	cups fat-free whipped topping

SAUCE

1	pkg. (10 oz.) frozen sweetened raspberries or sliced strawberries, thawed
1	Tbsp. cornstarch
1	Tbsp. sugar

1. In a small saucepan, sprinkle gelatin over cold water; let stand 1 minute. Add sugar; heat and stir over low heat until gelatin and sugar are completely dissolved. Transfer to a bowl; whisk in sour cream and vanilla. Refrigerate 10 minutes.

2. Fold in whipped topping. Pour into a 4-cup mold coated with cooking spray. Refrigerate, covered, for 4 hours or until firm.

3. For the sauce, drain berries, reserving syrup. Add enough water to the syrup to measure ¾ cup. In a small saucepan, mix cornstarch, sugar and the syrup mixture until smooth. Bring to a boil; cook and stir until thickened, about 2 minutes. Cool slightly. Stir in drained berries; refrigerate until serving.

4. To serve, unmold dessert onto a serving plate. Serve with sauce.

1 PIECE: *176 cal., 0 fat (0 sat. fat), 1mg chol., 37mg sod., 33g carb. (30g sugars, 2g fiber), 3g pro.*

CANDY CANE COFFEE CAKES

I make my festive-looking coffee cakes at Christmas and for breakfast company. My husband doesn't usually care for apricots, but he loves these.
—Kelley Winship, West Rutland, VT

- -

PREP: 40 min. + rising • **BAKE:** 15 min.
MAKES: 3 coffee cakes (12 slices each)

2	cups sour cream
2	pkg. (¼ oz. each) active dry yeast
½	cup warm water (110° to 115°)
¼	cup butter, softened
⅓	cup sugar
2	tsp. salt
2	large eggs, room temperature, beaten
5¼ to 6	cups all-purpose flour
1½	cups (12 oz.) finely chopped dried apricots
1½	cups finely chopped well-drained maraschino cherries
2	Tbsp. butter, melted

ICING

2	cups confectioners' sugar
2 to 3	Tbsp. water

1. In a saucepan, heat sour cream until lukewarm. Set aside. In a large bowl, dissolve yeast in warm water. Add sour cream, butter, sugar, salt, eggs and 2 cups flour. With an electric mixer, beat until smooth. Stir in just enough of the remaining flour to form a soft dough.

2. Turn out onto a floured surface and knead until smooth and elastic. Place in a greased bowl, turning once to grease top. Cover and let rise in a warm place until doubled, about 1 hour.

3. Punch dough down; divide into 3 equal parts. On a lightly floured surface, roll each part into a 15x6-in. rectangle. Place on greased baking sheets. With scissors, make 2-in. cuts at ½-in. intervals on the long sides of each rectangle. Combine apricots and cherries; spread one-third of the mixture down the center of each rectangle.

4. Crisscross strips over filling. Stretch dough to 22 in. and curve to form canes. Let rise until doubled, about 45 minutes.

5. Bake at 375° for 15-20 minutes. While warm, brush canes with melted butter. Combine the icing ingredients and drizzle over tops.

DIPPED CHERRY COOKIES

Our children and grandchildren declared this festive, flavorful cookie a keeper. We gave a batch to our mail carrier to thank her for trudging through so much snow, and she requested the recipe.
—Ruth Anne Dale, Titusville, PA

PREP: 30 min. • **BAKE:** 10 min./batch + standing
MAKES: about 4 dozen

2½ cups all-purpose flour
 ¾ cup sugar, divided
  1 cup cold butter, cubed
 ½ cup finely chopped maraschino cherries, patted dry
 12 oz. white baking chocolate, finely chopped, divided
 ½ tsp. almond extract
  2 tsp. shortening
     Coarse sugar and red edible glitter

1. Preheat oven to 325°. In a bowl, combine flour and ½ cup sugar; cut in butter until crumbly. Knead in cherries, ⅔ cup white chocolate and the almond extract until the dough forms a ball.
2. Shape into ¾-in. balls. Place 2 in. apart on ungreased baking sheets. Flatten slightly with a glass dipped in the remaining sugar. Bake 10-12 minutes or until edges are lightly browned. Remove to wire racks to cool completely.
3. In a microwave, melt shortening and the remaining white chocolate; stir until smooth.
4. Dip half of each cookie into chocolate; allow excess to drip off. Place on waxed paper; sprinkle with coarse sugar and edible glitter. Let stand until set. Store in an airtight container.
1 SERVING: *108 cal., 6g fat (4g sat. fat), 11mg chol., 34mg sod., 12g carb. (7g sugars, 0 fiber), 1g pro.*

CHERRY UPSIDE-DOWN CAKE

This cake is a staple in our house and it's always welcomed at neighborhood and family gatherings. Served warm with some vanilla ice cream and/or whipped cream, it really puts the cherry on top of a good meal.
—Nicole Nutter, Prosser, WA

PREP: 25 min. • **BAKE:** 35 min. + cooling • **MAKES:** 20 servings

 ⅓ cup butter, cubed
2¼ cups sugar, divided
  1 lb. fresh dark sweet cherries, pitted and halved
     (about 2 cups)
 ¾ cup shortening
  2 large eggs, room temperature
  1 Tbsp. vanilla extract
2¼ cups all-purpose flour
  2 tsp. baking powder
  1 tsp. salt
1½ cups 2% milk

1. Preheat oven to 350°. Place butter in a 13x9-in. baking pan; heat in oven until butter is melted, 2-3 minutes. Remove pan from oven; tilt carefully to coat bottom and sides with butter. Immediately sprinkle with ¾ cup sugar. Arrange cherries in a single layer over the sugar, cut side down.
2. In a large bowl, cream shortening and the remaining 1½ cups sugar until crumbly. Add eggs, 1 at a time, beating well after each addition. Beat in vanilla. In another bowl, whisk flour, baking powder and salt; add to the creamed mixture alternately with milk, beating well after each addition. (The batter may appear curdled.) Spoon over cherries.
3. Bake until a toothpick inserted in center comes out clean, 35-40 minutes. Cool 10 minutes before inverting onto a serving plate. Serve warm.
1 PIECE: *266 cal., 11g fat (4g sat. fat), 28mg chol., 207mg sod., 39g carb. (26g sugars, 1g fiber), 3g pro.*

HONEY CRAN-RASPBERRY PIE

This is my son's recipe—it was given to him when he got married. The pie is quite tart, but it pairs well with your favorite vanilla ice cream or a dollop of whipped cream.
—Beverly Batty, Forest Lake, MN

PREP: 30 min. + chilling
BAKE: 45 min. + cooling • **MAKES:** 8 servings

- 1 large egg, room temperature
- 3 to 4 Tbsp. ice water, divided
- 1 Tbsp. cider vinegar
- 2 cups all-purpose flour
- ¾ tsp. salt
- ½ cup butter-flavored shortening
- ¼ cup lard
- 1¼ cups plus 2 Tbsp. sugar, divided
- 5 Tbsp. quick-cooking tapioca
- 3 cups fresh or frozen cranberries, halved
- 2½ cups fresh or frozen unsweetened raspberries, thawed
- ⅓ cup honey
- 1 tsp. almond extract
- ½ tsp. ground cinnamon
  Dairy-free vanilla ice cream, optional

1. In a small bowl, whisk egg, 3 Tbsp. ice water and vinegar until blended. In a large bowl, mix flour and salt; cut in shortening and lard until crumbly. Gradually add the egg mixture, tossing with a fork, until the dough holds together when pressed. If mixture is too dry, slowly add more ice water, a teaspoon at a time, just until mixture comes together.
2. Divide dough in half. Shape each into a disk; wrap in plastic. Refrigerate 1 hour or overnight.
3. On a lightly floured surface, roll 1 half of dough to a ⅛-in.-thick circle; transfer to a 9-in. deep-dish pie plate. Trim pastry even with rim. Refrigerate 30 minutes.
4. Meanwhile, preheat oven to 425°. In a large bowl, mix 1¼ cups sugar and tapioca. Add cranberries, raspberries, honey and almond extract; toss to coat evenly. Let stand 15 minutes.
5. Pour filling into pie plate. Roll remaining dough to a ⅛-in.-thick circle. Place over filling. Trim, seal and flute edge. Cut slits in top. Combine cinnamon and the remaining 2 Tbsp. sugar; sprinkle over top. Place pie on a baking sheet; bake 10 minutes.

6. Reduce oven setting to 350°. Bake until crust is golden brown and filling is bubbly, 35-40 minutes. Cool pie on a wire rack. If desired, serve with ice cream.
1 PIECE: *532 cal., 20g fat (6g sat. fat), 29mg chol., 233mg sod., 86g carb. (49g sugars, 5g fiber), 5g pro.*

SORBET TRIO

This recipe is a refreshing way to cool down and provide a light finish to a fancy meal—with no ice cream maker needed! They look and taste like a lot more work than they really are.
—Rebecca Taylor, Manteca, CA

PREP: 40 min. + freezing • **MAKES:** 3½ qt.

- 3 cups water, divided
- 1½ cups sugar, divided
- 6 tsp. grated lemon zest, divided
- 1 cup lemon juice, divided
- 1½ cups carbonated mineral water, divided
  Salt
- ½ cup minced fresh mint, coarsley chopped
- 3 cups fresh or frozen blueberries
  Lemon peel strips, fresh raspberries and mint sprigs, optional

1. For lemon sorbet, in a small heavy saucepan, bring 1 cup water, ½ cup sugar and 2 tsp. lemon zest to a boil. Cook and stir until sugar is dissolved; cool. Add ½ cup lemon juice, ½ cup mineral water and a dash of salt. Transfer to an 8-in. square dish.
2. For mint sorbet, in a small heavy saucepan, bring 1 cup water, ½ cup sugar and 2 tsp. lemon zest and mint to a boil. Cook and stir until sugar is dissolved; cool. Strain. Add ¼ cup lemon juice, ½ cup mineral water and a dash of salt. Transfer to another 8-in. square dish.
3. For blueberry sorbet, in a small heavy saucepan, bring 1 cup water, ½ cup sugar, 2 tsp. lemon zest and blueberries to a boil. Cook and stir until sugar is dissolved; cool. Cover and process for 2-3 minutes or until blended. Strain and discard seeds and pulp. Add ¼ cup lemon juice, ½ cup mineral water and a dash of salt. Transfer to an 11x7-in. dish.
4. Freeze sorbets for 1 hour or until edges begin to firm; stir. Freeze 3 hours longer or until firm.
5. Just before serving, transfer sorbets separately to a food processor; cover and process for 1-2 minutes or until smooth. Scoop each flavor into serving dishes. Garnish as desired.
¾ CUP: *83 cal., 0 fat (0 sat. fat), 0 chol., 1mg sod., 21g carb. (20g sugars, 1g fiber), 0 pro.*

SLOW-COOKER CHERRY PEAR BUCKLE

I added pears to my cherry cobbler recipe to create this delightful slow-cooked buckle. You could also add fresh plums and berries to your cherries. You'll love this pretty and old-fashioned dessert.
—Mary Anne Thygesen, Portland, OR

PREP: 20 min. • **COOK:** 4½ hours
MAKES: 8 servings

- 6   medium pears, peeled and sliced
- 4   cups fresh or frozen pitted dark sweet cherries, thawed
- 1   cup sugar
- ¼   cup tapioca flour
- 1¾ cups all-purpose flour
- ¼   cup old-fashioned oats
- 3   tsp. baking powder
- ½   tsp. salt
- ¼   cup cold butter
- ¾   cup 2% milk
- 2   tsp. cinnamon sugar
       Sweetened whipped cream

1. Line the inside of a 5-qt. slow cooker with a double thickness of heavy-duty foil; spray foil with cooking spray. In a large bowl, combine pears, cherries, sugar and tapioca flour; spoon into slow cooker. Cook, covered, on high 4-5 hours or until mixture is bubbly.
2. Meanwhile, combine the flour, oats, baking powder and salt. Cut in butter until crumbly. Stir in the milk. Drop by tablespoonfuls over pear mixture; sprinkle with cinnamon sugar. Cover and cook until a toothpick inserted in center of topping comes out clean, 30-45 minutes longer. Serve with whipped cream.
1 SERVING: *411 cal., 7g fat (4g sat. fat), 17mg chol., 386mg sod., 86g carb. (48g sugars, 6g fiber), 5g pro.*

VERY MERRY CRANBERRY BISCOTTI

This is the perfect hostess gift to take with you as you make your rounds visiting over the holidays. Pack into a festive Christmas tin and top with a pretty bow.
—Darlene King, Regina, SK

PREP: 30 min. • **BAKE:** 45 min. + cooling
MAKES: about 3 dozen

- 3   large eggs, room temperature
- 1   cup sugar
- 1   tsp. vanilla extract
- 2½   cups all-purpose flour
- ½   tsp. baking soda
- ½   tsp. baking powder
- ½   tsp. salt
- 1   cup ground almonds
- 1   cup dried cranberries, chopped

1. Preheat oven to 350°. Beat eggs, sugar and vanilla until well-blended. In another bowl, whisk together flour, baking soda, baking powder and salt; gradually stir into egg mixture. Stir in ground almonds and cranberries (mixture will be stiff).
2. Divide dough in half. Using lightly floured hands, shape each portion into a 9x3-in. rectangle on a parchment-lined baking sheet. Bake until lightly browned, about 25 minutes.
3. Cool on pans on wire racks until firm. Reduce oven setting to 325°. Transfer baked rectangles to a cutting board. Using a serrated knife, cut diagonally into ½-in. slices. Place on baking sheets, cut side down.
4. Bake until lightly browned, 8-10 minutes per side. Remove to wire racks; cool completely. Store in an airtight container.

RED VELVET CHEESECAKE

This cheesecake will become a fixture on your holiday menu. The red velvet filling is spiked with cocoa, baked in a chocolate cookie crust, and topped with fluffy cream cheese frosting. Decadent and divine!
—Karen Dively, Chapin, SC

- -

PREP: 30 min. • **BAKE:** 1 hour + chilling
MAKES: 16 servings

- 17 **chocolate cream Oreo cookies, crushed**
- ¼ **cup butter, melted**
- 1 **Tbsp. sugar**

FILLING
- 3 **pkg. (8 oz. each) cream cheese, softened**
- 1½ **cups sugar**
- 1 **cup sour cream**
- ½ **cup buttermilk**
- 3 **Tbsp. baking cocoa**
- 2 **tsp. vanilla extract**
- 4 **large eggs, room temperature, lightly beaten**
- 1 **bottle (1 oz.) red food coloring**

FROSTING
- 3 **oz. cream cheese, softened**
- ¼ **cup butter, softened**
- 2 **cups confectioners' sugar**
- 1 **tsp. vanilla extract**

1. Preheat oven to 325°. Place a greased 9-in. springform pan on a double thickness of heavy-duty foil (about 18 in. square). Securely wrap foil around pan.

2. In a small bowl, combine cookie crumbs, butter and sugar. Press onto the bottom of the prepared pan.

3. In a large bowl, beat cream cheese and sugar until smooth. Beat in the sour cream, buttermilk, cocoa and vanilla. Add eggs; beat on low speed just until combined. Stir in food coloring. Pour over crust. Place the springform pan in a larger baking pan; add 1 in. of hot water to the larger pan.

4. Bake until the center is just set and the top appears dull, 60-70 minutes. Remove springform pan from water bath. Cool on a wire rack for 10 minutes. Carefully run a knife around the edge of pan to loosen; cool 1 hour longer. Refrigerate overnight, covering cake when completely cooled. Remove sides of pan.

5. For frosting, in a small bowl, beat cream cheese and butter until fluffy. Add confectioners' sugar and vanilla; beat until smooth. Frost top of cheesecake. Refrigerate until serving.

1 SLICE: *463 cal., 29g fat (17g sat. fat), 131mg chol., 276mg sod., 46g carb. (39g sugars, 1g fiber), 7g pro.*

CAST-IRON CHRISTMAS BREAKFAST

On Christmas morning, why not treat the family to a special country-style breakfast? Cast iron is perfect for recipes both sweet and savory, turning out satisfying dishes with a decidedly traditional touch.

BANANA-HAZELNUT PAIN PERDU DUET

The ultimate special breakfast at our house is French toast with warm bananas and Nutella. Pass it around with confectioners' sugar, maple syrup and fresh mint.
—Charlene Chambers, Ormond Beach, FL

TAKES: 30 min. • **MAKES:** 4 servings

- 8 slices French bread (½ in. thick)
- ¼ cup cream cheese, softened
- ¼ cup Nutella
- 1 medium banana, halved lengthwise and sliced
- 4 tsp. brown sugar
- 4 large eggs
- 1 cup 2% milk
- ¼ cup hazelnut liqueur
- 2 tsp. ground cinnamon
- 2 tsp. vanilla extract
- 2 Tbsp. butter
  Optional toppings: Confectioners' sugar, maple syrup, fresh mint leaves, additional banana slices and additional Nutella

1. On each of 4 bread slices, spread cream cheese and Nutella to within ½ in. of edges. Top with banana slices, brown sugar and the remaining bread. In a shallow bowl, whisk eggs, milk, liqueur, cinnamon and vanilla.

2. In a large cast-iron or other heavy skillet, heat butter over medium-low heat. Dip both sides of sandwiches in egg mixture, allowing each side to soak for 30 seconds. Place sandwiches in skillet; toast until golden brown, 4-5 minutes on each side. If desired, serve with toppings.

1 STUFFED FRENCH TOAST: 469 cal., 23g fat (10g sat. fat), 221mg chol., 340mg sod., 48g carb. (29g sugars, 3g fiber), 13g pro.

COUNTRY-STYLE TREE GARLAND

Make a garland for your tree with your choice of fabric—a gingham check gives a down-home look, but you can choose any pattern you like. Cut 3 strips of fabric 2 yd. long and 5⅞ in. wide. Place 2 strips right sides together and sew 1 short end together with a ¼-in. seam. Repeat with the third piece to create 1 long strip. Fold the strip lengthwise on itself with the right sides together and sew a ¼-in. seam along the cut edge; leave the short ends open to create a long tube. Turn tube right side out. Tie 1 end with a short piece of yarn, then fill the tube with table tennis balls—you'll need about 92 balls for a 6-yd. garland. Tie a short piece of yarn between each ball and at the end of the tube.

SAUSAGE JOHNNYCAKE

Here's a nice, hearty breakfast with plenty of old-fashioned flavor. I serve it to my bed-and-breakfast customers, who always love the cake's savory middle and maple syrup topping. It makes a fine start to a family weekend or holiday morning.
—Lorraine Guyn, Calgary, AB

PREP: 20 min. • **BAKE:** 30 min.
MAKES: 6 servings

- 1 cup cornmeal
- 2 cups buttermilk
- 12 uncooked breakfast sausage links
- 1⅓ cups all-purpose flour
- ¼ cup sugar
- 1½ tsp. baking powder
- ½ tsp. baking soda
- ½ tsp. salt
- ⅓ cup shortening
- 1 large egg, lightly beaten
- ½ tsp. vanilla extract
   Maple syrup

1. Preheat oven to 400°. In a small bowl, combine cornmeal and buttermilk; let stand for 10 minutes.
2. Meanwhile, in a 9-in. cast-iron or other ovenproof skillet over medium heat, cook sausage until no longer pink; drain on paper towels. Arrange 8 links in a spokelike pattern in the same skillet. Cut the remaining links in half; place them between the whole sausages.
3. In a large bowl, combine flour, sugar, baking powder, baking soda and salt. Cut in shortening until the mixture resembles coarse crumbs.
4. Stir egg and vanilla into the cornmeal mixture; add to the dry ingredients and stir just until blended. Pour batter over the sausages.
5. Bake for 30-35 minutes or until a toothpick inserted in the center comes out clean. Serve warm with syrup.
1 SLICE: *481 cal., 23g fat (7g sat. fat), 64mg chol., 940mg sod., 53g carb. (13g sugars, 2g fiber), 15g pro.*

SHAKSHUKA

Shakshuka is a dish of poached eggs with tomatoes, onion and cumin. I first had it while traveling through Southeast Asia, and it's been my favorite way to eat eggs since.
—Ezra Weeks, Calgary, AB

TAKES: 30 min. • **MAKES:** 4 servings

- 2 Tbsp. olive oil
- 1 medium onion, chopped
- 1 garlic clove, minced
- 1 tsp. ground cumin
- 1 tsp. pepper
- ½ to 1 tsp. chili powder
- ½ tsp. salt
- 1 tsp. Sriracha chili sauce or hot pepper sauce, optional
- 2 medium tomatoes, chopped
- 4 large eggs
   Chopped fresh cilantro
   Whole pita breads, toasted

1. In a large cast-iron or other heavy skillet, heat oil over medium heat. Add onion; cook and stir until tender, 4-6 minutes. Add garlic, seasonings and, if desired, chili sauce; cook 30 seconds longer. Add tomatoes; cook until the mixture is thickened, stirring occasionally, 3-5 minutes.
2. With the back of the spoon, make 4 wells in the vegetable mixture; break an egg into each well. Cook, covered, until egg whites are completely set and the yolks begin to thicken but are not hard, 4-6 minutes. Sprinkle with cilantro; serve with pita bread.
1 SERVING: *159 cal., 12g fat (3g sat. fat), 186mg chol., 381mg sod., 6g carb. (3g sugars, 2g fiber), 7g pro.*
DIABETIC EXCHANGES: *1½ fat, 1 medium-fat meat, 1 vegetable.*

4. Roll up dough jelly-roll style, starting with a short side; seal seams. Cut roll crosswise into 12 slices. Place cut side down in a greased 12-in. cast-iron skillet. Cover and let rise in a warm place until doubled, about 30 minutes.
5. Combine topping ingredients; sprinkle over rolls. Bake at 350° for 35-40 minutes or until golden brown. Cool on a wire rack.
6. In a small bowl, combine confectioners' sugar, extract and enough milk to achieve drizzling consistency; drizzle over rolls.
1 ROLL: *482 cal., 13g fat (6g sat. fat), 61mg chol., 308mg sod., 83g carb. (37g sugars, 2g fiber), 8g pro.*

STUFFED HASH BROWNS
Ever since we met, my husband has made me hash browns with bacon, pepper jack and sour cream. We share it when we have guests, too.
—Ann Ciszak Pazar, Anchorage, AK

- -

PREP: 15 min. • **COOK:** 10 min./batch
MAKES: 4 servings

1 pkg. (20 oz.) refrigerated shredded hash brown potatoes
¼ cup finely chopped onion
½ tsp. salt
¼ tsp. pepper
4 Tbsp. olive oil, divided
½ cup pepper jack cheese
½ cup crumbled cooked bacon
½ cup sour cream
2 green onions, thinly sliced

1. Toss potatoes with onion, salt and pepper. In a small cast-iron or other heavy skillet, heat 2 tsp. oil over medium heat. Add 1 cup potato mixture, pressing down to flatten with spatula. Cook, without stirring, until bottom is golden brown, 4-5 minutes. Drizzle with 1 tsp. oil; flip. Cook until bottom is golden brown, 4-5 minutes, sprinkling with 2 Tbsp. cheese and 2 Tbsp. bacon during the last minute of cooking.
2. Fold hash browns in half; slide onto plate and keep warm. Repeat with the remaining ingredients. Top with sour cream and green onions.
1 SERVING: *410 cal., 27g fat (9g sat. fat), 26mg chol., 791mg sod., 30g carb. (3g sugars, 3g fiber), 13g pro.*

ALMOND STREUSEL ROLLS
Try my prizewinning pastry! These rolls are so popular, they often don't even cool completely before the pan is empty.
—Perlene Hoekema, Lynden, WA

- -

PREP: 40 min. + rising
BAKE: 35 min. + cooling • **MAKES:** 1 dozen

2 pkg. (¼ oz. each) active dry yeast
¾ cup warm water (110° to 115°)
¾ cup warm whole milk (110° to 115°)
¼ cup butter, softened
½ cup sugar
2 large eggs, room temperature
1 tsp. salt
5¼ to 5½ cups all-purpose flour
FILLING
½ cup almond paste
¼ cup butter, softened
½ cup packed brown sugar
¼ tsp. almond extract
TOPPING
3 Tbsp. sugar
1 Tbsp. all-purpose flour
1 Tbsp. butter
ICING
1½ cups confectioners' sugar
¼ tsp. almond extract
1 to 2 Tbsp. whole milk

1. In a large bowl, dissolve yeast in warm water. Add the milk, butter, sugar, eggs, salt and 2 cups flour. Beat until smooth. Stir in enough of the remaining flour to form a soft dough.
2. Turn onto a floured surface; knead until smooth and elastic, about 6-8 minutes. Place in a greased bowl, turning once to grease top. Cover and let rise in a warm place until doubled, about 1 hour.
3. Punch dough down; roll out to a 15x10-in. rectangle. In a large bowl, beat filling ingredients until smooth. Spread over dough.

ORANGE SPICED HAM STEAK

I turn orange marmalade, mustard and just a hint of ginger into a glaze for ham that comes together super quick but feels exceptional. And that makes it perfect for when I'm entertaining guests for brunch!
—Connie Moore, Medway, OH

TAKES: 15 min. • **MAKES:** 4 servings

1	bone-in fully cooked ham steak (about 1 lb.)
¼	cup orange marmalade
2	Tbsp. water
1	Tbsp. butter
1	Tbsp. prepared mustard
1	tsp. corn syrup
⅛	to ¼ tsp. ground ginger

1. In a large greased cast-iron or other heavy skillet, brown ham for 3-4 minutes on each side; remove and set aside.
2. In the same skillet, combine remaining ingredients; bring to a boil. Add ham; cook, covered, until heated through, 1-2 minutes.
2 OZ. COOKED HAM: *188 cal., 8g fat (4g sat. fat), 51mg chol., 885mg sod., 16g carb. (14g sugars, 0 fiber), 14g pro.*

Holiday Helper
Marmalade has come to be almost exclusively associated with oranges, and the preserves with their signature rind are a holiday staple. But marmalade was originally made from—and gets its name from—quince! *Marmalade* means "quince jam" in Portuguese. The citrusy spread is delicious on breakfast breads, but its slightly bitter tang makes it an amazing complement for savory dishes like this one.

DILLED SALMON OMELETS WITH CREME FRAICHE

This is one of the biggest hits on our inn's menu. It has so much flavor, with the dill and rich salmon, that it will impress everyone.
—Susan Goodman, Wilmington, VT

PREP: 15 min. • **COOK:** 5 min./batch
MAKES: 6 servings

12	large eggs
2	Tbsp. 2% milk
	Salt and pepper to taste
2	Tbsp. butter
1	lb. salmon fillets, cooked and flaked
3	cups shredded Swiss cheese
2	Tbsp. snipped fresh dill
¾	cup creme fraiche or sour cream
6	fresh dill sprigs

1. In a large bowl, whisk the eggs, milk, salt and pepper until blended.
2. For each omelet, in an 8-in. cast-iron or other ovenproof skillet, melt 1 tsp. butter over medium heat. Pour ½ cup of the egg mixture into the pan. Sprinkle with ⅓ cup salmon, ½ cup cheese and 1 tsp. snipped dill. As the eggs set, lift the edges, letting uncooked portion flow underneath. Cook until eggs are nearly set.
3. Broil 6 in. from the heat until eggs are completely set, 1-2 minutes. Fold omelet in half; transfer to a plate. Top with 2 Tbsp. creme fraiche and a dill sprig. Repeat for remaining omelets.
1 OMELET: *632 cal., 48g fat (24g sat. fat), 553mg chol., 374mg sod., 4g carb. (3g sugars, 0 fiber), 44g pro.*

SAVORY APPLE-CHICKEN SAUSAGE

These easy, healthy sausages taste great and make an elegant brunch dish. The recipe is also very versatile: It can be doubled or tripled for a crowd, and the sausage freezes well either cooked or raw.
—Angela Buchanan, Longmont, CO

TAKES: 25 min. • **MAKES:** 8 patties

- 1 **large tart apple, peeled and diced**
- 2 **tsp. poultry seasoning**
- 1 **tsp. salt**
- ¼ **tsp. pepper**
- 1 **lb. ground chicken**

1. In a large bowl, combine the first 4 ingredients. Crumble chicken over the mixture and mix well. Shape into eight 3-in. patties.

2. In a large, greased cast-iron or other heavy skillet, cook the patties over medium heat until no longer pink, 5-6 minutes on each side. Drain if necessary.

1 SAUSAGE PATTY: *92 cal., 5g fat (1g sat. fat), 38mg chol., 328mg sod., 4g carb. (3g sugars, 1g fiber), 9g pro.*
DIABETIC EXCHANGES: *1 medium-fat meat.*

VERY VANILLA FRENCH TOAST

These French toast slices have creamy vanilla flavor from convenient pudding mix, plus a hint of cinnamon. We like to top them with fresh berries. As a change of pace, try making this with butterscotch pudding instead of vanilla.
—Linda Bernhagen, Plainfield, IL

TAKES: 10 min. • **MAKES:** 4 servings

- 1 **cup whole milk**
- 1 **pkg. (3 oz.) cook-and-serve vanilla pudding mix**
- 1 **large egg**
- ½ **tsp. ground cinnamon**
- 8 **slices Texas toast**
- 2 **tsp. butter**
  Optional: Confectioners' sugar and fresh berries

1. In a large bowl, whisk the milk, pudding mix, egg and cinnamon for 2 minutes or until well blended. Dip toast in pudding mixture, coating both sides.

2. In a large cast-iron or other heavy skillet, melt butter over medium heat. Cook bread on both sides until golden brown. If desired, srve with confectioners' sugar and berries.

2 SLICES: *336 cal., 8g fat (3g sat. fat), 65mg chol., 562mg sod., 57g carb. (21g sugars, 2g fiber), 9g pro.*

ROLLED BUTTERMILK BISCUITS

I scribbled down this recipe when our family visited The Farmers' Museum in Cooperstown, New York, more than 25 years ago. I must have gotten it right, because these biscuits turn out wonderful every time!
—Patricia Kile, Elizabethtown, PA

PREP: 20 min. • **BAKE:** 15 min. • **MAKES:** 8 biscuits

- 2 cups all-purpose flour
- 3 tsp. baking powder
- ½ tsp. baking soda
- ¼ tsp. salt
- 3 Tbsp. cold butter
- ¾ to 1 cup buttermilk
- 1 Tbsp. fat-free milk

1. Preheat oven to 450°. In a large bowl, combine the flour, baking powder, baking soda and salt; cut in butter until mixture resembles coarse crumbs. Stir in enough buttermilk just to moisten dough.

2. Turn onto a lightly floured surface; knead 3-4 times. Pat or roll to ¾-in. thickness. Cut with a floured 2½-in. biscuit cutter. Place in a large ungreased cast-iron or other ovenproof skillet.

3. Brush with milk. Bake until golden brown, 12-15 minutes.

1 BISCUIT: 162 cal., 5g fat (3g sat. fat), 12mg chol., 412mg sod., 25g carb. (1g sugars, 1g fiber), 4g pro.

DIABETIC EXCHANGES: 1½ starch, 1 fat.

NEW ORLEANS BEIGNETS

These sweet French doughnuts are square instead of round and have no hole in the middle. They're a traditional part of breakfast in New Orleans and just the thing for a special morning treat.
—Beth Dawson, Jackson, LA

PREP: 25 min. + chilling • **COOK:** 5 min./batch • **MAKES:** 4 dozen

- 1 pkg. (¼ oz.) active dry yeast
- ¼ cup warm water (110° to 115°)
- 1 cup evaporated milk
- ½ cup canola oil
- ¼ cup sugar
- 1 large egg
- 4½ cups self-rising flour
  - Oil for deep-fat frying
  - Confectioners' sugar

1. In a large bowl, dissolve yeast in warm water. Add milk, oil, sugar, egg and 2 cups flour. Beat until smooth. Stir in enough remaining flour to form a soft dough (dough will be sticky). Do not knead. Cover and refrigerate overnight.

2. Punch dough down. Turn onto a floured surface; roll into a 16x12-in. rectangle. Cut into 2-in. squares.

3. In a deep cast-iron or electric skillet, heat 1 in. oil to 375°. Fry squares, in batches, until golden brown on both sides. Drain on paper towels. Roll warm beignets in confectioners' sugar.

1 BEIGNET: 104 cal., 5g fat (1g sat. fat), 6mg chol., 142mg sod., 14g carb. (5g sugars, 0 fiber), 2g pro.

UPSIDE-DOWN BACON PANCAKE

Make a big impression when you present one family-sized bacon pancake. The brown sugar adds sweetness that complements the salty bacon. If you can fit more bacon in the skillet and want to add more, go for it.
—Mindie Hilton, Susanville, CA

TAKES: 30 min. • **MAKES:** 6 servings

- 6 bacon strips, coarsely chopped
- ¼ cup packed brown sugar
- 2 cups complete buttermilk pancake mix
- 1½ cups water
  Optional: Maple syrup and butter

1. Preheat oven to 350°. In a large cast-iron or other ovenproof skillet, cook bacon over medium heat until crisp. Remove bacon to paper towels with a slotted spoon. Remove drippings, reserving 2 Tbsp. Return bacon to pan with the reserved drippings; sprinkle with brown sugar.

2. In a small bowl, combine pancake mix and water just until moistened. Pour into pan.

3. Bake until a toothpick inserted in the center comes out clean, 18-20 minutes. Cool for 10 minutes before inverting onto a serving plate. Serve warm, with maple syrup and butter if desired.

1 SLICE: *265 cal., 9g fat (3g sat. fat), 12mg chol., 802mg sod., 41g carb. (13g sugars, 1g fiber), 6g pro.*

BLACK BEAN & WHITE CHEDDAR FRITTATA

This is one of my favorite comfort foods for breakfast or even a quick dinner. I like to make it with lime salsa. But if you're looking for something with more kick, use hot salsa or add some chipotle pepper.
—Aysha Schurman, Ammon, ID

PREP: 20 min. • **COOK:** 15 min.
MAKES: 6 servings

- 6 large eggs
- 3 large egg whites
- ¼ cup salsa
- 1 Tbsp. minced fresh parsley
- ¼ tsp. salt
- ¼ tsp. pepper
- 1 Tbsp. olive oil
- ⅓ cup finely chopped green pepper
- ⅓ cup finely chopped sweet red pepper
- 3 green onions, finely chopped
- 2 garlic cloves, minced
- 1 cup canned black beans, rinsed and drained
- ½ cup shredded white cheddar cheese
  Optional toppings: Minced fresh cilantro, sliced ripe olives and additional salsa

1. Preheat broiler. In a large bowl, whisk the first 6 ingredients until blended.

2. In a 10-in. cast-iron or other heavy skillet, heat oil over medium-high heat. Add peppers and green onions; cook and stir until peppers are tender, 3-4 minutes. Add garlic; cook 1 minute longer. Stir in beans. Reduce heat to medium; stir in egg mixture. Cook, uncovered, 4-6 minutes or until nearly set. Sprinkle with cheese.

3. Broil 3-4 in. from heat 3-4 minutes or until light golden brown and eggs are completely set. Let stand for 5 minutes. Cut into wedges. If desired, serve with toppings of your choice.

1 WEDGE: *183 cal., 10g fat (4g sat. fat), 196mg chol., 378mg sod., 9g carb. (2g sugars, 2g fiber), 13g pro.*
DIABETIC EXCHANGES: *2 medium-fat meat, ½ starch, ½ fat.*

HERBED SAUSAGE GRAVY OVER CHEESE BISCUITS

The crowd at my house loves anything with biscuits, and this rich sausage gravy is the best we've ever tasted! It's a real favorite of my husband and two toddlers.
—Lynn Crosby, Homerville, OH

- -

PREP: 20 min. • **BAKE:** 15 min
MAKES: 4 servings

2¼ cups all-purpose flour
3 tsp. baking powder
½ tsp. salt
½ cup 2% milk
¼ cup canola oil
½ tsp. dried oregano
1 oz. part-skim mozzarella cheese, cut into 8 cubes (about ½-in.)

GRAVY
½ lb. bulk pork sausage
¾ cup 2% milk
1 tsp. dried oregano
¼ cup all-purpose flour
1 cup cold water

1. Preheat oven to 450°. Whisk flour, baking powder and salt. Stir in milk and oil just until moistened. Turn onto a lightly floured surface; knead gently 8-10 times. Roll to ½-in. thickness; cut with a floured 2½-in. biscuit cutter. Place a pinch of oregano in the center of each biscuit; top with a cheese cube.

2. Moisten edge of dough with water and pull up over cheese, forming a pouch; pinch tightly to seal. Place seam side down on a lightly greased baking sheet, pressing down lightly. Bake until golden brown, 12-15 minutes.

3. Meanwhile, in a large cast-iron or other heavy skillet, cook sausage over medium heat until no longer pink; drain. Stir in milk and oregano. Mix flour and water until smooth; add to sausage mixture. Bring to a boil; cook and stir until thickened, about 2 minutes. Serve gravy with biscuits.

2 BISCUITS WITH ½ CUP GRAVY: *626 cal., 31g fat (8g sat. fat), 46mg chol., 1132mg sod., 65g carb. (4g sugars, 2g fiber), 20g pro.*

FIESTA SCRAMBLED EGGS

I love to fix this spicy scrambled egg dish for friends and family. It's almost a meal in itself, but I serve it with muffins or biscuits, fresh fruit juice and coffee.
—Kay Kropff, Canyon, TX

- -

TAKES: 30 min. • **MAKES:** 6 servings

½ cup chopped onion
¼ cup chopped sweet red pepper
1 jalapeno pepper, seeded and chopped
8 bacon strips, cooked and crumbled
8 large eggs, lightly beaten
1 cup shredded cheddar cheese, divided
½ tsp. salt
⅛ tsp. pepper
Salsa

In a large cast-iron or other heavy skillet, saute the onion and peppers until tender. Sprinkle with bacon. Pour eggs over the top; sprinkle with ½ cup cheese, salt and pepper. Cook over medium heat, stirring occasionally, until eggs are completely set. Sprinkle with the remaining cheese. Serve with salsa.

¾ CUP: *222 cal., 16g fat (8g sat. fat), 311mg chol., 529mg sod., 3g carb. (2g sugars, 0 fiber), 15g pro.*

MOM'S FRIED APPLES

Mom often made these rich cinnamon-sugar apples when I was growing up. The recipe is very dear to me, and it's a trip down memory lane whenever I prepare them.
—Margie Tappe, Prague, OK

PREP: 15 min. • **COOK:** 30 min. • **MAKES:** 8 servings

½   cup butter, cubed
6   medium unpeeled tart red apples, sliced
¾   cup sugar, divided
¾   tsp. ground cinnamon

1. Melt butter in a large cast-iron or other heavy skillet. Add apples and ½ cup sugar; stir to mix well. Cover and cook over low heat for 20 minutes or until apples are tender, stirring frequently.
2. Add cinnamon and the remaining sugar. Cook and stir over medium-high heat 5-10 minutes longer.
1 SERVING: *235 cal., 12g fat (7g sat. fat), 31mg chol., 116mg sod., 35g carb. (31g sugars, 3g fiber), 0 pro.*

COUNTRY PEAR PUFF PANCAKE

This sweet, gooey pancake is dressed up with caramelized pears and baked until golden. It's a delicious change of pace for mornings.
—Steffany Lohn, Brentwood, CA

PREP: 20 min. • **BAKE:** 20 min. • **MAKES:** 4 servings

5   Tbsp. butter, divided
3   medium pears, peeled and sliced
½   cup packed brown sugar, divided
1   Tbsp. lemon juice
½   cup all-purpose flour
½   cup 2% milk
3   large eggs, beaten
2   Tbsp. maple syrup
1   tsp. vanilla extract
⅛   tsp. salt
½   tsp. ground cinnamon
¼   tsp. ground nutmeg
    Whipped cream, optional

1. Preheat oven to 450°. In a 10-in. cast-iron or other ovenproof skillet, melt 3 Tbsp. butter over medium heat. Add pears; cook and stir until tender, about 5 minutes. Stir in ¼ cup brown sugar and lemon juice.
2. In a bowl, whisk the flour, milk, eggs, syrup, vanilla and salt until smooth; pour over pears. Bake until puffy, 10-12 minutes.
3. Meanwhile, in a microwave-safe bowl, melt the remaining butter. Stir in cinnamon, nutmeg and the remaining brown sugar. Spread over pancake. Bake until golden brown, 8-10 minutes. Cut into wedges and serve immediately. If desired, top with whipped cream.
1 SLICE: *468 cal., 19g fat (11g sat. fat), 181mg chol., 265mg sod., 68g carb. (48g sugars, 5g fiber), 8g pro.*

SKILLET CINNAMON ROLLS

I love using cast iron to get a nice crust on these cinnamon rolls! The skillet also makes an impressive serving dish to set on the table without it appearing that you tried too hard.
—Danielle Williams, Newport, RI

- -

PREP: 50 min. + rising • **BAKE:** 20 min.
MAKES: 1 dozen

- 1 **pkg. (¼ oz.) active dry yeast**
- 1 **cup warm whole milk (110° to 115°)**
- ¼ **cup sugar**
- ¼ **cup butter, softened**
- 1 **large egg yolk, room temperature**
- 1½ **tsp. vanilla extract**
- ¾ **tsp. salt**
- ½ **tsp. ground nutmeg**
- 2¾ **to 3¼ cups all-purpose flour**

FILLING

- 8 **bacon strips, chopped**
- ½ **cup packed brown sugar**
- 1 **Tbsp. maple syrup**
- 2 **tsp. ground cinnamon**
- ½ **tsp. ground nutmeg**

FROSTING

- 2 **cups confectioners' sugar**
- ½ **cup butter, softened**
- 2 **Tbsp. whole milk**
- 1 **Tbsp. maple syrup**

1. In a small bowl, dissolve yeast in warm milk. In a large bowl, combine sugar, butter, egg yolk, vanilla, salt, nutmeg, yeast mixture and 1 cup of the flour; beat on medium speed 2 minutes. Stir in enough of the remaining flour to form a soft dough (dough will be sticky).

2. Turn onto a floured surface; knead until smooth and elastic, 6-8 minutes. Place in a greased bowl, turning once to grease the top. Cover and let rise in a warm place until doubled, about 1 hour.

3. In a 10-in. cast-iron or other ovenproof skillet, cook bacon over medium-low heat until crisp. Remove with a slotted spoon; drain on paper towels. Discard drippings, reserving 3 Tbsp.

4. In the same skillet, combine brown sugar, syrup, cinnamon, nutmeg and 2 Tbsp. of the reserved bacon drippings; cook and stir until blended. Remove from pan and let cool to room temperature. Wipe out skillet; grease with remaining bacon drippings.

5. Punch dough down. Roll into an 18x12-in. rectangle. Sprinkle the brown sugar mixture and bacon to within ½ in. of edges. Roll up jelly-roll style, starting with a short side; pinch seams to seal. Cut crosswise into 12 rolls.

6. Place rolls, cut side down, in prepared skillet. Cover and let rise in a warm place until doubled, about 45 minutes. Preheat oven to 400°. Bake on a lower oven rack, until golden brown, 18-20 minutes. Cool for 20 minutes; do not cool completely.

7. In a small bowl, beat the frosting ingredients until smooth. Spread over warm rolls. Serve warm.

1 CINNAMON ROLL: *424 cal., 18g fat (10g sat. fat), 57mg chol., 356mg sod., 59g carb. (36g sugars, 1g fiber), 6g pro.*

2. Shape ¼ cupfuls of egg mixture into twelve 3-in.-long logs. Place bread crumbs and eggs in separate shallow bowls. Roll logs in crumbs to coat, then dip in egg and roll again in crumbs, patting to help the coating adhere. In a deep cast-iron or electric skillet, heat oil to 375°. Fry in batches until golden brown, about 3 minutes, turning occasionally. Drain on paper towels.

2 CROQUETTES: *381 cal., 27g fat (8g sat. fat), 303mg chol., 348mg sod., 18g carb. (3g sugars, 1g fiber), 15g pro.*

LOADED BREAKFAST POTATOES

My kids love loaded potatoes in restaurants, so I modified them to make at home. Using the microwave for the potatoes will save you about 10 minutes. I also use thin-skinned red potatoes instead of russets to save on peeling time.
—Tena Kropp, Aurora, IL

TAKES: 30 min. • **MAKES:** 6 servings

- 1½ lbs. red potatoes, cubed
- ¼ lb. bacon strips, chopped
- ¾ cup cubed fully cooked ham
- 1 cup shredded cheddar cheese
- ½ tsp. salt
- ¼ tsp. pepper
  Sour cream

1. Place potatoes in a microwave-safe dish and cover with water. Cover and microwave on high for 4-5 minutes or until tender.

2. Meanwhile, in a large cast-iron or other heavy skillet, cook bacon over medium heat until crisp. Remove to paper towels with a slotted spoon.

3. Drain potatoes; saute in drippings until lightly browned. Add the ham, cheese, salt, pepper and bacon. Cook and stir over medium heat until cheese is melted. Serve with sour cream.

¾ CUP: *273 cal., 16g fat (8g sat. fat), 45mg chol., 776mg sod., 19g carb. (1g sugars, 2g fiber), 13g pro.*

EGG & ASPARAGUS BREAKFAST CROQUETTES

Trying to come up with something new for a hot breakfast, I decided that this was a smart way to combine the whole meal. They're so good on their own, or with hollandaise on top and sprinkled with paprika for a fancier version.
—Barbara J. Miller, Oakdale, MN

PREP: 30 min. + chilling • **COOK:** 5 min./batch
MAKES: 6 servings

- 3 Tbsp. butter
- 3 Tbsp. all-purpose flour
- ¾ cup 2% milk
- 6 hard-boiled large eggs, chopped
- ½ cup chopped fresh asparagus
- ½ cup chopped green onions
- ⅓ cup shredded cheddar cheese
- 1 Tbsp. minced fresh tarragon
- ¼ tsp. salt
- ¼ tsp. pepper
- 1¾ cups panko bread crumbs
- 3 large eggs, beaten
  Oil for deep-fat frying

1. In a large saucepan, melt butter over medium heat. Stir in the flour until smooth; cook and stir until lightly browned, 1-2 minutes. Gradually whisk in milk; cook and stir until thickened (mixture will be thick). Stir in the next 7 ingredients. Refrigerate for 2 hours.

HOLIDAY FRUITS, NUTS & BERRIES

Want to give your menus a traditional touch? In these recipes, dried and seasonal fruits bring sweetness and complex flavors. The earthy taste and crunch of nuts add the finishing touches to old-fashioned holiday goodness.

ORANGE POMEGRANATE SALAD WITH HONEY

I discovered this fragrant salad in a cooking class. If you can, try to find orange flower water (also called orange blossom water), which perks up the orange segments. But orange juice adds a nice zip, too!
—Carol Richardson Marty, Lynwood, WA

TAKES: 15 min. • **MAKES:** 6 servings

- 5 medium oranges or 10 clementines
- ½ cup pomegranate seeds
- 2 Tbsp. honey
- 1 to 2 tsp. orange flower water or orange juice

1. Cut a thin slice from the top and bottom of each orange; stand orange upright on a cutting board. With a knife, remove peel and outer membrane from oranges. Cut crosswise into ½-in. slices.
2. Arrange orange slices on a serving platter; sprinkle with pomegranate seeds. In a small bowl, mix honey and orange flower water; drizzle over fruit.
⅔ CUP: *62 cal., 0 fat (0 sat. fat), 0 chol., 2mg sod., 15g carb. (14g sugars, 0 fiber), 1g pro.*
DIABETIC EXCHANGES: *1 fruit.*

OVERNIGHT BAKED OATMEAL

My husband and I once spent a long weekend at a bed-and-breakfast not far from home. The owners shared this recipe with me, which I made my own after a couple of simple changes.
—Jennifer Cramer, Lebanon, PA

PREP: 10 min. + chilling • **BAKE:** 45 min. • **MAKES:** 8 servings

- 2 large eggs, room temperature, lightly beaten
- 3 cups 2% milk
- ¾ cup packed brown sugar
- ¼ cup canola oil
- 1½ tsp. ground cinnamon
- 1 tsp. salt
- 2 cups old-fashioned oats
- ¼ cup dried blueberries
- ¼ cup dried cherries
- ¼ cup sliced almonds

1. In a large bowl, whisk together first 6 ingredients. Stir in oats, blueberries and cherries. Transfer to a greased 8-in. square baking dish. Refrigerate, covered, 8 hours or overnight.
2. Preheat oven to 350°. Remove oatmeal from refrigerator while the oven heats. Stir oatmeal; sprinkle with almonds. Bake, uncovered, until golden brown and a thermometer reads 160°, 40-50 minutes. Serve warm.
½ CUP: *331 cal., 13g fat (2g sat. fat), 54mg chol., 364mg sod., 46g carb. (30g sugars, 4g fiber), 8g pro.*

HOLIDAY AMBROSIA CAKE

*This is from an old recipe that came to me
as a typical fruitcake. I added pineapple,
coconut and pineapple juice, which made
it really moist, with a tropical taste.*
—Dotty Stodulski, North Port, FL

PREP: 40 min. • **BAKE:** 50 min. + cooling
MAKES: 12 servings

- ½   cup butter, softened
- 1   cup sugar
- 4   large eggs, room temperature
- 1   tsp. coconut extract
- 2½ cups all-purpose flour
- 1   tsp. baking powder
- ½   tsp. salt
- ½   cup unsweetened pineapple juice
- 2¼ cups sweetened shredded coconut
- 1½ cups chopped candied pineapple
- 1   cup chopped macadamia nuts
- 1   cup golden raisins
- ½   cup chopped dried mangoes
- ½   cup chopped green candied cherries
- ½   cup chopped red candied cherries

COCONUT GLAZE
- 1   cup confectioners' sugar
- 2   Tbsp. coconut milk or 2% milk
- ¼   tsp. coconut extract
- ¼   tsp. vanilla extract

1. Preheat oven to 350°. In a large bowl,
cream butter and sugar until light and
fluffy, 5-7 minutes. Add eggs, 1 at a time,
beating well after each addition. Beat in
extract. Combine flour, baking powder
and salt; add to the creamed mixture
alternately with pineapple juice, beating
well after each addition. Fold in the
coconut, pineapple, macadamia nuts,
raisins, mangoes and candied cherries.
2. Transfer to a greased and floured 10-in.
fluted tube pan. Bake until a toothpick
inserted in the center comes out clean,
50-60 minutes. Cool cake for 10 minutes
before removing from pan to a wire rack
to cool completely.
3. In a small bowl, combine confectioners'
sugar, coconut milk and extracts. Drizzle
over cool cake.

1 SLICE: *613 cal., 25g fat (13g sat. fat), 91mg
chol., 331mg sod., 95g carb. (65g sugars,
4g fiber), 7g pro.*

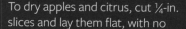

A FRUITFUL YULE

Add classic appeal and rustic charm
to your holiday decor by skipping
the tinsel and grabbing an apple
instead! This wreath started with
a 14-in. dried grapevine wreath
from a craft store, which was then
embellished with dried apples,
citrus and artificial berries.

To dry apples and citrus, cut ¼-in.
slices and lay them flat, with no
edges overlapping, on a parchment-lined baking sheet.
Brush immediately with lemon juice after cutting to preserver the
color—or leave as is for a more rustic look. Bake citrus fruits at 180°,
apples at 200°. Turn slices every 1-2 hours; dab with a paper towel after
turning to remove any juice. Remove the fruit from the oven while it's
still a little moist, and air-dry for 24 hours. For decorative effect, coat
the dried slices with a clear gloss sealer or metallic, translucent or
other acrylic paint.

1 Tbsp. butter
1 cup chopped walnuts
1 medium apple, peeled and finely chopped
3 Tbsp. dried cranberries
1 Tbsp. minced fresh parsley
1 Tbsp. olive oil
1 garlic clove, minced
1 pork tenderloin (1½ lbs.)
⅓ cup apple butter
½ tsp. salt
½ tsp. ground coriander

SAUCE
1 cup red currant jelly
1 shallot, finely chopped
2 Tbsp. cranberry juice
2 Tbsp. honey
1 Tbsp. dried currants
1 Tbsp. cider vinegar

1. Preheat oven to 350°. In a large heavy skillet, melt butter. Add walnuts; cook and stir over medium heat until toasted, about 2 minutes. Remove ½ cup for serving. Add apple to the remaining walnuts; cook and stir 1 minute longer. Cool slightly.
2. Place the cranberries, parsley, oil, garlic and apple mixture in a food processor; cover and process until finely chopped.
3. Cut a lengthwise slit down the center of the roast to within ½ in. of bottom. Open roast so it lies flat; cover with plastic wrap. Flatten to ½-in. thickness. Remove wrap; spread apple butter on 1 long side of the tenderloin to within ¼ in. of edges. Top with apple mixture. Close meat; tie with kitchen string. Place on a rack in a shallow roasting pan; rub with salt and coriander.
4. Bake at 350° until a thermometer inserted into center of stuffing reads 165° and thermometer inserted in pork reads at least 145°, 55-65 minutes. Let stand for 10 minutes before slicing.
5. Meanwhile, in a small saucepan, combine the sauce ingredients; bring to a boil. Reduce heat; simmer, uncovered, until slightly thickened, 12-14 minutes. Serve sauce with pork; top with the reserved walnuts.
3 OZ. COOKED PORK WITH 3 TBSP. SAUCE: *513 cal., 21g fat (4g sat. fat), 68mg chol., 260mg sod., 59g carb. (51g sugars, 2g fiber), 26g pro.*

HAZELNUT HOT CHOCOLATE

Vanilla beans and Frangelico liqueur give this hot chocolate a sophisticated flavor. With such a rich, dense taste, it could even be served as a dessert.
—*Michael Compean, Fountain Hills, AZ*

TAKES: 25 min.
MAKES: 22 servings

3 vanilla beans
9 cups whole milk
2¾ cups heavy whipping cream, divided
16 oz. bittersweet chocolate, divided
½ cup Nutella
2 Tbsp. dark brown sugar
1 Tbsp. sugar
¼ tsp. salt
¾ cup hazelnut liqueur
¼ cup chopped hazelnuts, toasted
Cinnamon sticks, optional

1. Split vanilla beans in half lengthwise. With a sharp knife, scrape the beans to remove the seeds. Set the seeds aside; discard the beans.
2. In a large saucepan, heat the milk and ¾ cup cream over medium heat just until the mixture comes to a simmer.
3. Chop 15 oz. chocolate. In a large heatproof bowl, combine the chopped chocolate, Nutella, sugars, salt and vanilla seeds. Pour the warm milk mixture over chocolate mixture. Let stand for 1 minute.
4. Meanwhile, whip the remaining cream and shave the remaining chocolate. Whisk the chocolate mixture until smooth; stir in liqueur. Serve with whipped cream, shaved chocolate and chopped hazelnuts. Garnish with a cinnamon stick if desired.
½ CUP: *299 cal., 20g fat (10g sat. fat), 29mg chol., 88mg sod., 26g carb. (22g sugars, 2g fiber), 6g pro.*

APPLE & WALNUT STUFFED PORK TENDERLOIN WITH RED CURRANT SAUCE

My special roasted pork tenderloin is stuffed with two of our favorite ingredients, walnuts and apples, which give it both sweetness and texture. The comforting, elegant entree is my family's most requested pork dish.
—*Gloria Bradley, Naperville, IL*

PREP: 35 min. • **BAKE:** 55 min.
MAKES: 6 servings

DRIED CHERRY & SAUSAGE DRESSING

Apples and dried cherries add a sweet-tart flavor to my homemade stuffing. It makes a holiday dinner one to remember.
—Connie Boll, Chilton, WI

PREP: 40 min. • **BAKE:** 45 min.
MAKES: 20 servings

- 1   loaf (1 lb.) unsliced Italian bread
- ¼   cup cherry juice blend or unsweetened apple juice
- 1   cup dried cherries
- 1   lb. bulk Italian sausage
- 2   celery ribs, chopped
- 1   medium onion, chopped
- 2   medium Granny Smith apples, chopped
- ½   cup chopped fresh parsley
- ½   cup butter, melted
- 1   tsp. Italian seasoning
- 1   tsp. fennel seed
- 1   tsp. rubbed sage
- ½   tsp. salt
- ¼   tsp. pepper
- 2   large eggs
- 2   cups chicken stock

1. Preheat oven to 375°. Cut bread into 1-in. cubes; transfer to two 15x10x1-in. baking pans. Bake 10-15 minutes or until toasted. Cool slightly.
2. In a small saucepan, bring juice to a boil. Stir in cherries. Remove from heat; let stand 10 minutes. Drain.
3. Meanwhile, in a large skillet, cook sausage, celery and onion over medium heat 8-10 minutes or until sausage is no longer pink and vegetables are tender, breaking up sausage into crumbles; drain. Transfer to a large bowl; stir in apples, parsley, butter, seasonings, bread cubes and drained cherries. In a small bowl, whisk eggs and stock; pour over the bread mixture and toss to coat.
4. Transfer to a greased 13x9-in. baking dish (dish will be full). Bake, covered, 30 minutes. Bake, uncovered, 15-20 minutes or until golden brown.
¾ CUP: 204 cal., 11g fat (5g sat. fat), 43mg chol., 422mg sod., 21g carb. (8g sugars, 1g fiber), 6g pro.

MEDITERRANEAN APRICOT PHYLLO BITES

Apricot and almonds make these flaky little bites a delicious ending to a meal or a special treat in the evening.
—Taste of Home *Test Kitchen*

PREP: 30 min. • **BAKE:** 10 min.
MAKES: 2½ dozen

- ½   cup unblanched almonds
- ½   cup chopped dried apricots
- 1   Tbsp. plus ½ cup butter, melted, divided
- 2   Tbsp. honey
- ¼   tsp. grated lemon zest
- ¼   tsp. almond extract
- 20   sheets phyllo dough (14x9 in.)

1. Place almonds and apricots in a food processor; cover and process until finely chopped. In a small bowl, combine 1 Tbsp. butter, honey, lemon zest and extract; add almond mixture and stir until blended.
2. Lightly brush one sheet of phyllo with the remaining butter; place another sheet of phyllo on top and brush with butter. (Keep the remaining phyllo covered with plastic wrap and a damp towel to prevent it from drying out.) Cut the two layered sheets into three 14x3-in. strips.
3. Place 1½ tsp. filling in lower corner of each strip. Fold dough over filling, forming a triangle. Fold triangle up, then fold triangle over, forming another triangle. Continue folding, like a flag, until you come to the end of the strip. Brush the end of the dough with butter and press onto the triangle to seal. Turn triangle and brush top with melted butter. Repeat.
4. Place triangles on a greased baking sheet. Bake at 375° for 10-12 minutes or until golden brown. Cool on a wire rack. Sprinkle with confectioners' sugar.
1 SERVING: 74 cal., 5g fat (2g sat. fat), 9mg chol., 56mg sod., 7g carb. (3g sugars, 1g fiber), 1g pro.
DIABETIC EXCHANGES: *½ starch, ½ fat.*

THYME & FIG GOAT CHEESE SPREAD

When I started growing herbs in my garden it took me a while to find a good way to use thyme, but this easy appetizer spread lets it shine. I usually garnish it with a sprig of thyme, slivered almonds and chopped figs.
—Laura Cox, Columbia, MO

TAKES: 15 min. • **MAKES:** 1½ cups

- 1 **cup crumbled goat cheese**
- ½ **cup sour cream**
- 1 **Tbsp. honey**
- ½ **tsp. minced fresh thyme**
- ½ **cup chopped dried figs**
- ¼ **cup slivered almonds**
  Additional minced fresh thyme, optional
  Assorted crackers, French bread baguette, slices or assorted fresh vegetables

In a small bowl, beat cheese, sour cream, honey and thyme until smooth; stir in figs and almonds. Sprinkle with additional thyme if desired. Refrigerate until serving. Serve with crackers, baguette slices or vegetables.

2 TBSP.: *81 cal., 6g fat (3g sat. fat), 14mg chol., 49mg sod., 7g carb. (5g sugars, 1g fiber), 3g pro.*

Holiday Helper

The ingredients in this recipe are simple and straightforward but, when combined, make an elegant-tasting spread. If you don't have fresh thyme on hand, use ¼ tsp. dried thyme.

SWISS CHERRY BRUSCHETTA

This recipe is a spinoff a cherry chicken main dish my husband adores. The combination of sweet, tart and salty flavors provides a contrast that's hard to resist.
—Shelly Platten, Amherst, WI

TAKES: 30 min. • **MAKES:** 16 servings

- 2 **large onions, chopped**
- 1 **garlic clove, minced**
- 4 **tsp. olive oil**
- 1 **Tbsp. balsamic vinegar**
- 1 **tsp. brown sugar**
- ½ **tsp. garlic salt**
- 2½ **cups pitted dark sweet cherries, coarsely chopped**
- 16 **slices French bread (½ in. thick), lightly toasted**
- 1½ **cups shredded Swiss cheese**
- 2 **Tbsp. minced fresh parsley**

1. In a large skillet, saute onions and garlic in oil until tender, about 6 minutes. Add the vinegar, brown sugar and garlic salt; reduce heat. Cook until onions are caramelized, 3-4 minutes. Stir in the cherries; cook until sauce is syrupy, about minutes longer.

2. Place toasted bread on a baking sheet; spoon cherry mixture evenly over toast. Sprinkle with cheese and parsley. Broil 3-4 in. from the heat until cheese is melted, 1-2 minutes.

1 PIECE: *115 cal., 4g fat (2g sat. fat), 9mg chol., 154mg sod., 15g carb., 1g fiber, 4g pro.*

FIG-CARROT STUFFED KABOCHA SQUASH

While searching for a new winter squash variety, I stumbled upon kabocha squash— it really wowed me. The flavor and texture are rich and beautiful, and this recipe, which I improvised, really suits the squash well.
—Caitlin Stephens-North, Malden, MA

PREP: 25 min. • **BAKE:** 45 min.
MAKES: 4 servings

- 1   medium kabocha squash (about 3 lbs.)
- ½   tsp. fennel seed
- ¼   tsp. ground fenugreek
- ¼   tsp. pepper
      Dash ground nutmeg
      Dash ground cloves
- 1   Tbsp. olive oil
- ½   tsp. salt

STUFFING

- 3   medium carrots, finely chopped
- 2   shallots, chopped
- 1   Tbsp. olive oil
- 5   fresh or dried figs, cut into eighths
- ½   cup water
- ¼   tsp. salt
- ¼   tsp. ground cinnamon
- ¼   tsp. pepper
      Dash ground nutmeg
      Dash ground cloves
- 3   Tbsp. chopped pecans

1. Preheat oven to 400°. Wash squash; cut into 4 wedges. Remove loose fibers and seeds from the inside and discard.
2. In a spice grinder or with a mortar and pestle, combine fennel seed, fenugreek, pepper, nutmeg and cloves; grind until seeds are crushed.
3. Brush squash with oil. Sprinkle with salt and ¾ tsp. spice mixture. Place in an ungreased 15x10x1-in. baking sheet. Bake, uncovered, for 35-40 minutes or until tender.
4. Meanwhile, in a large skillet, saute carrots and shallots in oil until tender. Stir in the figs, water, salt, cinnamon, pepper, nutmeg, cloves and remaining spice mixture. Bring to a boil. Reduce heat; simmer, uncovered, for 8-10 minutes or until liquid is evaporated and figs are tender. Stir in pecans.

5. Fill squash with stuffing. Bake 10-15 minutes longer or until heated through.
1 STUFFED WEDGE: *299 cal., 11g fat (1g sat. fat), 0 chol., 489mg sod., 52g carb. (19g sugars, 13g fiber), 5g pro.*

BROWNIE BOURBON BITES

Chocolate and chopped pecans flavor these simple, spirited treats. Make a double batch so you can give some as gifts and savor the rest!
—Paula Kirchenbauer, Newton, NJ

PREP: 25 min. + chilling
BAKE: 10 min. + cooling
MAKES: about 2 dozen

- ½   cup butter, softened
- ½   cup packed brown sugar
- ¼   cup bourbon
- 1   cup all-purpose flour
- 3   Tbsp. baking cocoa
- ½   cup miniature semisweet chocolate chips
- 1   cup coarsely chopped pecans

1. In a small bowl, cream butter and brown sugar until light and fluffy, 5-7 minutes. Beat in bourbon. Combine flour and cocoa; gradually add to creamed mixture, beating until smooth. Stir in chocolate chips. Cover and refrigerate for 1-2 hours.
2. Shape into 1-in. balls; roll in pecans. Place 2 in. apart on ungreased baking sheets. Bake at 350° until cookies are set, 8-10 minutes. Cool for 5 minutes before carefully removing from pans to wire racks to cool completely. Store in an airtight container.
1 COOKIE: *110 cal., 7g fat (3g sat. fat), 9mg chol., 35mg sod., 10g carb. (6g sugars, 1g fiber), 1g pro.*

2 cups fresh or frozen cranberries, thawed
4 celery ribs, sliced
1 medium onion, chopped
2½ cups apple cider or juice
3 Tbsp. brown sugar
4 garlic cloves, minced
4 tsp. grated orange zest
1 Tbsp. beef or chicken bouillon granules
1 tsp. dried rosemary, crushed, or dried thyme
6 Tbsp. all-purpose flour
¾ cup water
5 cups chopped cooked pork
4 sheets refrigerated pie crust

1. Adjust oven rack to lower third of oven; preheat oven to 450°. In a large saucepan, combine the first 9 ingredients; bring to a boil. Reduce heat; simmer, uncovered, until berries pop, about 10 minutes.
2. In a small bowl, mix flour and water until smooth; stir into cranberry mixture. Return to a boil, stirring constantly; cook and stir until thickened, 1-2 minutes. Stir in pork; remove from heat.
3. On a work surface, unroll crusts. Roll each into a 14-in. circle. Using a 5-in. disposable foil potpie pan as a guide (top side down), cut out sixteen 6-in. crust circles, rerolling scraps as needed.
4. Press 1 crust circle firmly into bottom and up the sides of each of eight 5-in. disposable foil pans. Divide the pork mixture evenly among pans. Place the remaining crust circles over tops, pressing bottom and top crusts together firmly; flute edges. Cut slits in crusts.
5. Place potpies on baking sheets. Bake until crust is golden brown and filling is bubbly, 30-35 minutes.
FREEZE OPTION: *Tightly cover unbaked potpies and freeze. To use, bake frozen pies on baking sheets in a preheated 425° oven until golden brown and a thermometer inserted in center reads 165°, 40-45 minutes.*
1 POTPIE: *727 cal., 34g fat (14g sat. fat), 98mg chol., 746mg sod., 73g carb. (19g sugars, 2g fiber), 30g pro.*

PRETTY CRANBERRY COFFEE CAKE

Cranberries make this coffee cake a beautiful quick bread that's perfect for the holidays. For extra shimmer, we add a drizzle of almond-flavored glaze.
—Darlene Brenden, Salem, OR

- -

PREP: 20 min. • **BAKE:** 1 hour
MAKES: 16 servings

1 cup butter, softened
1 cup sugar
2 large eggs, room temperature
1 tsp. almond extract
2 cups all-purpose flour
1 tsp. baking powder
1 tsp. baking soda
½ tsp. salt
1 cup sour cream
1 can (14 oz.) whole-berry cranberry sauce
½ cup chopped walnuts
OPTIONAL GLAZE
⅓ cup confectioners' sugar
½ tsp. almond extract
2 to 4 tsp. warm water

1. Preheat oven to 350°. In a large bowl, cream butter and sugar until light and fluffy, 5-7 minutes. Add eggs, 1 at a time, beating well after each addition. Beat in extract. In a second bowl, whisk flour, baking powder, baking soda and salt; add to the creamed mixture alternately with the sour cream, beating well after each addition.
2. Spoon a third of the batter into a greased 9-in. square baking pan. Top with a third of the cranberry sauce. Repeat layers twice. Sprinkle with walnuts.
3. Bake 60-65 minutes or until a toothpick inserted in cake portion comes out clean. Cool on a wire rack.
4. If desired, make the glaze: In a small bowl, mix confectioners' sugar, extract and enough water to reach a drizzling consistency. Spoon over cooled cake.
1 PIECE: *305 cal., 17g fat (9g sat. fat), 63mg chol., 295mg sod., 35g carb. (19g sugars, 1g fiber), 4g pro.*

INDIVIDUAL PORK & CRANBERRY POTPIES

My neighbor gave me this recipe years ago, and I love how these pies are different from the usual chicken potpie. The flavor combination in these pies is perfect for the cold winter months, but freezing them allows my family to enjoy them any time of year.
—Mary Shenk, DeKalb, IL

- -

PREP: 45 min. • **BAKE:** 15 min.
MAKES: 8 servings

CHRISTMAS CRANBERRIES

Bourbon adds bite to this holiday standby. These jars make lovely gifts when wrapped in a vintage tea towel, cinched with ribbon and adorned with small ornaments.
—Becky Jo Smith, Kettle Falls, WA

PREP: 35 min. • **PROCESS:** 15 min.
MAKES: 4 half-pints

- 2 **pkg. (12 oz. each) fresh or frozen cranberries, thawed**
- 1½ **cups sugar**
- 1 **cup orange juice**
- ¼ **cup bourbon**
- 3 **tsp. vanilla extract**
- 1 **tsp. grated orange zest**

1. In a large saucepan, combine the cranberries, sugar, orange juice and bourbon. Bring to a boil. Reduce heat; simmer, uncovered, until berries pop and mixture has thickened, 18-22 minutes.

2. Remove from heat. Stir in vanilla and orange zest. Ladle hot mixture into 4 hot half-pint jars, leaving ¼-in. headspace. Remove air bubbles and adjust headspace, if necessary, by adding hot mixture. Wipe rims. Center lids on jars; screw on bands until fingertip tight.

3. Place jars into canner with simmering water, ensuring that they are completely covered with water. Bring water to a boil; process for 15 minutes. Remove the jars and cool.

2 TBSP.: *54 cal., 0 fat (0 sat. fat), 0 chol., 0 sod., 13g carb. (11g sugars, 1g fiber), 0 pro.*

MOROCCAN SPICED FRUIT & NUT BREAD

Red pepper flakes combined with the cinnamon and allspice give each slice of this bread a subtle hint of warmth.
—Donna-Marie Ryan, Topsfield, MA

PREP: 30 min. • **BAKE:** 50 min. + cooling
MAKES: 1 loaf (16 slices) and ½ cup butter

- ½ **cup chopped dried apricots**
- ½ **cup chopped dates**
- ¼ **cup orange juice**
- 2 **cups all-purpose flour**
- ½ **cup sugar**
- ¼ **cup packed brown sugar**
- 2 **tsp. baking powder**
- ¾ **tsp. salt**
- ½ **tsp. ground cinnamon**
- ¼ **tsp. ground allspice**
- ¼ **tsp. crushed red pepper flakes**
- 2 **large eggs, room temperature**
- ¾ **cup 2% milk**
- ¼ **cup unsalted butter, melted**
- 1 **Tbsp. grated orange zest**
- ⅓ **cup sweetened shredded coconut**
- ¼ **cup chopped pecans**

ORANGE BUTTER

- ½ **cup unsalted butter, softened**
- 4 **tsp. confectioners' sugar**
- 2 **tsp. grated orange zest**
- 4 **tsp. orange juice**

1. Preheat oven to 350°. In a small saucepan, combine apricots, dates and orange juice; bring to a boil. Cook, uncovered, 1 minute. Remove from heat; let stand, covered, 10 minutes.

2. In a large bowl, whisk flour, sugars, baking powder, salt and spices. In a another bowl, whisk eggs, milk, melted butter and orange zest until blended. Add to flour mixture; stir just until moistened. Fold in coconut, pecans and apricot mixture.

3. Transfer to a greased 9x5-in. loaf pan. Bake 50-55 minutes or until a toothpick inserted in center comes out clean. Cool in pan 10 minutes before removing to a wire rack to cool.

4. In a small bowl, beat the remaining ingredients until blended. Serve bread with orange butter.

1 SLICE WITH 1½ TSP. BUTTER: *238 cal., 12g fat (6g sat. fat), 50mg chol., 186mg sod., 32g carb. (18g sugars, 2g fiber), 3g pro.*

RACK OF LAMB WITH FIGS

I've been making this rack of lamb for years. My grandma gave me the recipe because she knew how much I love figs. And the toasted walnuts sprinkled on top give it just the right finishing touch.
—Sylvia Castanon, Long Beach, CA

PREP: 30 min. • **BAKE:** 45 min.
MAKES: 8 servings

- 2 racks of lamb (2 lbs./8 ribs each)
- 1 tsp. salt, divided
- 1 cup water
- 1 small onion, finely chopped
- 1 Tbsp. canola oil
- 1 garlic clove, minced
- 2 Tbsp. cornstarch
- 1 cup port wine, or ½ cup grape juice plus ½ cup reduced-sodium beef broth
- 10 dried figs, halved
- ¼ tsp. pepper
- ½ cup coarsely chopped walnuts, toasted
  Chopped fresh parsley, optional

1. Preheat oven to 375°. Rub lamb with ½ tsp. salt. Place meat side up on a rack in a greased roasting pan. Bake, uncovered, for 45-60 minutes or until the meat reaches desired doneness (for medium-rare, a thermometer should read 135°; medium, 140°; medium-well, 145°).
2. Remove to a serving platter; cover loosely with foil. Add 1 cup water to roasting pan; stir to loosen browned bits from pan. Using a fine sieve, strain mixture; set drippings aside.
3. In a small saucepan, saute onion in oil until tender. Add garlic; cook 1 minute longer. Stir in cornstarch until blended; gradually add the wine, drippings, figs, pepper and the remaining salt. Bring to a boil. Reduce heat to medium-low; cook, uncovered, until figs are tender and sauce is thickened, about 10 minutes, stirring occasionally.
4. Sprinkle walnuts over lamb; serve with the fig sauce. If desired, top with chopped parsley.
2 CHOPS: *363 cal., 16g fat (4g sat. fat), 66mg chol., 362mg sod., 23g carb. (14g sugars, 3g fiber), 23g pro.*

SPECIAL RAISIN PIE

When I first made this pie, I thought it was great. Then I entered it at the county fair and I guess the judges agreed—it won first place! This makes an open lattice crust; for the tight lattice shown, make another half batch of pastry.
—Laura Fall-Sutton, Buhl, ID

PREP: 40 min. • **BAKE:** 35 min. + cooling
MAKES: 8 servings

- 2½ cups raisins
- 2 cups water
- ⅓ cup packed brown sugar
- ⅓ cup sugar
- ⅛ tsp. salt
- 2 Tbsp. plus 1½ tsp. cornstarch
- ¼ cup cold water
- 2 Tbsp. lemon juice
- 1 Tbsp. orange juice
- 2 tsp. grated orange zest
- 1 tsp. grated lemon zest
- ½ tsp. rum extract
  Pastry for double-crust pie (9 in.)
- 2 Tbsp. butter

1. In a small saucepan, combine raisins and water. Bring to a boil; cook 2 minutes. Add sugars and salt; cook until sugars are dissolved. Combine cornstarch and cold water until smooth; gradually stir into the pan. Cook and stir for 2 minutes or until thickened and bubbly. Remove from the heat; stir in the juices, zests and extract.
2. Roll out half of the pastry to fit a 9-in. pie plate; transfer pastry to pie plate. Fill with raisin mixture. Dot with butter.
3. Roll out remaining pastry; make a lattice crust. Trim, seal and flute edges. Bake at 375° for 35-40 minutes or until the crust is golden brown and the filling is bubbly, covering edges with foil during the last 10 minutes. Cool pie on a wire rack. Refrigerate leftovers.
1 PIECE: *481 cal., 17g fat (8g sat. fat), 18mg chol., 266mg sod., 82g carb. (46g sugars, 2g fiber), 3g pro.*
PASTRY FOR DOUBLE-CRUST PIE (9 INCHES): *Combine 2½ cups all-purpose flour and ½ tsp. salt; cut in 1 cup cold butter until crumbly. Gradually add ⅓-⅔ cup ice water, tossing with a fork until dough holds together when pressed. Divide dough in half. Shape each into a disk; wrap. refrigerate 1 hour or overnight.*

DUCK BREASTS WITH APRICOT CHUTNEY

Savory duck breasts are a distinctive choice for a special holiday dinner.
—Taste of Home Test Kitchen

- -

PREP: 30 min. • **BAKE:** 30 min. + cooling
MAKES: 12 servings

- 1½ cups orange juice
- ⅔ cup sugar
- 2 pkg. (6 oz. each) dried apricots, chopped
- ½ cup dried cherries
- ½ cup golden raisins
- 2 tsp. minced fresh gingerroot
- ¾ tsp. ground coriander
- ¾ tsp. ground cumin
- ¼ tsp. salt
- ¼ tsp. pepper
- ⅛ tsp. ground cloves
- 2 tsp. lemon juice
  DUCK
- 12 duck breast halves with skin (5 oz. each)
- 1½ tsp. salt
- ¼ tsp. pepper
- 2 Tbsp. olive oil
  ORANGE SAUCE
- ¼ tsp. minced garlic
- ½ cup Marsala wine
- ½ tsp. cornstarch
- ½ cup orange juice
- ⅓ cup chicken broth
- 2 Tbsp. grated orange zest
- 3 Tbsp. cold butter
- 1 Tbsp. minced fresh basil

1. For chutney, in a saucepan, combine orange juice and sugar. Cook and stir over medium heat until sugar is dissolved, about 3 minutes. Add apricots, cherries, raisins, gingerroot, coriander, cumin, salt, pepper and cloves. Bring to a boil. Reduce heat to low; cook until apricots are tender, about 10 minutes. Transfer to a bowl; stir in lemon juice. Let stand at room temperature for at least 2 hours.

2. Season both sides of duck breasts with salt and pepper. In a large skillet, saute duck, skin side down, in oil until skin is browned; turn and cook for 1 minute longer. Set aside 1 Tbsp. drippings.

3. Place duck on a greased rack in a shallow roasting pan. Bake at 350° until meat reaches desired doneness (for medium, a thermometer should read 165°; well-done, 180°), 30-35 minutes.

4. For orange sauce, saute garlic in the reserved drippings for 1 minute. Add wine; bring to a boil. Cook and stir until reduced by half. In a bowl, combine the cornstarch, orange juice, broth and orange zest until blended. Stir into wine mixture. Bring to a boil. Reduce heat; simmer, uncovered, for 5 minutes. Remove from heat. Add butter and basil; whisk until smooth. Remove skin from duck if desired before slicing. Serve with orange sauce and chutney.

1 DUCK BREAST HALF WITH ¼ CUP CHUTNEY AND 1 TBSP. SAUCE: *525 cal., 30g fat (11g sat. fat), 81mg chol., 456mg sod., 44g carb. (38g sugars, 3g fiber), 18g pro.*

QUINOA, FIG & HONEY-BALSAMIC PARFAIT

This recipe is special to me because of the two main ingredients, quinoa and figs. Quinoa is gluten-free, which is good for those who have food allergies, like my daughter. And I love fresh ripe figs when they are in season. Enjoy this for breakfast or dessert.
—Dawn Hutchins, St. Johns, FL

TAKES: 30 min. • **MAKES:** 4 servings

- 1　cup water
- ½　cup quinoa, rinsed
- ¼　cup balsamic vinegar
- 1　tsp. vanilla extract
- ¼　tsp. ground cinnamon
- ⅛　tsp. salt
- ¼　cup honey
- 8　fresh figs, quartered
- 1　cup (8 oz.) vanilla yogurt

1. In a small saucepan, bring water to a boil. Add quinoa. Reduce heat; simmer, covered, 12-15 minutes or until liquid is absorbed. Remove from heat; fluff with a fork.
2. Meanwhile, place vinegar in a small saucepan. Bring to a boil; cook 1-2 minutes or until liquid is reduced by half.
3. In a small bowl, mix cooked quinoa, vanilla, cinnamon and salt. Layer half of quinoa mixture, half of honey, balsamic vinegar, half of figs and half of yogurt into 4 parfait glasses. Top with the remaining quinoa mixture, honey, yogurt and figs.
1 PARFAIT: *272 cal., 2g fat (1g sat. fat), 3mg chol., 117mg sod., 59g carb. (43g sugars, 4g fiber), 7g pro.*

BISHOP'S BREAD

This bread is packed with cherries, chocolate and nuts—a fresh alternative to fruitcake. I give away many loaves at Christmas.
—Yvonne Wheeler, Minneapolis, MN

PREP: 15 min. • **BAKE:** 2 hours + cooling • **MAKES:** 1 loaf (16 slices)

- 1　cup sugar
- 3　large eggs, room temperature
- ½　tsp. almond extract
- ½　tsp. vanilla extract
- 1½　cups all-purpose flour
- 1½　tsp. baking powder
- 1　tsp. salt
- 1　cup whole almonds
- 1　cup chopped walnuts
- 1　cup chopped dates
- ½　cup each red and green maraschino cherries, drained and halved
- 1　milk chocolate candy bar with almonds (7 oz.), broken into bite-sized pieces

1. Preheat oven to 300°. In a large bowl, beat sugar, eggs and extracts. In another bowl, combine the flour, baking powder and salt; stir in almonds, walnuts, dates, cherries and candy bar. Stir into egg mixture until blended.
2. Pour into a greased and floured 9x5-in. loaf pan. Press down firmly to eliminate air spaces. Bake for 2 hours. Cool 10 minutes before removing from pan to a wire rack.
1 SLICE: *320 cal., 15g fat (3g sat. fat), 37mg chol., 225mg sod., 43g carb. (28g sugars, 3g fiber), 7g pro.*

COOKIE PLATTER PARTY

Cookies are as much a part of the Christmas season as the ornaments on the tree! With these four fabulous plates of carefully chosen cookies, you'll have the ideal collection for any party.

Beginner Baker

You don't need to be an expert to create a share-worthy spread—kids will love to make these easy recipes!

CINNAMON STAR CUTOUTS

My grandmother made these aromatic cinnamon stars every Christmas when I was a child. I have such fond memories of helping her in the kitchen.
—Jean Jones, Peachtree City, GA

PREP: 15 min. + chilling
BAKE: 15 min./batch
MAKES: 5 dozen

- 1 cup butter, softened
- 2 cups sugar
- 2 large eggs, room temperature
- 2¾ cups all-purpose flour
- ⅓ cup ground cinnamon

1. In a large bowl, cream the butter and sugar until light and fluffy. Add eggs, 1 at a time, beating well after each addition. Combine flour and cinnamon; gradually add to the creamed mixture and mix well. Cover and refrigerate for 1 hour or until easy to handle.
2. Preheat oven to 350°. On a lightly floured surface, roll out dough to ¼-in. thickness. Cut with a 2½-in. star-shaped cookie cutter dipped in flour. Place 1 in. apart on ungreased baking sheets.
3. Bake 15-18 minutes or until edges are firm and bottoms of cookies are lightly browned. Remove to wire racks to cool.
1 COOKIE: 78 cal., 3g fat (2g sat. fat), 15mg chol., 33mg sod., 12g carb. (7g sugars, 0 fiber), 1g pro.

SWEETHEART COOKIES

These rounds filled with fruit preserves were blue-ribbon winners at the county fair two years running. A family favorite, they never last beyond Christmas!
—Pamela Esposito, Smithville, NJ

PREP: 25 min. • **BAKE:** 15 min./batch • **MAKES:** 2 dozen

- ¾ cup butter, softened
- ½ cup sugar
- 1 large egg yolk, room temperature
- 1½ cups all-purpose flour
- 2 Tbsp. raspberry or strawberry preserves
  Confectioners' sugar, optional

1. In a bowl, cream butter and sugar. Add egg yolk; mix well. Stir in the flour by hand. On a lightly floured surface, gently knead dough for 2-3 minutes or until thoroughly combined.
2. Roll into 1-in. balls. Place 2 in. apart on greased baking sheets. Using the end of a wooden spoon handle, make an indention in the center of each. Fill each with ¼ tsp. preserves.
3. Bake at 350° for 13-15 minutes or until edges are lightly browned. Remove to wire racks. Dust warm cookies with confectioners' sugar if desired. Cool.
1 COOKIE: *102 cal., 6g fat (4g sat. fat), 23mg chol., 46mg sod., 11g carb. (5g sugars, 0 fiber), 1g pro.*

WHIPPED SHORTBEAD

This version of shortbread melts in your mouth. Mostly I make it for the holidays, but I'll also prepare it year-round for wedding showers and afternoon teas.
—Jane Ficiur, Bow Island, Alberta

PREP: 50 min. • **BAKE:** 20 min./batch • **MAKES:** 18 dozen

- 3 cups butter, softened
- 1½ cups confectioners' sugar, sifted
- 1½ cups all-purpose flour
- 1½ cups cornstarch
  Nonpareils and/or halved candied cherries

1. Preheat oven to 300°. In a large bowl, cream butter and confectioners' sugar until light and fluffy, about 5 minutes. Gradually add flour and cornstarch, beating until well blended.
2. With hands lightly dusted with additional cornstarch, roll dough into 1-in. balls. Place 1 in. apart on ungreased baking sheets. Press lightly with a floured fork. Top with nonpareils or cherry halves.
3. Bake 20-22 minutes or until bottoms are lightly browned. Cool for 5 minutes before removing from pans to wire racks.
1 COOKIE: *39 calories, 3g fat (2g saturated fat), 7mg cholesterol, 20mg sodium, 4g carbohydrate (1g sugars, 0 fiber), 0 protein.*

BUTTER MINT COOKIES

These delicate and oh-so-easy cookies with a touch of mint were a big hit when I made them for a party at work!
—Anita Epitropou, Zion, IL

- -

PREP: 15 min. • **BAKE:** 10 min./batch • **MAKES:** 3 dozen

- 1   cup butter, softened
- ½   cup confectioners' sugar
- 1½   tsp. peppermint extract
- 1¾   cups all-purpose flour
-      Green colored sugar

1. Cream butter and confectioners' sugar until light and fluffy, 5-7 minutes. Beat in extract. Gradually add flour and mix well.
2. Roll tablespoonfuls of dough into balls. Place 1 in. apart on ungreased baking sheets; flatten with a glass dipped in colored sugar. Bake at 350° for 10-12 minutes or until firm. Remove to wire racks to cool.
1 COOKIE: *74 cal., 5g fat (3g sat. fat), 14mg chol., 41mg sod., 6g carb. (2g sugars, 0 fiber), 1g pro.*

CHOCOLATE FUDGE PEANUT BUTTER COOKIES

Five ingredients are all you'll need to whip up a batch of these melt-in-your-mouth goodies. They go over big with kids and adults alike.
—Elaine Stephens, Carmel, IN

- -

PREP: 20 min.
BAKE: 10 min./batch + cooling
MAKES: 3½ dozen

- 2   cans (16 oz. each) chocolate fudge frosting, divided
- 1   large egg, room temperature
- 1   cup chunky peanut butter
- 1½   cups all-purpose flour
-      Sugar

1. Preheat oven to 375°. Reserve 1 can plus ⅓ cup frosting for topping cookies. In a large bowl, mix egg, peanut butter and the remaining frosting until blended. Stir in flour just until moistened.
2. Drop dough by rounded tablespoonfuls 2 in. apart onto greased baking sheets. Flatten with a fork dipped in sugar.
3. Bake 7-9 minutes or until set. Remove from pans to wire racks to cool completely. Spread with reserved frosting.
1 COOKIE: *143 cal., 7g fat (1g sat. fat), 5mg chol., 79mg sod., 18g carb. (12g sugars, 1g fiber), 2g pro.*
DIABETIC EXCHANGES: *1 starch, 1 fat.*

One Cookie, Five Ways Platter

Starting with just one basic dough (p. 193), a talented baker turns everyday ingredients into five sensational sweets!

CRUMB-TOPPED DATE BARS

I use a basic dough as a starting point for a whole spread of cookies. Here, it doubles as a shortbread-like crust and crumbly topping for these sweet date bars.
—Gloria McBride, Payson, UT

PREP: 20 min. • **BAKE:** 25 min.
MAKES: 2 dozen

- 1 pkg. (8 oz.) chopped dates
- ½ cup sugar
- ½ cup water
- 1 Tbsp. lemon juice
- 2 cups Basic Cookie Dough

1. Preheat oven to 375°. In a saucepan, bring the dates, sugar, water and lemon juice to a boil. Reduce heat; simmer, uncovered, for 5 minutes, stirring occasionally. Remove from the heat; cool.
2. Press half of the cookie dough into a greased 9-in. square baking pan. Spread with the date mixture. Crumble remaining dough over filling. Bake for 25-30 minutes or until top is golden brown. Cool on a wire rack. Cut into bars.
1 BAR: *141 cal., 5g fat (3g sat. fat), 17mg chol., 77mg sod., 23g carb. (15g sugars, 1g fiber), 2g pro.*

JELLY SANDWICH COOKIES

To create the stained glass effect of these cookies, I sandwich jelly between two layers of basic dough. Your favorite raisin filling is excellent here, too.

PREP: 20 min. • **BAKE:** 10 min./batch
MAKES: about 2 dozen

2 cups Basic Cookie Dough
  Assorted jellies or jams

1. Preheat oven to 375°. On a lightly floured surface, roll out dough to ⅛-in. thickness. Cut with a 2½-in. round cookie cutter. Using a 1½-in. cookie cutter of your choice, cut out the center of half of the cookies.
2. Place whole cookies 2 in. apart on greased baking sheets. Spread with 1 tsp. jelly or jam; top with the cutout cookies. Pinch edges with a fork to seal. Bake for 10-12 minutes or until the edges are golden brown. Remove to wire racks to cool.
1 COOKIE: *98 cal., 5g fat (3g sat. fat), 17mg chol., 77mg sod., 12g carb. (4g sugars, 0 fiber), 1g pro.*

CHERRY SURPRISE COOKIES

I tuck a rich chocolate surprise into each of these cute bites. Candied cherries add a colorful finishing touch. The cookies are unusual but so easy to make.

TAKES: 20 min. • **MAKES:** 3 dozen

- 2 cups Basic Cookie Dough
- 36 chocolate stars or chocolate kisses
- 36 candied cherry halves

Preheat the oven to 375°. Drop cookie dough by heaping teaspoonfuls 2 in. apart onto greased baking sheets. Top each with a chocolate star and wrap dough around it. Top each with a candied cherry half. Bake for 10-12 minutes or until bottoms are lightly browned. Remove to wire racks to cool.

1 COOKIE: *96 cal., 5g fat (3g sat. fat), 12mg chol., 57mg sod., 13g carb. (7g sugars, 0 fiber), 1g pro.*

CHOCOLATE MALLOW COOKIES

Cocoa, marshmallows and ready-made frosting transform the basic dough into these delightful treats. Sometimes, I'll top each with a pecan half.

PREP: 20 min. • **BAKE:** 10 min./batch • **MAKES:** 40 cookies

- 2 cups Basic Cookie Dough
- ½ cup sugar
- ½ cup baking cocoa
- 1 large egg, room temperature
- ¼ cup 2% milk
- ½ cup chopped pecans
- 20 large marshmallows, halved
- 1 can (16 oz.) chocolate frosting

1. Preheat oven to 375°. Combine the cookie dough, sugar, cocoa, egg and milk; mix well. Stir in pecans. Drop by tablespoonfuls 2 in. apart onto ungreased baking sheets. Bake for 8 minutes. Press a marshmallow half onto the top of each cookie. Bake 2 minutes longer or until marshmallow is puffed. Remove to wire racks to cool.

2. Cut a hole in the corner of a pastry or plastic bag; insert a medium star tip. Fill bag with frosting. Pipe a star onto each cookie.

1 COOKIE: *140 cal., 6g fat (3g sat. fat), 15mg chol., 72mg sod., 21g carb. (14g sugars, 1g fiber), 1g pro.*

BASIC COOKIE DOUGH

Skip the store-bought stuff and learn how to make cookies from scratch—it's easy! Bake some right away, then pop the extra into the freezer for later.

TAKES: 15 min. • **MAKES:** 8 cups

- 2½ cups butter, softened
- 2 cups sugar
- 2 large eggs, room temperature
- ¼ cup 2% milk
- 2 tsp. vanilla extract
- 7½ to 8 cups (30 to 32 oz.) all-purpose flour
- 4 tsp. baking powder
- 1 tsp. salt

In a large bowl, cream butter and sugar until light and fluffy, about 5 minutes. Beat in eggs, milk and vanilla. In another bowl, whisk 7½ cups flour, baking powder and salt; gradually beat into creamed mixture, adding additional flour if necessary. Divide dough into four 2-cup portions. Refrigerate, covered, until needed.

4 TSP. DOUGH: *98 cal., 5g fat (3g sat. fat), 17mg chol., 91mg sod., 12g carb. (4g sugars, 0 fiber), 1g pro.*

CLASSIC SUGAR COOKIES

Use cookie cutters to cut seasonal shapes from a few cups of the basic dough. Prepared frosting and colored sugar make it a snap to decorate these classic cookies.

PREP: 10 min. • **BAKE:** 10 min./batch
MAKES: about 3 dozen

- 2 cups Basic Cookie Dough Colored sugar and frosting of your choice

On a lightly floured surface, roll out dough to ¼-in. thickness. Using 2½-in. cookie cutters, cut out desired shapes. Place 2 in. apart on ungreased baking sheets. Leave plain or sprinkle with colored sugar. Bake at 375° for 8-10 minutes or until the edges are golden brown. Remove to wire racks to cool. Frost plain cookies; sprinkle with colored sugar if desired.

1 COOKIE: *65 cal., 3g fat (2g sat. fat), 11mg chol., 51mg sod., 8g carb. (3g sugars, 0 fiber), 1g pro.*

Holiday Hostess with the Mostess

For elegant, showstopping cookies that will impress your guests, look no further!

RAINBOW COOKIES

(SHOWN BOTTOM ROW, CENTER)

I always bake these two weeks ahead. That allows the cookies enough time to mellow, leaving them moist and full of almond flavor!

—Mary Ann Lee, Clifton Park, NY

- -

PREP: 50 min. + chilling
BAKE: 10 min./batch + cooling
MAKES: about 8 dozen

- 1 can (8 oz.) almond paste
- 1 cup butter, softened
- 1 cup sugar
- 4 large eggs, separated, room temperature
- 2 cups all-purpose flour
- 6 to 8 drops red food coloring
- 6 to 8 drops green food coloring
- ¼ cup seedless red raspberry jam
- ¼ cup apricot preserves
- 1 cup semisweet chocolate chips

1. Preheat oven to 350°. Grease the bottoms of 3 matching 13x9-in. baking pans (or reuse 1 pan). Line the pans with waxed paper; grease the paper.
2. Place almond paste in a large bowl; break up with a fork. Cream with butter, sugar and egg yolks until light and fluffy, 5-7 minutes. Stir in flour. In another bowl, beat egg whites until soft peaks form. Fold into dough, mixing until thoroughly blended.
3. Divide dough into 3 portions (about 1⅓ cups each). Color 1 portion with red food coloring and 1 with green; leave the remaining portion uncolored. Spread each portion into the prepared pans. Bake until edges are light golden brown, 10-12 minutes.

4. Invert onto wire racks; remove waxed paper. Place another wire rack on top and turn over. Let cool completely.
5. Place the green layer on a large piece of plastic wrap. Spread evenly with raspberry jam. Top with uncolored layer and spread with apricot jam. Top with the pink layer. Bring plastic wrap over layers. Slide onto a baking sheet and set a cutting board or a heavy, flat pan on top to compress layers. Refrigerate overnight.
6. The next day, melt chocolate in a microwave; stir until smooth. Spread over top layer; allow to harden. With a sharp knife, trim the edges. Cut into ½-in. strips across the width; then cut each strip into 4-5 pieces. Store cookies in airtight containers.
1 COOKIE: *61 cal., 3g fat (2g sat. fat), 13mg chol., 19mg sod., 7g carb. (5g sugars, 0 fiber), 1g pro.*

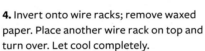

CANDY STEPS UP!

Use candies—like the Coconut Chocolate Candies on this tray—to create a pretty barrier between soft cookies and hard, crunchy ones. (See p. 97 for recipe.)

CINNAMON CRACKLE COOKIES

A blend of cinnamon, nutmeg and citrus peel gives these sugar cookies an excellent spiced flavor.
—Vicki Lair, Albert Lea, MN

PREP: 15 min. • **BAKE:** 10 min./batch
MAKES: 7 dozen

½ cup butter, softened
½ cup shortening
1 cup sugar
½ cup packed brown sugar
1 large egg, room temperature
1 tsp. vanilla extract
½ tsp. almond extract
2½ cups all-purpose flour
1 Tbsp. ground cinnamon
2 tsp. baking soda
2 tsp. cream of tartar
2 tsp. ground nutmeg
2 tsp. grated orange zest
1 tsp. grated lemon zest
½ tsp. salt
    Additional sugar

1. Preheat oven to 350°. In a large bowl, cream butter, shortening and sugars until light and fluffy, 5-7 minutes. Beat in egg and extracts. Combine flour, cinnamon, baking soda, cream of tartar, nutmeg, orange and lemon zest and salt; gradually add to the creamed mixture.
2. Shape into 1-in. balls; roll in sugar. Place 2 in. apart on ungreased baking sheets. Bake for 10-15 minutes or until lightly browned. Remove to wire racks to cool.
1 COOKIE: *50 cal., 2g fat (1g sat. fat), 5mg chol., 54mg sod., 7g carb. (4g sugars, 0 fiber), 0 pro.*

PEPPERMINT STARS

I make these buttery mint cookies each Christmas because they're my daughter's favorite. They're called stars, but you can use whatever cookie cutter design you like!
—Lois White, Brookfield, MO

PREP: 40 min. + chilling
BAKE: 10 min./batch + cooling
MAKES: 4½ dozen

¾ cup butter, softened
1 cup sugar
2 large eggs, room temperature
2½ cups all-purpose flour
1 tsp. baking powder
½ tsp. salt
¾ cup peppermint candies (about 25 pieces), finely crushed
GLAZE
2 cups confectioners' sugar
3 Tbsp. 2% milk
⅛ tsp. peppermint extract
    Red or green food coloring, optional

1. In a large bowl, cream butter and sugar. Beat in eggs. Combine flour, baking powder and salt; add to creamed mixture. Stir in crushed candies. Cover and refrigerate for 1 hour.
2. On a lightly floured surface, roll dough to ⅛-in. thickness. Cut into shapes with a floured 2½-in. star cookie cutter. Place 2 in. apart on greased baking sheets. Bake at 325° for 10-12 minutes or until lightly browned. Remove to wire racks to cool.
3. For glaze, in a small bowl, combine confectioners' sugar, milk and extract; stir until smooth. Tint with food coloring if desired. Spread over cookies.
1 COOKIE: *84 cal., 3g fat (2g sat. fat), 14mg chol., 55mg sod., 14g carb. (9g sugars, 0 fiber), 1g pro.*
DIABETIC EXCHANGES: *2 starch, 1 fat.*

ROSETTES

These traditional deep-fried favorites are crisp and delicious with a delicate, lacy look. Dipping the edges into icing helps defines the beautiful pattern.
—Iola Egle, Bella Vista, AR

PREP: 20 min. • **COOK:** 30 min.
MAKES: about 4 dozen

2 large eggs
2 tsp. sugar
1 cup 2% milk
3 tsp. vanilla extract
1 cup all-purpose flour
¼ tsp. salt
    Oil for deep-fat frying
ICING
2 cups confectioners' sugar
1 tsp. vanilla extract
1 to 3 Tbsp. water

1. In a small bowl, beat eggs and sugar; stir in milk and vanilla. Combine flour and salt; gradually add to batter until smooth.
2. Heat 2½ in. of oil to 375° in a deep-fat fryer or electric skillet. Place rosette iron in hot oil, then dip in batter, three-fourths up the sides of iron (do not let batter run over the top of the iron). Immediately place in hot oil; loosen rosette with fork and remove iron.
3. Fry rosettes 1-2 minutes on each side or until golden brown. Remove to paper towel-lined wire racks. Repeat with the remaining batter.
4. For icing, combine the confectioners' sugar, vanilla and enough water to achieve a dipping consistency. Dip edges of rosettes into icing; let dry on wire racks.
1 ROSETTE: *50 cal., 2g fat (0 sat. fat), 8mg chol., 18mg sod., 7g carb. (5g sugars, 0 fiber), 1g pro.*

FROSTED GINGERBREAD NUT COOKIES

I received the recipe for these soft ginger cookies from a dear friend, who has since passed away. This comforting classic satisfies my sweet tooth and brings back lovely memories.
—Karyn Rogers, Hemet, CA

- -

PREP: 15 min. • **BAKE:** 10 min./batch + cooling • **MAKES:** 5 dozen

- ½ cup butter, softened
- ⅔ cup sugar
- 1 large egg, room temperature
- ½ cup molasses
- 2¾ cups all-purpose flour
- 1 tsp. baking soda
- 1 tsp. ground cinnamon
- 1 tsp. ground ginger
- ½ tsp. salt
- ¼ tsp. ground cloves
- ½ cup buttermilk
- ½ cup chopped walnuts
- FROSTING
- 1½ cups confectioners' sugar
- 4½ tsp. butter, softened
- ½ tsp. vanilla extract
- 2 to 3 Tbsp. half-and-half cream
- Walnuts halves, optional

1. Preheat oven to 350°. In a large bowl, cream butter and sugar until light and fluffy, 5-7 minutes. Beat in egg and molasses. Combine the flour, baking soda, cinnamon, ginger, salt and cloves; add to creamed mixture alternately with buttermilk, beating well after each addition. Stir in chopped walnuts.
2. Drop by tablespoonfuls 2 in. apart onto greased baking sheets. Bake for 10-12 minutes or until edges are firm. Remove to wire racks to cool.
3. For frosting, in a small bowl, combine the confectioners' sugar, butter, vanilla and enough cream to achieve desired consistency. Frost cooled cookies. Top each with a walnut half if desired.
1 COOKIE: *74 cal., 3g fat (1g sat. fat), 8mg chol., 62mg sod., 12g carb. (7g sugars, 0 fiber), 1g pro.*

FESTIVE MERINGUE CHRISTMAS TREES

These meringues are eye-catching on the dessert table at a holiday party, and they taste heavenly! Look no further for the perfect treat to get you into the Christmas spirit.
—Jenni Sharp, Milwaukee, WI

- -

PREP: 20 min. • **BAKE:** 3 hours + standing
MAKES: about 26 meringues

- 3 large egg whites
- 1½ tsp. clear or regular vanilla extract
- ¼ tsp. cream of tartar
- Dash salt
- ⅔ cup sugar
- Green food coloring
- Assorted sprinkles
- Star nonpareils
- Confectioners' sugar, optional

1. Place egg whites in a large bowl; let stand at room temperature for 30 minutes.
2. Preheat oven to 200°. Add vanilla, cream of tartar and salt to the egg whites; beat on medium speed until foamy. Gradually add sugar, 1 Tbsp. at a time, beating on high after each addition until the sugar is dissolved. Continue beating until stiff glossy peaks form, about 7 minutes. Tint with green food coloring and mix thoroughly.
3. Cut a small hole in the tip of a pastry bag; insert a large #828 open star tip. Transfer meringue to bag. Pipe 2-in.-diameter tree shapes 2 in. apart onto parchment-lined baking sheets; top with sprinkles and a star nonpareil.
4. Bake until firm to the touch, about 3 hours. Turn off oven and open door all the way; leave meringues in oven until cool. Remove meringues from parchment. If desired, sprinkle lightly with confectioners' sugar. Store in an airtight container at room temperature.
1 MERINGUE: *23 cal., 0 fat (0 sat. fat), 0 chol., 12mg sod., 5g carb. (5g sugars, 0 fiber), 0 pro.*

WHITE CHOCOLATE RASPBERRY THUMBPRINTS

When I pass around the cookie tray, all eyes land on these fancy thumbprints. The white chocolate filling and dab of jewel-toned jam will satisfy even the most discriminating sweet tooth.
—Agnes Ward, Stratford, ON

- -

PREP: 25 min. + chilling • **BAKE:** 10 min./batch + cooling
MAKES: about 3 dozen

- ¾   cup butter, softened
- ½   cup packed brown sugar
- 2   large eggs, separated, room temperature
- 1¼   cups all-purpose flour
- ¼   cup baking cocoa
- 1¼   cups finely chopped pecans or walnuts

FILLING
- 4   oz. white baking chocolate, coarsely chopped
- 2   Tbsp. butter
- ¼   cup seedless raspberry jam

1. In a large bowl, cream butter and brown sugar until light and fluffy, 5-7 minutes. Beat in egg yolks. Combine flour and cocoa; gradually add to the creamed mixture and mix well. Cover and refrigerate for 1-2 hours or until easy to handle.
2. In a shallow bowl, whisk egg whites until foamy. Place nuts in another shallow bowl. Shape dough into 1-in. balls. Dip into egg whites, then roll in nuts.
3. Using a wooden spoon handle, make an indentation in center of each cookie. Place 1 in. apart on greased baking sheets. Bake at 350° for 8-10 minutes or until set. Remove to wire racks to cool completely.
4. In a microwave, melt white chocolate and butter; stir until smooth. Spoon about ½ tsp. filling into each cookie. Top each with about ¼ tsp. jam. Store in an airtight container.
1 COOKIE: 120 cal., 8g fat (4g sat. fat), 22mg chol., 43mg sod., 11g carb. (7g sugars, 1g fiber), 2g pro.

ALMOND BISCOTTI

I've learned to always bake a double batch of these crisp dunking cookies, because one batch goes too fast!
—H. Michaelsen, St. Charles, IL

- -

PREP: 15 min. • **BAKE:** 35 min. + cooling • **MAKES:** about 3½ dozen

- ½   cup butter, softened
- 1¼   cups sugar, divided
- 3   large eggs
- 1   tsp. anise extract
- 2   cups all-purpose flour
- 2   tsp. baking powder
    Dash salt
- ½   cup chopped almonds
- 2   tsp. milk

1. In a large bowl, cream butter and 1 cup sugar until light and fluffy, 5-7 minutes. Add eggs, 1 at a time, beating well after each addition. Beat in extract. Combine dry ingredients; gradually add to creamed mixture and mix well. Stir in almonds.
2. Line a baking sheet with foil and grease the foil. Divide dough in half; shape each portion into a 12x3-in. rectangle on the foil. Brush with milk; sprinkle with the remaining sugar.
3. Bake at 375° for 15-20 minutes or until golden brown and firm to the touch. Lift foil with rectangles onto a wire rack; cool for 15 minutes. Reduce heat to 300°.
4. Transfer rectangles to a cutting board; cut diagonally with a serrated knife into ½-in. slices. Place cut side down on ungreased baking sheets.
5. Bake for 10 minutes. Turn and bake 10 minutes longer or until firm. Remove to wire racks to cool. Store in an airtight container.
1 COOKIE: 207 cal., 9g fat (4g sat. fat), 50mg chol., 129mg sod., 29g carb. (16g sugars, 1g fiber), 4g pro.

The Ultimate Chocolate Collection

Four delectable cookies designed to please the chocolate lovers in your life!

JUMBO BROWNIE COOKIES

Bring these deeply fudgy cookies to a party, and you're sure to make a friend. A little espresso powder in the dough makes them over-the-top good.
—*Rebecca Cababa, Las Vegas, NV*

PREP: 20 min. • **BAKE:** 15 min./batch
MAKES: about 1½ dozen

- 2⅔ cups (16 oz.) 60% cacao bittersweet chocolate baking chips
- ½ cup unsalted butter, cubed
- 4 large eggs, room temperature
- 1½ cups sugar
- 4 tsp. vanilla extract
- 2 tsp. instant espresso powder, optional
- ⅔ cup all-purpose flour
- ½ tsp. baking powder
- ¼ tsp. salt
- 1 pkg. (11½ oz.) semisweet chocolate chunks

1. Preheat oven to 350°. In a large saucepan, melt chocolate chips and butter over low heat, stirring until smooth. Remove from the heat; let cool until mixture is warm.
2. In a small bowl, whisk the eggs, sugar, vanilla and, if desired, espresso powder until blended. Whisk into chocolate mixture. In another bowl, mix the flour, baking powder and salt; add to the chocolate mixture, mixing well. Fold in chocolate chunks; let stand until mixture thickens slightly, about 10 minutes.
3. Drop by ¼ cupfuls 3 in. apart onto parchment-lined baking sheets. Bake until set, 12-14 minutes. Cool on pans 1-2 minutes. Remove to wire racks to cool completely.
1 COOKIE: *350 cal., 19g fat (11g sat. fat), 60mg chol., 65mg sod., 48g carb. (40g sugars, 3g fiber), 4g pro.*

SLICE & BAKE CHOCOLATE PECAN COOKIES

Toasting the pecans makes a huge difference in the taste of these cookies. The double chocolate drizzle also satisfies my cravings for chocolate. They are so fancy looking, your guests will think they came from the best baker in town!
—*Lindsay Weiss, Overland Park, KS*

- -

PREP: 45 min. + chilling • **BAKE:** 10 min./batch + cooling
MAKES: 8 dozen

1½	cups butter, softened
2¼	cups confectioners' sugar
1	large egg, room temperature
3	tsp. vanilla extract
3¼	cups all-purpose flour
½	cup baking cocoa
½	tsp. baking powder
1⅔	cups chopped pecans, toasted
1	cup semisweet chocolate chips
1	cup white baking chips

1. In a large bowl, cream butter and confectioners' sugar until light and fluffy, 5-7 minutes. Beat in egg and vanilla. Combine the flour, cocoa and baking powder; gradually add to creamed mixture and mix well. Stir in pecans. Shape dough into four 6-in. logs; wrap and refrigerate for 2 hours or until firm.
2. Preheat oven to 375°. Unwrap the dough and cut into ¼-in. slices. Place slices 2 in. apart on ungreased baking sheets. Bake for 10-12 minutes or until firm. Remove to wire racks to cool.
3. In a microwave, melt semisweet chocolate chips; stir until smooth. Drizzle over cookies. Repeat with white chips. Let stand until set. Store in an airtight container.
1 COOKIE: *86 cal., 6g fat (3g sat. fat), 10mg chol., 25mg sod., 9g carb. (5g sugars, 0 fiber), 1g pro.*
DIABETIC EXCHANGES: *1 fat, ½ starch.*

CHOCOLATE-COVERED CHERRY COOKIES

Although these cookies require a little extra effort, they're worth it. I make them for every family gathering—and they never last long!
—*Marie Kinyon, Mason, MI*

- -

PREP: 30 min. • **BAKE:** 10 min./batch
MAKES: 4 dozen

½	cup butter
1	cup sugar
1	large egg, room temperature
1½	tsp. vanilla extract
1½	cups all-purpose flour
½	cup baking cocoa
¼	tsp. salt
¼	tsp. baking powder
¼	tsp. baking soda
48	maraschino cherries, blotted dry

FROSTING

1	cup (6 oz.) semisweet chocolate chips
½	cup sweetened condensed milk
1	to 3 tsp. maraschino cherry juice

1. In a bowl, cream butter and sugar until light and fluffy, 5-7 minutes; beat in egg and vanilla. Combine dry ingredients; gradually add to creamed mixture (batter will be very firm). Shape into 48 balls, about 1 in. round, and place on ungreased baking sheets. Push 1 cherry halfway into each ball.
2. For frosting, melt chocolate chips in milk in a small saucepan over low heat, stirring constantly. Remove from the heat; add cherry juice and stir until smooth.
3. Bake at 350° for 10-12 minutes. Spoon 1 tsp. frosting over each cherry while the cookie is still warm. Cool on wire racks.
1 COOKIE: *89 cal., 3g fat (2g sat. fat), 10mg chol., 43mg sod., 15g carb. (11g sugars, 0 fiber), 1g pro.*

PEPPERMINT CREAM SANDWICH COOKIES

My mother and I made these crisp sandwich cookies with perky peppermint filling together at the holidays. They are a perfect addition to any party.
—Donna Williamson, Round Rock, TX

PREP: 35 min. + chilling
BAKE: 10 min./batch + cooling
MAKES: 2 dozen

- 1½ cups butter, softened
- 1½ cups sugar
- 2 large eggs, room temperature
- 3 cups all-purpose flour
- ⅔ cup baking cocoa
- 2 tsp. instant espresso powder
- ½ tsp. salt

FILLING
- ½ cup butter, softened
- 1 tsp. peppermint extract
- 1 tsp. vanilla extract
- 2½ cups confectioners' sugar
- 1 Tbsp. 2% milk
- Red food coloring, optional

1. In a large bowl, cream butter and sugar until light and fluffy, 5-7 minutes. Beat in eggs. In another bowl, whisk flour, cocoa, espresso powder and salt; gradually beat into the creamed mixture.

2. Divide dough in half. Shape each half into a disk; cover. Refrigerate for 1 hour or until firm enough to roll.

3. Preheat oven to 350°. On a lightly floured surface, roll 1 portion of dough to ¼-in. thickness. Cut with a floured 2½-in. fluted round cookie cutter. Place cutouts 1 in. apart on parchment-lined baking sheets. Bake 10-12 minutes or until firm. Remove from pans to wire racks to cool completely. Repeat with the remaining dough.

4. In a large bowl, beat butter and extracts until creamy. Beat in confectioners' sugar, alternately with milk, until smooth. Tint as desired with food coloring. Spread frosting on the bottoms of half of the cookies; cover with remaining cookies. Store in an airtight container in the refrigerator.

1 SANDWICH COOKIE: *304 cal., 16g fat (10g sat. fat), 56mg chol., 178mg sod., 38g carb. (25g sugars, 1g fiber), 3g pro.*

MRS. CLAUS' HOSTESS GIFTS

During the season of giving, there's nothing like homemade goodies from your kitchen to show you care. These edible, beautiful gifts are perfect for co-workers, neighbors and teachers.

GINGERBREAD SPICE JELLY

I've made batches of this simple jelly, a winner at our county fair, to give as gifts for many years. When the jars are empty, people return them for a refill.
—Robin Nagel, Whitehall, MT

PREP: 15 min. + standing
PROCESS: 10 min. • **MAKES:** 5 half-pints

 2½ **cups water**
 18 **gingerbread spice tea bags**
 4½ **cups sugar**
 ½ **cup unsweetened apple juice**
 2 **tsp. butter**
 2 **pouches (3 oz. each)**
    liquid fruit pectin

1. In a large saucepan, bring water to a boil. Remove from heat; add tea bags. Cover and steep 30 minutes.
2. Discard tea bags. Stir in the sugar, apple juice and butter. Bring to a full rolling boil over high heat, stirring constantly. Stir in pectin. Continue to boil the mixture for 1 minute, stirring constantly.
3. Remove from heat; skim off the foam. Ladle the hot mixture into 5 hot half-pint jars, leaving ¼-in. headspace. Wipe rims. Center lids on jars; screw on bands until fingertip tight.
4. Place jars into canner with simmering water, ensuring that they are completely covered with water. Bring to a boil; process for 10 minutes. Remove jars and cool. (Jelly may take up to 2 weeks to set.)
NOTE: *This recipe was tested with Celestial Seasonings Gingerbread Spice tea bags.*
2 TBSP.: *91 cal., 0 fat (0 sat. fat), 1mg chol., 2mg sod., 23g carb. (23g sugars, 0 fiber), 0 pro.*

CHOCOLATE-COVERED PRETZELS

These fun recipe came from my grandma, who loves to make candy and treats for my students. I have followed in her footsteps and make these for co-workers and for other family members.
—Aimee Worth, Fair Oaks, CA

PREP: 1 hour + chilling • **MAKES:** 20 pretzels

- 20 medium pretzel twists (about 5 oz.)
- 12 oz. milk chocolate candy coating disks, melted
    Colored sprinkles
- 12 oz. white candy coating disks, melted

1. Dip 10 pretzels in milk chocolate, allowing excess to drip off. Place on waxed paper. Decorate half the pretzels with sprinkles. Chill for 10 minutes or until set.
2. Dip the remaining 10 pretzels in white candy coating, allowing excess to drip off. Place on waxed paper. Decorate half the pretzels with sprinkles. Chill for 10 minutes or until set.
3. Drizzle the plain white-coated pretzels with milk chocolate. Drizzle the plain milk chocolate-coated pretzels with the white candy coating. Chill for 10 minutes or until set. Store pretzels in an airtight container.

1 PRETZEL: *207 cal., 10g fat (9g sat. fat), 1mg chol., 143mg sod., 28g carb. (23g sugars, 0 fiber), 1g pro.*
CHOCOLATE-COVERED SANDWICH COOKIES: *Use an 18-oz. package of cream-filled chocolate sandwich cookies in place of the pretzels. Makes 4 dozen.*

WRAP UP SLICE-AND-BAKE COOKIE DOUGH

Jars of homemade cookie mix make thoughtful hostess gifts—and prepared cookie dough does, too! Use your favorite slice-and-bake cookie recipe and shape the dough into a log, just as if you were going to slice it yourself. Then wrap it—first in waxed paper, and then candy-style in crepe paper or tissue. Tie off the ends with fluffy yarn or ribbon and you have an adorable treat. Don't forget to include the baking directions on the label!

ROASTED CURRY CHICKPEAS

We coat chickpeas with simple seasonings to make a low-fat snacking sensation. It rivals calorie-laden varieties sold in stores and makes an unusual, giftable treat.
—Taste of Home *Test Kitchen*

TAKES: 30 min. • **MAKES:** 1 cup

- 1 can (15 oz.) chickpeas or garbanzo beans
- 2 Tbsp. olive oil
- 1 tsp. salt
- ¼ tsp. pepper
- 2 tsp. curry powder
- ½ tsp. crushed red pepper flakes

Rinse and drain chickpeas; place on paper towels and pat dry. Place in a greased 15x10x1-in. baking pan; drizzle with oil and sprinkle with seasonings. Toss to coat. Bake at 450° until crispy and golden brown, 25-30 minutes.
¼ CUP: *162 cal., 9g fat (1g sat. fat), 0 chol., 728mg sod., 17g carb. (3g sugars, 5g fiber), 4g pro.*

GOOD-NIGHT SANTA CAPPUCCINO MIX

I enjoy this sweetly indulgent mix all through the year, and I love to bag it up to give as gifts during the holidays.
—Carol Witczak, Tinley Park, IL

TAKES: 5 min. • **MAKES:** 8 servings (1½ cups cappuccino mix)

- 1 cup powdered nondairy creamer
- ½ cup instant coffee granules
- ½ cup sugar
- ¾ tsp. ground cinnamon
- ¼ tsp. ground cardamom
- ⅛ tsp. ground nutmeg

ADDITIONAL INGREDIENT (FOR EACH SERVING)

- 1 cup hot water

1. In a small bowl, mix the first 6 ingredients. Store in an airtight container in a cool, dry place for up to 6 months.
2. To prepare cappuccino mix: Place 3 Tbsp. mix in a coffee mug. Stir in 1 cup hot water.
1 CUP PREPARED CAPPUCCINO: *120 cal., 3g fat (3g sat. fat), 0 chol., 1mg sod., 21g carb. (13g sugars, 0 fiber), 0 pro.*

GINGERBREAD TRUFFLES

I never received compliments on my baking until I brought my gingerbread truffles to a party. Every Christmas, family, friends and co-workers ask me to make these.
—Angela Randjelovic, Independence, OH

PREP: 50 min. • **COOK:** 10 min. + chilling • **MAKES:** 3 dozen

 14 oz. white baking chocolate, chopped
 ½ cup heavy whipping cream
 1 tsp. ground cinnamon
 ½ tsp. ground ginger
 ¼ tsp. ground cloves
 1 pkg. (10 oz.) dark chocolate chips
 5 tsp. shortening
 3 Tbsp. crystallized ginger

1. Place white chocolate in a small bowl. In a small saucepan, bring whipping cream just to a boil. Pour hot cream over white chocolate; whisk until smooth. Stir in the cinnamon, ginger and cloves. Cool to room temperature, stirring occasionally. Cover and refrigerate until firm but not hard, about 3 hours.
2. Shape mixture into ¾-in. balls. Place on waxed paper-lined baking sheets. Refrigerate for at least 1 hour.
3. In a microwave, melt chocolate chips and shortening; stir until smooth. Dip truffles in chocolate; allow excess to drip off. Place on waxed paper. Sprinkle with crystallized ginger. Store in an airtight container in the refrigerator.
1 TRUFFLE: *113 cal., 7g fat (5g sat. fat), 4mg chol., 12mg sod., 13g carb. (12g sugars, 1g fiber), 1g pro.*

SPICY-SWEET PUPPY CHOW

This variation on regular puppy chow replaces peanut butter with Nutella and chipotle for a delicious spicy-sweet combination.
—Taste of Home *Test Kitchen*

PREP: 20 min. + standing • **MAKES:** 5 cups

 4 cups Rice Chex
 1 cup miniature pretzels
 ½ cup Nutella
 ½ to 1 tsp. chipotle chili powder
 ½ cup confectioners' sugar
 ¼ cup baking cocoa

1. In a large bowl, combine Chex and pretzels; set aside.
2. Place Nutella in a small microwave-safe bowl. Microwave on high for 45 seconds. Stir in chili powder until well blended. Pour over the cereal mixture and toss to coat.
3. Combine confectioners' sugar and cocoa in a large bowl; add the cereal mixture and toss to coat. Spread onto waxed paper; let stand until set. Store mixture in an airtight container.
¾ CUP: *261 cal., 8g fat (1g sat. fat), 0 chol., 261mg sod., 47g carb. (24g sugars, 2g fiber), 4g pro.*

SPICY OATMEAL COOKIE MIX

Brown sugar and spice and everything nice—like cinnamon, coconut, oats and chips—are layered in pretty jars of yummy, ready-to-bake cookie mix for a quick and easy gift. Remember to include preparation instructions and a list of any additional ingredients needed with your gift tag.
—Taste of Home *Test Kitchen*

- -

PREP: 15 min. • **BAKE:** 10 min./batch
MAKES: 4 cups mix (about 3½ dozen cookies)

- 1   cup all-purpose flour
- 1   tsp. ground cinnamon
- ¾   tsp. baking soda
- ¼   tsp. salt
- ⅛   tsp. ground nutmeg
- ½   cup packed brown sugar
- ½   cup sugar
- 1   cup old-fashioned oats
- ½   cup milk chocolate chips
- ½   cup butterscotch chips
- ½   cup sweetened shredded coconut

ADDITIONAL INGREDIENTS

- ½   cup butter, softened
- 1   large egg, room temperature
- ¾   tsp. vanilla extract

1. In a small bowl, combine the first 5 ingredients. In a 1-qt. glass jar, layer the flour mixture, brown sugar, sugar, oats, chips and coconut, packing well between each layer. Cover and store in a cool, dry place up to 6 months.
2. To prepare cookies: Preheat oven to 350°. In a large bowl, beat butter, egg and vanilla. Add cookie mix and mix well.
3. Drop by rounded teaspoonfuls 2 in. apart onto ungreased baking sheets. Bake 9-11 minutes or until golden brown. Cool 2 minutes before removing to wire racks.
1 COOKIE: *90 cal., 4g fat (3g sat. fat), 11mg chol., 63mg sod., 12g carb. (8g sugars, 0 fiber), 1g pro.*

CHOCOLATE-DIPPED PRETZEL RODS

Kids of all ages enjoy making and eating these fun treats. The decorated pretzels make a pretty gift presented in a cellophane bag or a glass jar.
—Kay Waters, Benld, IL

- -

PREP: 25 min. + standing
MAKES: about 4½ dozen

- 3   cups chopped toasted almonds
- 2   pkg. (14 oz. each) caramels, unwrapped
- 2   Tbsp. water
- 2   pkg. (10 oz. each) pretzel rods
- 2   pkg. (10 to 12 oz. each) white baking chips
- 2   pkg. (10 to 12 oz. each) dark chocolate chips
     Assorted sprinkles, optional

1. Place almonds in a shallow dish. In a large glass measuring cup, microwave caramels and water on high until caramels are melted, stirring continuously.
2. Dip three-fourths of each pretzel into the caramel, allowing excess to drip off. (Reheat caramel in microwave if mixture becomes too thick for dipping.) Roll in almonds. Place on waxed paper until set.
3. In a microwave, melt white baking chips; stir until smooth. Dip half of the caramel-coated pretzels in white baking chips, allowing excess to drip off. Add sprinkles if desired; return to waxed paper to set. Repeat with chocolate chips and the remaining pretzels.
4. Store in airtight containers or wrap in cellophane gift bags and tie with ribbon.
1 PRETZEL: *245 cal., 12g fat (5g sat. fat), 3mg chol., 278mg sod., 34g carb. (22g sugars, 2g fiber), 5g pro.*

CHRISTMAS JAM

I have a passion for cooking, and it's probably my grandmother I can thank for it. She was a marvelous cook who could really stretch a food dollar!
—Jo Talvacchia, Lanoka Harbor, NJ

PREP: 25 min. • **PROCESS:** 10 min. • **MAKES:** about 14 half-pints

- 1 pkg. (40 oz.) frozen unsweetened strawberries, thawed or 2½ qt. fresh strawberries, hulled
- 1 lb. fresh or frozen cranberries, thawed
- 5 lbs. sugar
- 2 pouches (3 oz. each) liquid fruit pectin

1. Grind strawberries and cranberries in a food processor or grinder; place in a Dutch oven. Add sugar. Bring to a full rolling boil; boil for 1 minute. Remove from the heat; stir in pectin and return to a full rolling boil. Boil for 1 minute, stirring constantly. Remove from the heat.

2. Cool for 5 minutes; skim off foam. Carefully ladle hot mixture into hot half-pint jars, leaving ¼-in. headspace. Remove air bubbles; wipe rims and adjust lids. Process for 10 minutes in a boiling-water canner.

2 TBSP.: *84 cal., 0 fat (0 sat. fat), 0 chol., 0 sod., 22g carb. (21g sugars, 0 fiber), 0 pro.*

MRS. CLAUS COOKIE POPS

These cute Mrs. Claus pops would be a delight on a cookie platter or as a holiday gift or party favor.
—Taste of Home *Test Kitchen*

PREP: 45 min. + freezing • **MAKES:** 1 dozen

- 12 wooden pop sticks
- 12 double-stuffed Golden Oreo cookies
- 10 pink candy coating disks
- 2 pkg. (12 oz. each) white candy coating disks, divided
  Popped popcorn
  Black decorating icing
  Assorted holiday sprinkles

1. Insert a pop stick into the filling of each cookie; place on a waxed paper-lined baking sheet. To secure sticks, freeze until firm, about 15 minutes.

2. In a microwave, melt pink candy coating with 3 cups white candy coating, stirring until well blended. Dip cookies in coating, allowing excess to drip off (reheat coating as necessary). Attach popcorn for buns in Mrs. Claus' hair; return to baking sheets. Freeze until set, about 30 minutes.

3. Melt the remaining white candy coating. Dip popcorn and tops of cookies in white coating for hair; swirl with a small spatula to make curls. Return to baking sheets.

4. Transfer black icing to a pastry bag fitted with a small round pastry tip; pipe eyes and eyeglasses onto faces. Add decorations as desired, using melted coating to attach. Let stand at room temperature until set.

1 COOKIE POP: *385 cal., 21g fat (17g sat. fat), 2mg chol., 115mg sod., 49g carb. (46g sugars, 0 fiber), 1g pro.*

CANDY CANE HOT COCOA MIX

We make batches of this minty, malted milk-flavored hot chocolate to give as gifts. Be prepared—friends will return the jars for refills!
—Sara Tatham, Plymouth, NH

TAKES: 30 min.
MAKES: 6⅔ cups mix (20 servings)

- 1⅓ cups instant chocolate drink mix
- 1⅓ cups chocolate malted milk powder
- ⅓ cup baking cocoa
- 1 cup confectioners' sugar
- 6 Tbsp. powdered nondairy creamer
- 3 cups nonfat dry milk powder
- 1½ cups miniature semisweet chocolate chips
- 1 cup crushed candy canes (about 40 mini candy canes)

EACH SERVING
- ¾ cup hot water

1. In a large bowl, mix chocolate drink mix, malted milk powder and baking cocoa. In another bowl, mix confectioners' sugar and creamer.

2. In each of four 1-pint canning jars, layer ¾ cup nonfat dry milk powder, ¾ cup chocolate mixture, 3 Tbsp. chocolate chips, ⅓ cup confectioners' sugar mixture, 3 Tbsp. chocolate chips and ¼ cup candy canes, pouring ingredients through a large funnel or a waxed-paper cone. Press candy canes down to fit if needed.

3. Cover and store in a cool, dry place up to 2 months (mixture will settle).

4. To prepare hot cocoa: Transfer the contents of jar to a covered container; mix well. Place ⅓ cup combined mix in a mug; stir in ¾ cup hot water until blended.

1 SERVING PREPARED HOT COCOA: *315 cal., 6g fat (3g sat. fat), 2mg chol., 155mg sod., 63g carb. (53g sugars, 3g fiber), 6g pro.*

CHRISTMAS PICKLES

A dear family friend made these pickles for decades. I've adapted the recipe a bit over the years, but in my heart they are still "Dr. Rhodes' pickles." While they're delicious any time of year, the colors make them ideal for holiday gift-giving—and it's a tasty twist on the classic Christmas pickle tradition.
—Patricia Martin, Shelbyville, TN

PREP: 10 min. • **COOK:** 25 min. + chilling
MAKES: 6½ qt.

- 1 gallon whole dill pickles
- 11¼ cups sugar
- 1 cup white vinegar
- 1 Tbsp. mustard seed
- 1 Tbsp. whole cloves
- 3 to 4 jalapeno peppers, chopped
- 4 to 5 garlic cloves, minced
- 4 to 5 whole cinnamon sticks
- 1 lb. whole candied cherries
- 3 jars (15 oz. each) pearl onions, drained
- 1 tsp. olive oil

1. Drain pickles, reserving juice; set juice aside. Cut pickles into ½-in. slices; set aside. In a large stockpot, combine sugar, vinegar, mustard seed, cloves, peppers, garlic, cinnamon sticks and pickle juice.

2. Cook over medium heat until sugar is dissolved, about 10 minutes, stirring occasionally. Bring to a boil. Reduce heat; simmer, uncovered, 10 minutes. Remove from heat; cool slightly. Discard the cinnamon sticks.

3. In a large bowl, combine cherries, onions and pickle slices. Pour liquid over the pickle mixture. Stir in oil.

4. Cover and refrigerate for 48 hours, stirring occasionally. Divide mixture among jars. Cover and store in the refrigerator up to 1 month.

¼ CUP: *99 cal., 0 fat (0 sat. fat), 0 chol., 55mg sod., 25g carb. (23g sugars, 0 fiber), 0 pro.*

PARMESAN WALNUTS

I love this recipe as it's quick, easy and an alternative to high-calorie snacks. They're delicious right out of the jar or sprinkled on a salad as an alternative to croutons.
—Karen Orvis, Plainville, CT

- -

TAKES: 10 min. • **MAKES:** 4 servings

- 2 tsp. butter
- ½ cup coarsely chopped walnuts
- ⅛ tsp. cayenne pepper
- 1 Tbsp. grated Parmesan cheese

In a small heavy skillet, melt butter. Add walnuts and cayenne. Cook over medium heat until the walnuts are toasted, about 4 minutes. Remove from the heat; sprinkle with cheese. Spread on foil to cool.

2 TABLESPOONS: *118 cal., 12g fat (2g sat. fat), 6mg chol., 33mg sod., 2g carb. (0 sugars, 1g fiber), 3g pro.*
DIABETIC EXCHANGES: *2 fat.*

SUGARPLUM SPICE BREAD

I make Christmas Eve magical with hot cocoa and toasted slices of this fragrant fruit-studded bread. My son and I combined several recipes to come up with this winner. Baked as mini loaves, they make the perfect edible gift.
—Jackie Brown, Tully, NY

- -

PREP: 30 min. + rising • **BAKE:** 30 min.
MAKES: 8 mini loaves (5 slices per loaf)

- ¾ cup butter, softened
- ¾ cup sugar
- 4 large eggs, room temperature
- 5½ to 6 cups all-purpose flour
- 2 pkg. (¼ oz. each) quick-rise yeast
- 1½ tsp. ground cardamom
- 1 tsp. salt
- ¾ tsp. ground cinnamon
- ¼ tsp. ground nutmeg
- 1½ cups 2% milk
- 1 cup diced dried fruit
- ½ cup raisins
- ½ cup golden raisins

FROSTING
- 2 Tbsp. butter, softened
- 2 Tbsp. shortening
- 2 cups confectioners' sugar
- ½ tsp. vanilla extract
- 2 to 3 Tbsp. 2% milk

1. In a large bowl, cream butter and sugar. Add eggs, 1 at a time, beating well after each addition. Add 4 cups flour, the yeast, cardamom, salt, cinnamon and nutmeg. Heat milk to 120°-130°; add to creamed mixture and beat until moistened. Stir in enough of the remaining flour to form a firm dough. Turn onto a heavily floured surface. Sprinkle with fruit and raisins; knead until smooth and elastic, 6-8 minutes. Cover and let rise in a warm place until doubled, about 40 minutes.
2. Punch dough down. Turn onto a lightly floured surface; divide into 8 portions. Shape into loaves. Place in 8 greased 5x3x2-in. loaf pans. Cover and let rise until doubled, about 30 minutes. Bake at 350° for 30-35 minutes or until golden brown. Remove from pans to wire racks to cool.
3. For frosting, in a small bowl, cream butter and shortening. Gradually beat in confectioners' sugar, vanilla and enough milk to reach desired spreading consistency. Frost loaves.

1 SLICE: *174 cal., 5g fat (3g sat. fat), 29mg chol., 101mg sod., 29g carb. (15g sugars, 1g fiber), 3g pro.*

CRAN-RASPBERRY HONEY SPREAD

Honey gives this tangy spread its sweetness. I came up with the recipe way back when our family first took up beekeeping and we had a bumper crop.
—J. Fleming, Almonte, ON

PREP: 15 min. • **COOK:** 20 min. + processing
MAKES: 6 half-pints

- 2½ cups fresh or frozen sweetened raspberries, thawed
- 2 cups fresh or frozen cranberries, thawed
- 1 cup chopped peeled apple
- 2½ cups honey
- 1½ cups sugar
- 1 pouch (3 oz.) liquid fruit pectin

1. Pulse raspberries, cranberries and apple in batches in a food processor until almost smooth. Transfer to a Dutch oven.
2. Stir in honey and the sugar. Bring to a full rolling boil over high heat, stirring constantly. Stir in pectin. Continue to boil 1 minute, stirring constantly. Remove from heat; skim off foam.
3. Ladle hot mixture into 6 hot half-pint jars, leaving ¼ in. headspace. Remove air bubbles and adjust headspace, if necessary, by adding hot mixture. Wipe rims. Center lids on jars; screw on bands until fingertip tight.
4. Place jars into canner with simmering water, ensuring that they are completely covered with water. Bring to a boil; process for 10 minutes. Remove jars and cool.
*2 **TBSP.:** 84 cal., 0 fat (0 sat. fat), 0 chol., 1mg sod., 22g carb. (21g sugars, 1g fiber), 0 pro.*

CANDY CANE REINDEER

We had a blast creating these adorable candy cane stocking stuffers! Rudolph and his friends never looked sweeter than they do with pretzel antlers, candy eyes, and bright noses made with Red Hots.
—Taste of Home *Test Kitchen*

PREP: 30 min. + standing • **MAKES:** 1 dozen

- 8 oz. white candy coating, coarsely chopped
- 12 candy canes (6 in.)
- 12 miniature pretzels
- 12 Red Hots or milk chocolate M&M's
- 24 12 double candy eyes or 24 single candy eyes, black sugar pearls or miniature semisweet chocolate chips

1. In a microwave, melt candy coating; stir until smooth. Keep warm. Holding the curved end of a candy cane, use a spoon to drizzle coating over the straight part of cane. Gently shake off excess. Place on waxed paper to dry. Repeat with the remaining candy canes. Break pretzels in half to resemble antlers; set aside 24 pieces.
2. Attach Red Hots candy noses to the curved portion of each candy cane with melted candy coating, holding for about 10 seconds to help adhere. Use candy coating to attach candy eyes just above noses and pretzel antlers above eyes, holding each piece as needed to help adhere. Place in mugs or drinking glasses; let dry for about 1 hour.
*1 **CANDY CANE:** 201 cal., 6g fat (5g sat. fat), 0 chol., 124mg sod., 37g carb. (26g sugars, 0 fiber), 1g pro.*

CREAM CHEESE CANDIES

These homemade mints make an ideal last-minute addition to holiday treat trays. Pretty much everyone in my neighborhood has the recipe now!
—Katie Koziolek, Hartland, MN

PREP: 15 min. + standing • **MAKES:** about 6 dozen

3 oz. cream cheese, softened
¼ tsp. peppermint or almond extract
3 cups confectioners' sugar, divided
    Sugar or colored sugar, optional

1. Mix cream cheese and extract until blended. Beat in 1½ cups confectioners' sugar. Knead in remaining confectioners' sugar.
2. Shape into ½-in. balls. If desired, roll in sugar. Place on waxed paper. Flatten with a fork. Let stand until firm, 1-2 hours. Store between layers of waxed paper in an airtight container in the refrigerator.
1 PIECE: *24 cal., 0 fat (0 sat. fat), 1mg chol., 4mg sod., 5g carb. (5g sugars, 0 fiber), 0 pro.*

MOROCCAN SPICE BLEND

For years, we've enjoyed using this Moroccan spice blend to flavor everything from lamb stew to scrambled eggs. We love it so much, we package it up and give it as gifts so everyone can share.
—Carol Ward, Deming, NM

TAKES: 5 min. • **MAKES:** ¼ cup

1¼ tsp. ground allspice
2 tsp. ground nutmeg
1½ tsp. coarsely ground pepper
1½ tsp. ground mace
1 tsp. ground cinnamon
1½ tsp. ground cardamom
2 tsp. ground ginger
2 tsp. salt
1 tsp. ground turmeric
⅛ tsp. saffron threads or ½ tsp. additional ground turmeric

Combine all ingredients; store in an airtight container.
½ TSP.: *3 cal., 0 fat (0 sat. fat), 0 chol., 197mg sod., 1g carb. (0 sugars, 0 fiber), 0 pro.*

GINGERBREAD HOUSE PARTY

Bring friends together for a little light construction—building and decorating all things gingerbread, from houses to cookies. To feed your creativity, we've shared recipes for delicious snacks and gingerbread-flavored treats.

Building Memories

Let your imagination roam when building your own gingerbread house. Here are some ideas for creative candy decor to get you started.

Edible chocolate rocks make your house feel lifelike. Use them to craft a facade, door frame or walking path.

THE BLUEPRINT FOR SWEET SUCCESS

- Search your pantry for inspiration. Grab a bag of pretzels or a box of cereal, or raid your candy stash. Get creative adding fun details.
- Create a textured landscape around the house by blanketing the surface with shredded coconut. Sisel trees, found in craft and hobby shops, make a realistic addition to the scene.

- Build a sweet snowman by stacking marshmallows on a toothpick and adding details with tinted royal icing.
- Premade gingerbread house kits are available in craft stores and online, but you can use the Gingerbread Base recipe (p. 222) to design your own cutouts.

Use graham crackers to create custom additions, like a dormer, an entryway or a chimney.

Meringues make the perfect snowy peaks for rooftops.

Careful snipping turns sour gummy strips into bricks.

Pretzels of various shapes frame windows and doors, and cereal squares make fool-the-eye shingles.

GINGERBREAD BARN

This Christmas gingerbread barn will add a cheerful rustic touch to your holiday decor. Start with the Gingerbread Base and icing recipes (p. 222). If you plan to use your barn for display only, you can use white or hot glue instead of icing.
—Taste of Home *Test Kitchen*

PREP: 3 hours + standing
BAKE: 50 min. + cooling

    Gingerbread Base (p. 222)
    Icing (p. 222)
1 pkg. (14.4 oz.) graham crackers
3 cups Golden Grahams
1 thin butter ring cookie
    Decorating sprinkles and candies
1 sour candy belt
    Sugars and edible glitter
    Unsweetened shredded coconut
    Thin pretzel sticks and pretzel rods
    Sugar ice cream cones
2 large marshmallows
40 miniature marshmallows
2 black jelly beans
2 black candy coating disks
    Chocolate river stones
EQUIPMENT
    Heavy-duty cardboard
    Muffin tin
    Cardboard cake board
    (at least 17x22 in.)

1. Trace enlarged barn patterns onto cardboard; cut out. Cut out windows.
2. Line a baking sheet with foil; spray foil with cooking spray. With a lightly floured rolling pin, roll one-sixth of the gingerbread dough directly on foiled baking sheet into a rectangle about ¼ in. thick. Place a pattern on the dough. Using a sharp knife or pizza cutter, cut quantities noted on each pattern piece; remove pattern. Remove dough scraps; cover, refrigerate and reroll if needed.
3. Bake at 350° until edges just begin to brown, 12-14 minutes. Remove from oven; immediately replace patterns on cookies. Cut around edges to trim off excess cookie if necessary. Cool until firm, about 10 minutes. Remove to wire rack to cool completely. Repeat with the remaining dough and patterns.
4. For silo roof: Cut a 5-in. gingerbread circle. Turn a standard-size muffin tin upside down; spray bottom of 1 cup with cooking spray. Mold dough over and down cup sides and press together any cracks; trim excess. Bake until golden brown, 10 minutes. Cool for 10 minutes on tin, then cool completely on wire rack. Trim to fit cardboard roll (p. 222).
5. Cut out animal patterns and use the remaining dough for animal cutouts. Bake large cookies for 12-14 minutes, smaller ones 6-7 minutes.
6. For barn: Test cookie pieces to make sure they fit snugly. If necessary, trim with a serrated knife. Combine 4 tsp. water and ½ tsp. red food coloring. Carefully brush onto front, back and sides of barn. Let dry completely overnight.
7. Insert #10 tip into pastry bag; fill two-thirds full with icing. Squeeze a wide strip of icing onto the bottom edge of the back barn piece. Position on cardboard cake board about 7 in. from 1 short edge. Prop with small cans until icing is firm, 3-4 hours.
8. Squeeze icing onto the bottom edge of 1 side piece and onto 1 side edge of the back piece. Align at a right angle as tightly as possible; prop up. Repeat with the other side. For added stability, squeeze icing along the inside edges of all pieces and corners.
9. Squeeze icing onto the bottom and side edges of the front piece; position with other assembled pieces. Prop up; let dry completely.
10. To assemble roof: From heavy-duty cardboard, cut two 10½x3½-in. pieces (A). Also cut two 10½x2½-in. pieces (B). Tape 1 long edge of an A piece and a B piece together with masking tape; repeat to connect the other A and B pieces. Then, tape the A pieces together to form the center roof peak.
11. Squeeze icing onto the upper edges of the slant of the front and back edges of the barn. Carefully place roof so peak is centered between the front and back. (There will be a ¾-in. overhang on both.)
12. To cover roof, cut graham crackers to fit. Using icing, attach in rows, beginning from bottom. Use icing to attach the silo to the base at 1 corner of the barn.
13. To decorate barn: Using a #5 tip, outline windows and doors with white icing. For shutters, cut graham crackers to fit the window on front of barn. Pipe edges and diagonal line with white icing; dry completely. Attach shutters with icing.
14. For the door, cut a graham cracker into fourths. Secure 3 pieces together horizontally with icing; pipe icing around edges of door and make an "X" in center. Let dry completely. Adhere door to barn with icing.
15. Pipe icing onto roof to cover the graham crackers completely; decorate with coarse sugar and edible glitter.
16. Frost base around barn and silo. Use shredded coconut to create snow. To make path, pipe or spread a thin layer of icing onto board; immediately press in chocolate river stones.
17. Use icing to attach animals around the barn and to secure the wreath over the door. Place the fence where desired, and secure with icing. Pipe icing onto lower edge of silo; stand it at the corner of the barn. (See p. 222 for tips on making the silo and other design elements.)

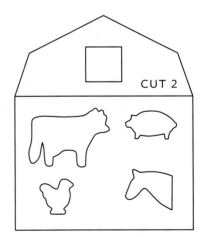

Photocopy patterns at 400% for correct size.

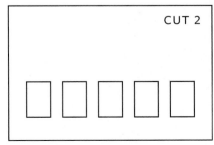

GINGERBREAD BASE

This recipe makes the ideal base for gingerbread-house construction. The recipe was designed for the barn shown on the previous page but can be used to make any design you please. Roll out to ¼ in. thick and bake cutouts at 350° for 12-14 minutes.
—Taste of Home *Test Kitchen*

- -

PREP: 20 min. + chilling
MAKES: 9-10 cups dough (enough for 1 barn and about 2 dozen large cookies)

2¼	cups shortening
2	cups sugar
2	large eggs, room temperature
1	cup molasses
⅔	cup light corn syrup
2	tsp. ground ginger
1½	tsp. ground cinnamon
1	tsp. ground cloves
8½	to 9 cups all-purpose flour

Beat shortening and sugar until fluffy, 5-7 minutes. Beat in eggs, molasses, corn syrup, ginger, cinnamon and cloves. Add flour, 1 cup at a time, until the dough can be formed into a ball. Turn onto a lightly floured surface. Knead until smooth and easy to handle; add more flour if needed. Cover; chill several hours or overnight.

ICING

When building a gingerbread house, this icing is an essential adhesive as well as decoration.
—Taste of Home *Test Kitchen*

- -

TAKES: 15 min.
MAKES: 8-9 cups

1½	cups butter, softened
1½	cups shortening
¾	cup water
3	Tbsp. vanilla extract
12	cups confectioners' sugar
	Assorted food paste colors

Cream butter and shortening. Add water and vanilla; beat until smooth. Gradually beat in sugar; mix well. Keep covered with a damp cloth. Tint portions with food coloring as directed or as desired.

DESIGN THE DETAILS

SILO

Coat a cardboard roll with icing; press Golden Grahams cereal into icing, alternating seams. Squeeze icing onto top edge of silo; carefully press on the silo roof (see Step 4, p. 220). Pipe icing onto roof; decorate with coarse sugar and edible glitter.

FENCE

Cut pretzel rods to desired size; using rods as posts, secure 3 pretzel sticks to 1 side of the rod with icing. Repeat until the fence is desired length; for corners, secure pretzel sticks at right angles. Dry until icing is firm, about 1 hour.

WREATH

Tint a portion of icing green; with a #67 leaf tip, decorate a butter ring cookie. Add sprinkles and decorating candies. Cut sour candy belt into a thin strip to make a bow, and attach to the wreath with icing.

SHEEP

For each sheep: Break 2 pretzel sticks in half; insert into a large marshmallow. Use icing to adhere mini marshmallows to large marshmallow; trim as needed. When body is set, use icing to secure a jelly bean to body for the head. Cut a black candy disk in half; trim to make ears and attach to jelly bean with icing. Pipe on icing for eyes, nose and mouth; let dry. Tint some icing light pink; pipe onto ears.

HORSES, CHICKENS & COWS

Use the patterns (p. 220) or your own shaped cutters to make cookies out of the Gingerbread Base recipe. Thin a small portion of icing with water and tint as desired for each animal; use to flood the surface of the cookies. Pipe on details as desired.

TREES

Use a serrated knife to score and cut sugar ice cream cones to desired heights. For taller trees, stack 2 cones. Tint a portion of icing with green food coloring; decorate trees using a #67 leaf tip. While icing is still wet, use tweezers to place sprinkles or candies as ornaments or lights. When dry, pipe white frosting at intervals for snow; sprinkle with white decorating sugar.

GARLIC-PARMESAN CHEESE BALL

This garlic cheese ball is one of our entertaining mainstays. It complements most meals and is so easy to prepare and dress up with a variety of garnishes.
—Susan Seymour, Valatie, NY

PREP: 10 min. + chilling • **MAKES:** about 2 cups

- 11   oz. cream cheese, softened
- ⅓   cup grated Parmesan cheese
- ¼   cup mayonnaise
- ½   tsp. dried oregano
- ¼   tsp. garlic powder or ½ to 1 tsp. minced garlic
- ¾   cup chopped walnuts, optional
       Assorted fresh vegetables and/or crackers

In a large bowl, combine the first 5 ingredients. Shape into a ball. Roll in walnuts if desired. Wrap tightly; chill 2 hours. Serve with vegetables and/or crackers.

2 TBSP.: *98 cal., 10g fat (5g sat. fat), 21mg chol., 109mg sod., 1g carb. (1g sugars, 0 fiber), 2g pro.*

MULLED GRAPE CIDER

I came up with this recipe one year when I was making grape jelly and ended up with 30 jars of delicious grape syrup instead! I simmered the syrup with spices to make this pretty drink.
—Sharon Harmon, Orange, MA

PREP: 20 min. • **COOK:** 3 hours • **MAKES:** 12 servings (3 qt.)

- 5   lbs. Concord grapes
- 8   cups water, divided
- 1½   cups sugar
- 8   whole cloves
- 4   cinnamon sticks (4 in.)
       Dash ground nutmeg

1. In a large saucepan, combine grapes and 2 cups water; bring to a boil, stirring constantly. Press through a strainer; reserve juice and discard skins and seeds.

2. Pour juice through a double layer of cheesecloth into a 5-qt. slow cooker. Add the sugar, cloves, cinnamon sticks, nutmeg and remaining water. Cover and cook on low for 3 hours. Discard cloves and cinnamon sticks.

1 CUP: *231 cal., 1g fat (0 sat. fat), 0 chol., 4mg sod., 59g carb. (56g sugars, 0 fiber), 1g pro.*

CRISP CARAWAY TWISTS

This appetizer is always a hit when I serve it on holidays or special occasions. The flaky cheese-filled twists (made with convenient puff pastry) bake to a crispy golden brown. When our big family gets together, I make two batches.
—*Dorothy Smith, El Dorado, AR*

TAKES: 30 min. • **MAKES:** about 1½ dozen

- 1 **large egg**
- 1 **Tbsp. water**
- 1 **tsp. country-style Dijon mustard**
- ¾ **cup shredded Swiss cheese**
- ¼ **cup finely chopped onion**
- 2 **tsp. minced fresh parsley**
- 1½ **tsp. caraway seeds**
- ¼ **tsp. garlic salt**
- 1 **sheet frozen puff pastry, thawed**

1. Preheat oven to 375°. In a small bowl, beat the egg, water and mustard; set aside. In another bowl, combine the cheese, onion, parsley, caraway seeds and garlic salt.

2. Unfold pastry sheet; brush with egg mixture. Sprinkle cheese mixture lengthwise over half of the pastry. Fold pastry over filling; press edges to seal. Brush top with remaining egg mixture. Cut widthwise into ½-in. strips; twist each strip several times.

3. Place twists 1 in. apart on greased baking sheets, pressing the ends down. Bake for 15-20 minutes or until golden brown. Serve warm.

1 TWIST: *90 cal., 5g fat (2g sat. fat), 15mg chol., 91mg sod., 8g carb. (0 sugars, 1g fiber), 3g pro.*

GINGERBREAD CARAMEL CRUNCH

If you love gingerbread, you won't be able to resist this crispy, crunchy popcorn. Munch it yourself or share it as a tasty gift!
—*Lynne Weigle-Snow, Alexandria, VA*

PREP: 25 min. • **BAKE:** 1 hour • **MAKES:** 3½ qt.

- 14 **cups air-popped popcorn**
- ¾ **cup packed brown sugar**
- ½ **cup butter, cubed**
- ¼ **cup light corn syrup**
- ¼ **cup molasses**
- 1½ **tsp. ground ginger**
- ½ **tsp. ground cinnamon**
- ¼ **tsp. salt**
- ½ **tsp. baking soda**
- ½ **tsp. vanilla extract**

1. Place popcorn in a large bowl coated with cooking spray; set aside. Butter the sides of a small heavy saucepan; add the brown sugar, butter, corn syrup, molasses, ginger, cinnamon and salt. Bring to a boil over medium heat, stirring constantly. Boil without stirring for 5 minutes.

2. Remove from the heat; stir in baking soda (mixture will foam). Stir in vanilla. Quickly pour over the popcorn and mix well.

3. Transfer to 2 greased 15x10x1-in. baking pans. Bake at 250° for 1 hour, stirring every 10 minutes. Remove from pans and place on waxed paper to cool. Store in an airtight container.

1 CUP: *167 cal., 7g fat (4g sat. fat), 17mg chol., 144mg sod., 27g carb. (16g sugars, 1g fiber), 1g pro.*

GINGERBREAD HOUSE COOKIES

This is my favorite molasses cookie. I use the recipe not only to create little houses for Christmas, but also to make bunnies for Easter and stars for the Fourth of July.
—Karen Haen, Sturgeon Bay, WI

PREP: 40 min. + chilling
BAKE: 10 min./batch + cooling
MAKES: 4 dozen

- 1 cup shortening
- ½ cup sugar
- ½ cup packed brown sugar
- 2 large eggs, room temperature
- 1 cup molasses
- 1 to 1½ tsp. grated orange zest
- 5½ cups all-purpose flour
- 3 tsp. baking soda
- ¾ tsp. salt
- ¾ tsp. ground ginger
- ¾ tsp. ground cinnamon
- ½ tsp. ground nutmeg
- ½ cup water
  Frosting and food coloring
  of your choice

1. In a large bowl, cream shortening and sugars until light and fluffy, 5-7 minutes. Add eggs, 1 at a time, beating well after each addition. Beat in molasses and orange zest. Combine flour, baking soda, salt and spices; add to creamed mixture alternately with water, mixing well after each addition. Cover and refrigerate for 3 hours or until easy to handle.
2. On a lightly floured surface, roll out dough to ¼-in. thickness. Cut with a 3½-in. gingerbread house cookie cutter dipped in flour. If desired, create windows using small cutters of various shapes.
3. Place 1 in. apart on greased baking sheets. Bake at 350° for 8-10 minutes or until edges are firm. Cool for 2 minutes before removing to wire racks. Tint frosting and decorate cooled cookies as desired.
1 COOKIE: *127 cal., 4g fat (1g sat. fat), 9mg chol., 85mg sod., 20g carb. (9g sugars, 0 fiber), 2g pro.*

GINGER-BREAD BUDDIES

A classic gingerbread man cookie cutter doesn't have to make cookie-cutter cookies! With a little imagination (and colored icing), you can make your cookies into almost anything—even a Yeti!

CHOCOLATE GINGERBREAD TOFFEE CAKE WITH GINGER WHIPPED CREAM

This cake literally stands above the rest—exactly what you need for a special-occasion dessert. With notes of ginger coming though in both the frosting and cake, it is absolutely delicious and worth the extra steps involved.
—Marie Rizzio, Interlochen, MI

PREP: 45 min. + chilling
BAKE: 30 min. + cooling
MAKES: 16 servings

- 2 cups heavy whipping cream
- 5 slices fresh gingerroot (⅛ in. thick)

CAKE

- 1½ cups dark chocolate chips
- ½ cup butter, softened
- 1½ cups packed brown sugar
- 3 large eggs, room temperature
- 2 tsp. vanilla extract
- 2¾ cups all-purpose flour
- 1 tsp. baking soda
- ¾ tsp. ground ginger
- ¾ tsp. ground cinnamon
- ½ tsp. salt
- ¼ tsp. ground allspice
- ¼ tsp. ground nutmeg
- 1 cup sour cream
- 1 cup hot water
- ½ cup molasses

GANACHE

- 1 pkg. (10 oz.) dark chocolate chips
- ¼ tsp. salt
- 1 can (14 oz.) sweetened condensed milk
- 2 Tbsp. butter
- 1 tsp. vanilla extract
- 2 Tbsp. heavy whipping cream

ASSEMBLY

- 6 Tbsp. confectioners' sugar
- 1 cup brickle toffee bits

1. In a small heavy saucepan, heat cream and gingerroot until bubbles form around sides of pan. Remove from the heat; let cool slightly. Cover and refrigerate for 8 hours or overnight.

2. Meanwhile, in a microwave, melt the chocolate; stir until smooth. Set aside. In a large bowl, cream butter and brown sugar until blended. Add eggs, 1 at a time, beating well after each addition. Beat in melted chocolate and the vanilla. Combine the flour, baking soda, ginger, cinnamon, salt, allspice and nutmeg; add to the creamed mixture alternately with the sour cream, beating well after each addition.

3. In a small bowl, combine the hot water and molasses; beat into batter. Transfer to 3 greased and floured 8-in. round baking pans.

4. Bake at 350° until a toothpick inserted in the center comes out clean, 30-35 minutes. Cool for 10 minutes before removing from pans to wire racks to cool completely.

5. Meanwhile, for ganache, place chocolate and salt in the top of a double boiler or a metal bowl over simmering water; cook and stir until melted, 2-3 minutes. Stir in the condensed milk until smooth. Remove from the heat; stir in butter and vanilla until butter is melted.

6. Cool, stirring occasionally, to room temperature or until ganache reaches a spreading consistency, about 45 minutes. Add cream; beat mixture until smooth, 2-3 minutes.

7. Strain the ginger-cream mixture into a large bowl, discarding the ginger slices. Beat until cream begins to thicken. Add confectioners' sugar; beat until stiff peaks form.

8. To assemble, place 1 cake layer on a serving plate; spread with half the ganache. Sprinkle with half of the toffee bits. Repeat layers once. Top with the remaining cake layer; spread ginger whipped cream over top and sides of cake. Refrigerate for at least 2 hours. Store leftovers in the refrigerator.

1 SLICE: *765 cal., 42g fat (25g sat. fat), 107mg chol., 409mg sod., 96g carb. (76g sugars, 3g fiber), 9g pro.*

WARM SPICED NUTS

I like to set out bowls of spiced nuts when hosting holiday parties. Sometimes I stir in M&M's to make it a sweet and salty snack.
—Jill Matson, Zimmerman, MN

PREP: 5 min. • **BAKE:** 30 min. • **MAKES:** 3 cups

- 1 cup pecan halves
- 1 cup unblanched almonds
- 1 cup unsalted dry roasted peanuts
- 3 Tbsp. butter, melted
- 4½ tsp. Worcestershire sauce
- 1 tsp. chili powder
- ½ tsp. garlic salt
- ¼ tsp. cayenne pepper

1. In a large bowl, combine the pecans, almonds and peanuts. Combine butter and Worcestershire sauce; pour over nuts and toss to coat.

2. Spread in a single layer in an ungreased 15x10x1-in. baking pan. Bake at 300° until browned, about 30 minutes, stirring occasionally.

3. Transfer warm nuts to a bowl. Combine the chili powder, garlic salt and cayenne; sprinkle over nuts and stir to coat. Serve warm, or allow to cool before storing in an airtight container.

¼ CUP: *231 cal., 22g fat (4g sat. fat), 8mg chol., 123mg sod., 7g carb. (2g sugars, 3g fiber), 6g pro.*

SWEET POTATO-GINGERBREAD MERINGUE PIE

This delicious pie showcases gingerbread flavor in the meringue instead of the crust. Baking it on the bottom rack gets the crust nice and crisp without parbaking it.
—Shannon Norris, Cudahy, WI

PREP: 1 hour + chilling
BAKE: 40 min. + broiling
MAKES: 10 servings

- 1¼ cups all-purpose flour
- 4½ tsp. sugar
  Dash salt
- 6 Tbsp. cold butter, cubed
- 1 large egg yolk, room temperature
- 4 to 6 Tbsp. ice water

FILLING
- 3 lbs. medium sweet potatoes
- 1⅓ cups sugar
- ⅔ cup butter, softened
- ½ tsp. pumpkin pie spice
  Dash salt
- 4 large eggs, room temperature, lightly beaten
- 2 tsp. vanilla extract

MERINGUE
- 1 cup sugar
- ⅓ cup water
- 1 Tbsp. molasses
  Dash salt
- 5 large egg whites, room temperature
- ¾ tsp. cream of tartar
- ¾ tsp. pumpkin pie spice
- ½ tsp. ground ginger

1. Pulse flour, sugar and salt in a food processor until blended. Add butter; pulse until butter is the size of peas. Combine egg yolk and 2 Tbsp. ice water; slowly add to processor until dough holds together, adding remaining ice water, if needed, 1 Tbsp. at a time. Shape dough into a disk; wrap and refrigerate 1 hour or overnight.

2. Preheat oven to 400°. Scrub sweet potatoes; pierce several times with a fork. Bake until tender, 45-50 minutes. Cool slightly; peel and mash to yield about 4 cups. Reduce oven setting to 350°.

3. On a lightly floured surface, roll dough to a ⅛-in.-thick circle; transfer to a 9-in. deep-dish pie plate. Trim to ½ in. beyond rim of plate; flute edge. Refrigerate for 30 minutes.

4. For filling, beat sugar, butter, pie spice and salt until blended. Add eggs and vanilla; beat in cooled sweet potatoes until smooth. Add filling to chilled crust. Bake on bottom rack until a knife inserted in center comes out clean, 40-45 minutes. Keep warm.

5. Meanwhile, for meringue, combine sugar, water, molasses and salt in a small saucepan over medium-high heat; using a pastry brush dipped in water, wash down the sides of the pan to eliminate sugar crystals. When the mixture comes to a boil, stop brushing. Cook without stirring until a thermometer reads 240° (soft-ball stage).

6. As molasses mixture cooks, preheat the broiler. Beat egg whites, cream of tartar and spices on medium speed until soft peaks form. While beating, gradually drizzle hot molasses mixture over the egg whites; continue beating until stiff glossy peaks form. Spread meringue over warm pie; broil 4-6 in. from heat until slightly browned, 1-2 minutes. Cool on a wire rack.

1 PIECE: *609 cal., 22g fat (13g sat. fat), 144mg chol., 663mg sod., 96g carb. (64g sugars, 5g fiber), 9g pro.*

Holiday Helper
For a picture-perfect meringue that doesn't weep or bead, make sure the filling is hot, and spread the meringue all the way out to the crust. If you'd prefer not to broil the meringue, use a kitchen torch instead.

GINGERBREAD AMARETTI COOKIES

These are classic Italian cookies with a new gingerbread twist! Don't overbake—they should be slightly chewy.
—Tina Zaccardi, Eastchester, NY

PREP: 20 min. • **BAKE:** 12 min./batch • **MAKES:** 2 dozen

- 1 can (8 oz.) almond paste
- ¾ cup sugar
- 1 Tbsp. baking cocoa
- 1 tsp. ground ginger
- ½ tsp. ground cinnamon
  Dash ground cloves
- 2 large egg whites, room temperature
- 2 Tbsp. molasses
- 1 cup pearl or coarse sugar

1. Preheat oven to 375°. Crumble almond paste into a food processor; add sugar, baking cocoa and spices. Pulse until combined. Add egg whites and molasses; process until smooth.
2. Drop by tablespoonfuls into pearl sugar; roll to coat. Place 2 in. apart on parchment-lined baking sheets. Bake until set, 10-12 minutes. Cool for 1 minute before removing from pans to wire racks. Store in an airtight container.
1 COOKIE: *107 cal., 3g fat (0 sat. fat), 0 chol., 6mg sod., 21g carb. (19g sugars, 1g fiber), 1g pro.*

SNAPPY COCKTAIL MEATBALLS

This recipe was given to me 20 years ago by a sweet German lady. The meatballs are easy to prepare and can be made ahead of time.
—Nancy Means, Moline, IL

TAKES: 30 min. • **MAKES:** About 5 dozen

- 2 large eggs, lightly beaten
- 1¼ cups soft bread crumbs
- 1 tsp. salt
- ½ tsp. garlic salt
- ½ tsp. onion powder
- ½ tsp. pepper
- 2 lbs. lean ground beef (90% lean)

SAUCE
- 1 can (28 oz.) diced tomatoes, undrained
- ½ cup packed brown sugar
- ¼ cup vinegar
- ½ tsp. salt
- 1 tsp. grated onion
- 10 gingersnaps, finely crushed

1. In a large bowl, combine the first 6 ingredients. Crumble beef over mixture and mix well. Shape into 1¼-in. balls. Place meatballs on a greased rack in a shallow baking sheet. Bake at 450° for 15 minutes. Drain on paper towels.
2. Combine tomatoes, brown sugar, vinegar, salt and onion in a large saucepan. Bring to a boil. Stir in gingersnaps; continue to boil until sauce is thick and clear. Reduce heat to simmer; add meatballs. Heat through.
1 MEATBALL: *43 cal., 2g fat (2g sat. fat), 16mg chol., 118mg sod., 4g carb. (3g sugars, 0 fiber), 3g pro.*

Getting Ready for the Holidays

PARTY TIMELINE

This useful checklist will help you budget your time wisely and keep your party on schedule.

1 MONTH PRIOR:

☐ Choose date and time.

☐ Set budget.

☐ Determine guest list.

3 WEEKS PRIOR:

☐ Send out invitations (ask about any food allergies).

☐ Check to make sure you have enough chairs, linens, serving dishes and utensils. Rent or buy more if needed.

☐ Arrange for a helper (this would be a good thing to ask an older child or teenager to do).

2 WEEKS PRIOR:

☐ Plan the menu; create a master shopping list.

☐ Make a large grocery shopping trip to buy nonperishables and ingredients for freezer-friendly dishes. Prepare and freeze any dishes that can be made in advance.

1 WEEK PRIOR:

☐ Follow up with any guests who haven't responded.

☐ Clean the house thoroughly; put away breakable items.

☐ Stock the bar.

☐ Choose the music.

2-3 DAYS PRIOR:

☐ Notify neighbors if cars will be parked on the street.

☐ Clean glassware, china and silverware. Clean and iron table linens.

☐ Think about the party space: Where will coats go? Where are the trash cans? How will people move around your house? Move furniture if necessary. Set up cleanup stations (salt, stain remover, club soda, clean cloths) to have at the ready.

☐ Put up decorations.

☐ Finish grocery shopping.

1 DAY PRIOR:

☐ Buy flowers.

☐ Finish as much of the cooking and prep work as possible.

☐ Do a quick cleanup of the house. Check the guest bathroom—empty trash and set out fresh hand towels.

DAY OF:

☐ Chill wine, set up the bar, and slice lemons and any other garnishes.

☐ Set the table and/or buffet.

☐ Finish any cooking.

☐ Set aside space for dirty dishes.

☐ Take out trash; have trash cans and extra garbage bags ready.

HOW TO SET THE TABLE

- The dinner plate is the center of the place setting; everything else is positioned around it. Arrange the flatware in the order in which it will be used.

- Forks go to the left of the plate. If you're serving a salad, place a small salad fork to the left of the dinner fork. Place the napkin under the forks or on the plate.

- The knife and spoons go to the right of the plate. Place the knife with the sharp edge toward the plate. The soupspoon goes outside of the teaspoon. If soup is to be served, set the bowl on the plate.

- The desert utensil—whether a fork or a spoon—can either be placed horizontally above the plate or be brought out when dessert is served.

- Smaller plates for salad or bread go above and to the left of the forks. Position the butter plate with the butter spreader across the plate.

- Cup and saucer go above the spoons with the handle to the right.

- Water and wine glasses go to the left of the coffee cup; the water glass goes on the left.

HOW MUCH FOOD & DRINK TO SERVE

Take the stress out of planning with our guide to how many drinks and how much food to stock, course by course. A good rule of thumb is to round up from these and err on the side of having too much—better to end up with a few leftovers than to leave your guests hungry.

APPETIZERS

On average, each guest will have about six appetizers (this number may double if you're having a cocktail-style event). Stock up on bulk items like nuts, pretzels and olives, both to supplement prepared appetizers and to set out before guests arrive.

Guests	Appetizer
5	30 appetizers
10	60 appetizers
20	120 appetizers

ENTREES AND SIDES

- Poultry, fish or meat: 6 oz. per serving
- Grains: 1½ oz. as a side dish, 2 oz. as a main dish casserole
- Potatoes: 5 oz.
- Vegetables: 4 oz.
- Beans: 2 oz.
- Pasta: 4 oz (main dish)
- Bread such as buns, rolls or cornbread: 1 to 2 pieces

DESSERTS

Guests	Cake/Tart/Pastry	Creamy Dessert	Ice Cream
5	5 slices	20 oz.	25 oz.
10	10 slices	40 oz.	50 oz.
20	20 slices	80 oz.	100 oz.

DRINKS

These guidelines are for parties that last two hours. Figure on 1 lb. of ice per guest.
(if serving one type of alcohol—if you're offering more, reduce the amount of each type)

Guests	Wine/Champagne	Beer	Spirits	Liqueurs	Nonalcoholic
5	3 bottles	15 bottles	1 bottle	1 bottle	5 (if serving alcohol as well) / 15 (if not)
10	5 bottles	30 bottles	2 bottles	1 bottle	10/30
20	10 bottles	60 bottles	4 bottles	2 bottles	20/60

Holiday Menus

Use these menu cards to record what you served at Christmas dinner and other seasonal gatherings. Make note of beverage pairings, ingredient substitutions or anything else you want to remember about your holiday menu.

OCCASION:

GUESTS:

FOOD:

DRINKS:

NOTES:

OCCASION:

GUESTS:

FOOD:

DRINKS:

NOTES:

OCCASION: _____

GUESTS:
_____
_____
_____
_____

FOOD:
_____
_____
_____
_____
_____
_____

DRINKS:
_____
_____

NOTES:
_____
_____
_____
_____
_____
_____

OCCASION: _____

GUESTS:
_____
_____
_____
_____

FOOD:
_____
_____
_____
_____
_____
_____

DRINKS:
_____
_____

NOTES:
_____
_____
_____
_____
_____
_____

Holiday Memories

FAMILY MILESTONES

What major events happened in your family this year? Births, weddings, graduations, a new home or job, or a particularly memorable vacation?

_____
_____
_____
_____
_____
_____
_____
_____
_____
_____
_____
_____
_____

MEMORIES OF THE FEAST

What was most memorable about the time spent around the holiday table? What things did your loved ones say or do that you want to remember? Ask your family a question—what are they most thankful for, or which dish was their favorite—and record their answers!

_____
_____
_____
_____
_____
_____
_____
_____
_____
_____
_____

SPECIAL PEOPLE

Who did you see this year that you haven't seen in a while? Who came to visit, or hosted you? Who sent a particularly lovely card, or a favorite gift?

_____

_____

_____

_____

_____

ALL ABOUT THE COOKIES!

What cookies did you make this year, and which were your favorites? Who is on your list for getting a cookie platter or box?

_____

_____

_____

_____

_____

FOR NEXT YEAR!

Whether there are things you want to repeat or things you wish you'd done differently, or gift ideas or new recipes you want to try, note them here and check back when planning for 2021!

_____

_____

_____

_____

RECIPE
INDEX

This index lists every recipe in the book in alphabetical order.
Just search for the titles when you want to find your favorites.
On page 240, you'll find an index of all the special bonus content—
including tips, how-tos and a little bit of Christmas history!

P. 86

P. 24

P. 107

BONUS CONTENT